D1104792

stellwagen

Stellwagen

The Making and Unmaking of
a National Marine Sanctuary

Peter Borrelli

University Press of New England
Hanover and London

For Jane

Published by University Press of New England,

One Court Street, Lebanon, NH 03766

www.upne.com

© 2009 by University Press of New England

Printed in U.S.A.

5 4 3 2 1

Library of Congress Cataloging-in-Publication Data

Borrelli, Peter.

Stellwagen: the making and unmaking of a national marine sanctuary / Peter Borrelli.

   p.   cm.

Includes bibliographical references and index.

ISBN 978-1-58465-714-9 (cloth : alk. paper)

1. Stellwagen Bank National Marine Sanctuary (Mass.) I. Title.

QH91.75.U6B67   2009

333.95′6160916345—dc22   2009012349

This book was published with the generous support of Furthermore: a program of the J. M. Kaplan Fund.

University Press of New England is a member of the Green Press Initiative. The paper used in this book meets their minimum requirement for recycled paper.

Contents

Map of Stellwagen Bank follows page xviii

Foreword

Rachel Carson once observed that, "The human race is challenged more than ever before to demonstrate our mastery—not over nature but of ourselves." Fifty years later, it is clear that we have failed to meet that challenge with respect to the marine environment. Our oceans are in trouble. Evidence of this sad truth can be found on the ocean bottom, in the diminished number of once-storied fish stocks, in the uncertainties faced by those who make their living from, live near, or otherwise enjoy coastal and ocean resources. We have shifted, irrevocably, from the luxury of treating the ocean as vast and limitless to the hard reality that we must restrain ourselves if we hope to continue to use the attractive array of goods, services, and intangible "quality of life" benefits that coastal and ocean environments provide.

The situation we are in is not surprising or unusual. For generations we humans have maintained a predictable relationship with the natural world. We discover, explore, utilize, exploit, divvy up, and partition. More people want more natural resources and develop increasingly sophisticated ways to access and process those resources. The result is strained and depleted ecosystems, direct contact between previously isolated users, and an accompanying ratcheting up of law and management to divide the shrinking pie and resolve conflicts.

Today, the expectations of abundant ocean resources, unrestricted activity, and limited government are being replaced. Just as we no longer traverse the American West in horse-drawn wagon trains observing herds of wild buffalo, we no longer fish from sail-powered boats nor witness the abundance of marine life that was one of the signature features of the New World. We now struggle to protect endangered marine mammals while developing more seafood for a hungry world. We also want renewable energy from the ocean. But we still lack basic information about what lies beneath the surface and how marine ecosystems function, while facing the urgent reality that climate change will further stress these already vulnerable systems.

The issues we face today demand a strong legal and management response.

However, ocean law and policy are in many ways playing "catch up" to the demand for more intensive management. The laws governing ocean activities are fractured among different agencies with different mandates. Among the current smorgasbord of ocean-related laws is one that sounds deceptively simple: the National Marine Sanctuaries Act.

Whenever I talk with people about National Marine Sanctuaries, they almost always assume that these places are fully protected marine equivalents of terrestrial wilderness areas, with little human activity or resource exploitation allowed. This is a logical conclusion, based on our understanding that a "sanctuary" is a place of refuge, as well as our collective experience with land-based parks or wilderness areas, where human use is regulated according to a site's unique set of qualities and sensitivities. Regardless of their level of understanding about the ocean, people are surprised to learn that National Marine Sanctuaries are *not* marine wilderness areas and they are not uniformly managed, with some Sanctuaries providing very little protection to resources within their boundaries and others providing much more.

Like many pieces of legislation, the Sanctuaries Act contains ambivalent or apparently contradictory language. Legislation is often drafted in attempts to please many constituents and win passage, ultimately posing more questions than providing answers. The burden of interpretation is then on administrators, who are vulnerable to both internal and external politics, and interest groups, which expend great energy in attempting to influence outcomes. When significant energy goes into arguing about what a law ought to be instead of actually applying it to resource management issues, citizens become confused, frustrated, and ambivalent, and managers become preoccupied with defending themselves. This has been the situation at the Gerry E. Studds Stellwagen Bank National Marine Sanctuary.

Application of the Sanctuaries Act is growing increasingly important, as we confront the truth that the ocean is no longer an endless expanse, and is in fact getting increasingly crowded. So we begin exercises in oceanic line-drawing, identifying which places are open or closed or somewhere in between, who's in and who's out, which activities are allowed and which are prohibited. In fact, the Sanctuaries Act provides important guidance for just such line-drawing or zoning exercises. We have seen the Act applied at the Florida Keys National Marine Sanctuary and the Channel Islands National Marine Sanctuary, where areas with varied levels of protection, including "no-take" zones, were successfully mapped out utilizing scientific information and stakeholder input. Yet we have also seen implementation of the very same law become a tedious exercise in stakeholder disenfranchisement, agency infighting, and inaction in the face of degrading resource conditions. This is the subject of Peter Borrelli's examination, *Stellwagen: The Making and Unmaking of a National Marine Sanctuary.*

Is this the best we can do? At a point in history when we need to act urgently to manage our activities in the ocean, is the Sanctuaries Act the right vehicle to execute comprehensive ecosystem-based management? Was President George W. Bush's protection of huge swaths of the Pacific Ocean as national monuments (under the Antiquities Act) an indication that the Sanctuaries Act may not be as important as previously thought to future marine management? The very flexibility of the Sanctuaries Act presents a great conundrum, with potential to accomplish innovative management at a time when we very much need it, but also so much room for interpretation that the debate of resource management issues — and not their resolution — gets the most attention. I remain optimistic that, with leadership and good judgment, the Act can play a vital role in sustainable ocean management; I am equally concerned that we may not have time for an extended debate about marine management, either by using the law as is, or by engaging in the often lengthy and unpredictable process of amending it. The experience of Stellwagen is both distressing and enlightening. It shows how difficult marine planning can be — and how important it is to keep one's eyes open to the complexity of the task.

Until our governance structure changes, the National Marine Sanctuaries Act remains one of our best means to manage our activities in the ocean in a sustainable manner. Appropriate implementation of the Act requires leadership both by government and private citizens. It has never been more important to utilize all avenues — even imperfect ones — to ensure long-term health and viability of marine ecosystems.

Susan E. Farady
Director, Marine Affairs Institute & Rhode Island Sea Grant
Legal Program, Roger Williams University School of Law,
and former chair of the Sanctuary Advisory Council,
Gerry E. Studds Stellwagen Bank National Marine Sanctuary

Acknowledgments

The idea for this book first came to me shortly after the untimely death of Gerry E. Studds in 2006. Studds was what we like to call today an Ocean Hero. The former Massachusetts congressman was on the forefront of marine conservation throughout his career, no more so than when he championed (along with Senator John Kerry) the cause of the Stellwagen Bank National Marine Sanctuary. His steadfast commitment to the marine environment and to ecologically rational public policy during several decades of political backlash to the environmental revolution of the sixties and seventies was an inspiration to many. He was an eternal optimist and always thought better of his colleagues and his constituents than they might have deserved. He believed fervently in the concept of the public trust and the notion that the sanctuary that now bears his name is the "people's sanctuary"—not just for the time being, not for the use and exploitation of a few, but for all the people for all time. I am grateful for his reinforcement of that old conservation lesson: that which was worth saving once is worth saving again and again.

I am also grateful to my former colleagues at the Provincetown Center for Coastal Studies whose knowledge of and dedication to the marine environment within the coastal waters of Massachusetts greatly influenced my thinking about the need for more aggressive conservation measures. Our time together was like a long ocean voyage of discovery. None of them, however, should be held responsible for my interpretations of science or public policy or for any shortcomings found in the pages that follow.

For a decade I served as a member of the federal Sanctuary Advisory Council (SAC), along with many fishermen, mariners, scientists, educators, and other citizens interested and concerned about the future of Stellwagen Bank. Though we did not always agree, I wish to thank them all for their time, effort, and insights. Special thanks must go to former SAC chairs John Williamson and Susan Farady. Their commitment to marine conservation and democratic process was an inspiration.

I owe a special thanks to my editor, Richard Pult, for his encouragement and guidance throughout this project and to the University Press of New England for agreeing to venture into the often stormy waters of ocean policy. Finally, I am grateful to Furthermore, the publishing program of the J. M. Kaplan Fund, for its financial assistance and to its president, Joan K. Davidson, who has encouraged and supported my work over the past thirty years.

Introduction

This is the story of a twenty-five-year-long effort to protect a biologically productive marine area in Massachusetts Bay known as Stellwagen Bank. But first a word of caution. To paraphrase the old saw about the making of laws and sausage, those interested in the marine environment and the greater public good may not want to read on, for the effort to protect Stellwagen Bank as a national marine sanctuary has been a largely unsuccessful process, leaving this observer to wonder if current laws and the people responsible for implementing them are capable of solving the crisis facing America's oceans.[1]

Twenty-five years ago, when concerned citizens and political leaders first recognized that something needed to be done to protect the coastal waters of Massachusetts, mineral extraction, pollution, habitat loss, collapsing fisheries, marine mammal disturbance, and urbanization all threatened Stellwagen. Today, the threats are much the same—only greater—with the addition of potential ecological turmoil caused by global warming. This is not to say that some progress has not been made. In the context of this small book, the cleanup of Boston Harbor, once considered to be the most polluted harbor in the nation, has been miraculous and awakened tens of thousands, if not millions, to the wonders of the marine environment. Indeed, throughout New England, public access to the ocean and awareness and concern for its health have never been greater. Still, the crisis grows.

In its 2003 report to the nation, the Pew Oceans Commission attributed the crisis not just to the usual list of problems for which some faltering remedies are in place, but to "a failure of both perspective and governance. We have failed to conceive of the oceans as our last public domain, to be managed holistically for the greater public good in perpetuity."[2]

The commission, which was chaired by Leon Panetta (who championed the cause of the Monterey Bay National Marine Sanctuary in the 1980s), went on to observe that the principal laws that are supposed to protect coastal zones, endangered marine mammals, ocean waters, and fisheries were enacted thirty years ago "on a crisis by crisis, sector by sector basis." Furthermore, most of those laws, dated and inadequate as they may be, have been under constant assault by a series of presidents and Congresses. As this book goes to press, the Bush administration has issued a ruling that would relieve federal agencies of some of the requirements of the Endangered Species Act, and Congress has for the umpteenth time failed to reauthorize the Marine Mammal Protection Act.

One of those early environmental building blocks was Title III of the Marine Protection, Research, and Sanctuaries Act (MPRSA), also known as the National Marine Sanctuaries Act (NMSA), signed into law on October 23, 1972, by President Richard Nixon (see appendix B for the complete text of the act).[3] The mission of the National Marine Sanctuary Program (NMSP) is to identify, designate, and comprehensively manage the nation's system of marine protected areas for the long-term benefit, use, and enjoyment of the public.[4] Though nominated in 1982, it was not until 1992 that an 842-square-mile area over and around Stellwagen Bank was designated as a national marine sanctuary (see appendix D). Ten years in the making, and as this study concludes, fifteen years in the unmaking.

Once envisioned as a key tool for protecting and managing the ocean, to date only thirteen sanctuaries have been created, representing less than 0.5 percent of the U.S. Exclusive Economic Zone, and since 2000 there has been a congressional moratorium on the creation of any new sanctuaries (see appendix C).[5] Several sanctuaries, notably one in the Florida Keys and California's Channel Islands, have set aside marine reserves where most human activity is prohibited, but for the most part marine sanctuaries continue to be used intensively.

As the story of Stellwagen Bank illustrates, some of the underlying premises of these laws — including the National Marine Sanctuaries Act itself — may be dated, while their administration is in need of major reform. That reform surely must begin with the removal of the National Oceanic and Atmospheric Administration (NOAA) from under the shadow of the Department of Commerce and with the creation of an independent oceans agency — a recommendation first made in 1969 by the Stratton Commission but rejected by President Nixon as a matter of political expedience (see chapter 3).

The Stellwagen Bank story is complicated by the realities of geography. First, it is out of sight of land, and for most citizens and politicians of the region, out of mind. Second, it is part of the larger Gulf of Maine ecosystem, posing challenging technical questions about how to protect it as a discrete area — assuming that a technical solution is even possible. Preserving or restoring the ecological integrity of Stellwagen Bank is one of those challenges. Creating and managing a sustainable fishery within Stellwagen Bank may be another.

After fifteen years of scientific study and endless wrangling over how best to manage Stellwagen Bank, it remains a sanctuary in name only. Even NOAA ranked the overall environmental quality of the sanctuary as fair-to-poor in a 2006 condition report.

It is ironic, given the region's rich maritime history, that so little concern has been given to the state of the sanctuary. While some regions of the country have come to appreciate their sanctuaries as public treasures and pressed for even stronger protections, New Englanders in the time-honored tradition of home rule and town meeting have feigned at pursuing consensus, while private interests have continued to use the sanctuary as if they owned it.

This book has two objectives. The first is to attempt to explain that protecting Stellwagen Bank is not about managing any one species of fish or whale or invertebrate — or of monitoring its disappearance, as the case may be — but about protecting habitat from human disturbance. The second is that marine protection, while it must be informed by science, is ultimately a matter of changing human behavior. As Aristotle wrote in *Politics* more than two thousand years ago, "Men pay most attention to what is their own: they care less about what is common; or, at any rate, they care for it only to the extent to which each is individually concerned. Even where there is no other cause for inattention, men are more prone to neglect their duty when they think that another is attending to it . . . ."[6]

And finally, the story has special interest because of the name now officially associated with it: that of the late Gerry E. Studds, whose career in Congress coincided with the development of virtually all the major pieces of legislation that currently define ocean policy in the United States. Upon his retirement in 1996 and in honor of his dedication to the protection of marine ecosystems, Congress renamed the sanctuary that he helped create the Gerry E. Studds Stellwagen Bank National Marine Sanctuary.

Studds served in the House of Representatives from 1973 to 1996 as Democratic representative of the Tenth Massachusetts District, which includes the coastal communities south of Boston known collectively as the South Shore, Cape Cod, and the islands of Martha's Vineyard and Nantucket. It would be disrespectful to think that Gerry Studds was simply in the right place at the right time. As a representative from a coastal district of the Bay State, having

an interest in the marine environment was a prerequisite to election. His predecessor was Representative Hastings Keith, a Republican and co-sponsor
with Senator John F. Kennedy of the legislation that created the Cape Cod
National Seashore, signed into law by President John F. Kennedy. But Studds
brought more than an interest to the job. He was a man of great intelligence,
quick to understand the crisis facing the nation's and world's oceans, and a
man of vision capable of imagining and effecting solutions. His colleagues
will long remember his eloquence, stentorian voice, and tenacity; as well as
his commitment to the lost art of bipartisanship.

Early in his congressional career, Studds became involved in the conservation and management of fisheries and was a co-sponsor of the original
Magnuson Fishery Conservation and Management Act (Magnuson Act),
passed in 1976. The law extended U.S. jurisdiction over fisheries resources
to the 200-mile limit, phased out foreign fishing within this area, and established the mechanism by which domestic fisheries have been managed ever
since. He remained on top of the issue of fisheries management throughout his career, sponsoring subsequent amendments to what later became
the Magnuson-Stevens Act and the Sustainable Fisheries Act of 1996. Over
the course of the next twenty-three years, he would also champion the cause
of wildlife protection and marine protected areas, playing a central role in
defending the Marine Mammal Protection Act, Endangered Species Act, and
National Marine Sanctuaries Act against weakening amendments.

Most of the political impetus for creating a system of ocean sanctuaries was
propelled by concerns about oil and gas exploration and development off the
coasts of California and Massachusetts. Today, with oil prices skyrocketing
and political pressure mounting to resume offshore exploration and development in areas such as Georges Bank and to site wind "farms" in shallow waters
in close proximity to major metropolitan areas, there will be renewed controversy over protections afforded existing sanctuaries, not to mention any
efforts to expand the system.

In the years preceding the designation of Stellwagen Bank, Studds consistently stated that one of the key reasons for creating the sanctuary was to protect a vital and historic fishing ground. Studds and other members of the New
England congressional delegation were strongly committed to what some
would call a multiple-use management strategy. In the case of Studds, it took
the form of a "promise" that many fishermen in the region to this day claim to
have been made to them personally.

That such a promise was made has never been questioned, but given Studds' equally firm commitment to rebuilding the region's sadly depleted fisheries, it would be naïve to think that it was an unconditional promise or that he had the authority to "give" what under law is a privilege, not a right. The promise was conditioned on the willingness and commitment of the fishing community to define and act on behalf of the common good.

Some time after retiring from Congress, Studds acknowledged that he and his colleagues probably had underestimated fishermen's opposition to change and the industry's utter denial that too many fishermen were still trying to catch too few fish. Studds believed that the Magnuson Act provided fishermen and government the mechanism for achieving sustainability, and that fishermen would be guided by their enlightened self-interest.

One would think that protection of Stellwagen Bank and sustainability would be twin objectives pursued simultaneously and harmoniously by all concerned. Not so. Difficulties arose the instant that Stellwagen Bank became a sanctuary, largely over jurisdictional authority. The National Marine Sanctuaries Act clearly granted lead-agency status over the management of commercial and recreational fisheries to the National Marine Fisheries Service (NMFS) and in the case of Stellwagen Bank to the New England Fisheries Management Council, one of nine the regional fisheries management councils created by the Magnuson Act. That authority is guarded fiercely.

Some effort has been made over the past five years to coordinate NOAA offices and programs. The slogan at headquarters in Silver Spring, Maryland, is that there is only one NOAA. But on many issues, NMFS and the Office of National Marine Sanctuaries could not be further apart; the former driven by the belief (and mandate) to manage the crisis of collapsing fisheries, the later trying to protect representative fragments of the ocean from further exploitation. By law, the Stellwagen Bank National Marine Sanctuary is required to review and if necessary amend its management plan every five years. Given the complexity of the issues and the number of people involved, it is possible that five years is too often. But the sanctuary's first management plan review has now dragged on for ten years, largely due to opposition within NOAA over the goals of the sanctuary.

A colleague and former state legislator once asked rhetorically in a gem of a little book about the governmental process, *Does the Citizen Stand a Chance?*[7] His answer was a resounding no. Those who believe that legislative bodies act in the interest of the common good or that government agencies do what they are legislatively mandated to do, are sorely misled. In the absence of strong and effective leadership, which more or less defines the past two decades of gridlock in Washington, D.C., agencies more or less set their own agendas in response to pressures from vested interests, euphemistically referred to these days as "stakeholders." Increasingly, it is left to the courts to set agencies back on track. Those who generalize that the nation has become too litigious need only look closely at how often agencies such as NOAA fail to meet public expectations within reasonable periods of time.

It is never too late to start over. The Pew Commission and U.S. Commission on Ocean Policy (2004) have addressed the need for a major overhaul of the federal bureaucracy aimed at strengthening and consolidating all ocean-related programs and authorities around the common theme of ecosystem-based management. With greater congressional leadership and administrative support, the sanctuary program could be strengthened and double in size in a decade.[8]

However, marine sanctuaries will never become a useful tool in ocean planning and management until Congress provides clear guidance on what uses are compatible at the time of designation. In its present form, the Sanctuaries Act promotes multiple use, a concept often interpreted to justify any and all uses, or what some cynically call multiple abuse. On Stellwagen Bank, it has fostered a business-as-usual attitude on the part of many users and a siege mentality on the part of the sanctuary staff.

At the same time, Congress needs to come to grips with the reality that the goals of the Sustainable Fisheries Act may never be met and that the time is fast approaching when the management of fisheries and allocation of fishing rights must be carried out in radically different ways. The National Marine Sanctuaries Act represents an early effort to zone the ocean, but as the story of Stellwagen Bank illustrates, Congress and several administrations stopped short of fulfilling their public trust obligations to protect the oceans for all people for generations to come. Instead, they yielded to various interests that continue to exploit the resources of the oceans as though they were limitless, giving nothing back in the process and leaving few places in a natural state.

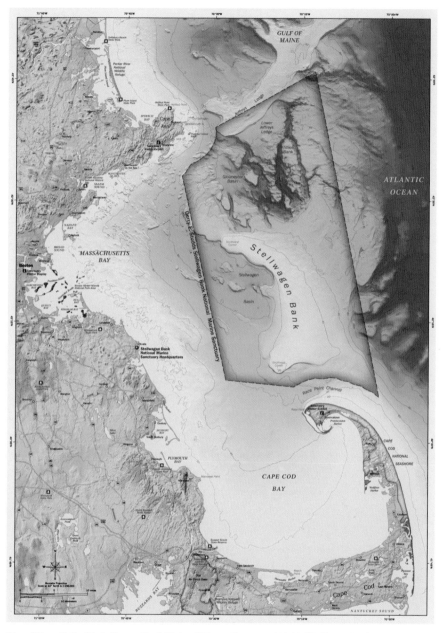

Map of Gerry E. Studds Stellwagen Bank National Marine Sanctuary. *NOAA / Stellwagen Bank National Marine Sanctuary*

PART I

DISCOVERY

Chapter 1

Middle Bank

On October 22, 1854, Navy Lieutenant Henry S. Stellwagen, commander of the Coast Survey Steamer *Bibb*, reported:

> I consider I have made an important discovery in the location of a 15 fathom bank lying in a line between Cape Cod and Cape Ann — with 40 and 50 fathoms inside and 35 fathoms outside it. It is not on any chart I have been able to procure. We have traced nearly five miles in width and over six miles in length, it no doubt extending much further.[1]

The Coast Survey

At the time of his "discovery," Stellwagen was on loan to the Coast Survey (the earliest forerunner of today's National Oceanic and Atmospheric Administration) and assigned to mapping the entrance to Massachusetts Bay.

While Massachusetts Bay may not seem like a particularly treacherous body of water when viewed from an airplane window or ferry, the rocky, island-studded entrance to Boston Harbor is tricky to navigate in a boat even in fair weather. Add a stiff wind or one of New England's famous nor'easters and poor visibility and you have the makings of a shipwreck. To this day, should you be so lucky as to be in the vicinity, the best refuge for fishing vessels, tankers, and even military vessels is Provincetown Harbor.

Stellwagen went on to report that:

> knowledge of it [Middle Bank] will highly benefit commanders of vessels bound in during thick weather by day or night. By it they can not only ascertain their distance to the eastward of the coast, but by attention to the lead after passing inside, a good idea of latitude may be obtained.[2]

By "attention to the lead," Stellwagen was referring to the practice of taking soundings or measurements of the depth of water by lowering overboard lead weights attached to a long marked line. In recognition of the navigational importance of the survey and thoroughness and dedication of Stellwagen's work under adverse conditions, Alexander Bache, superintendent of the Coast Survey at the time, named it Stellwagen's Bank. Over time, it simply became Stellwagen Bank.

The adverse conditions about which Bache received regular reports mostly had to do with the *Bibb*, one of the first in a series of steam cutters built in the 1840s for government survey and revenue work. During its initial sea trials, the *Bibb* took on water so rapidly that it had to be run aground to prevent it from sinking.[3] It was beset with mechanical problems throughout its relatively short commission. Originally designed to use a steam-driven horizontal paddle wheel and sails, it was soon refitted with a more efficient side-wheel propulsion system.

Stellwagen's talents as a hydrographer extended to inventing a sounding device equipped with a steel cup for collecting sediment samples. The invention, called a Stellwagen Cup, won him the Scott Premium Medal from the Franklin Institute.

Following his successful survey of Massachusetts Bay, Stellwagen resumed his military career in 1856, advancing to the rank of captain in 1862 and playing a significant role in the Civil War. A *New York Times* obituary on July 20, 1866, noted that while in command of the *Mercedita*, Captain Stellwagen had made some of the most important captures of the war during the Southern Blockade. His capture of Fort White, which guarded the entrance to Winyah Bay leading into Georgetown, South Carolina, helped secure the coast for Sherman's crushing March to the Sea.

Throughout his adventuresome career, which included assignments in the Mediterranean in pursuit of pirates, along the African coast to help control the slave trade, and in Mexico where he fought under Commodore Perry at the fall of Vera Cruz during the Mexican War, Stellwagen made drawings and watercolor sketches of historic if not artistic interest.

Cyprian Southack

While history has recognized Stellwagen's claim to Middle Bank, the work of another naval cartographer by the name of Captain Cyprian Southack

(1662–1745) deserves some attention. During the late seventeenth and early eighteenth century, the primary concern of the English Admiralty in North America was holding the French in check. For this, the English required accurate maps of English and French settlements and military outposts, as well as detailed charts of the coasts of New England, Nova Scotia, and New Brunswick. To fulfill this need, William Fisher and John Thornton published the first English atlas of charts and sailing instructions in 1689, called *The English Pilot, The Fourth Book*. Although *The English Pilot's* publishing standards and accuracy has been the subject of criticism, it remained the principal navigational manual for North America for the next 105 years.[4]

The English Pilot relied heavily on shipmasters for new charts, and among those most heavily relied upon and plagiarized was Captain Cyprian Southack, who sailed the Sea of New England for decades as an English privateer, naval commander, fisherman, and even a diplomat for more than fifty years.[5]

Throughout his travels, Southack compiled extensive notes about harbors, shoals, currents, and the sea floor, which he produced in an atlas format called the *New England Coasting Pilot* (1730–1734). *The English Pilot* reproduced several versions of Southack's charts, which gave them broader circulation and effectively made them the "official" charts of the area. The last of many editions of *The English Pilot* was published in 1794.

Stellwagen claims not to have seen or been "able to procure" any charts of Massachusetts Bay showing the bank that he surveyed. However, several soundings in Massachusetts Bay appear in Southack's highly detailed map of 1731 entitled "Correct Map of the Sea Coast of New England," which appeared in the *New England Coasting Pilot* and subsequent editions of *The English Pilot*.[6] And on a line between Cape Cod and Cape Ann there appears a 15-fathom bank—just as Stellwagen reported in 1854—marked by Southack as Barren Bank.

While the accuracy of Southack's charts do not measure up to the standards of the Coast Survey more than a century later, his work may have been the best of its day. His knowledge of the New England coast was extensive and he was a keen observer. His charts are filled with interesting, detailed, handwritten notes. The 1731 map even includes notations about the seafloor of Massachusetts Bay, noting the presence of "coarse sands and stones" to the north of the bank, "brown coarse sand" to the east, and "gray owse" in the deeper areas to the west in what we now know as Stellwagen Basin. Contemporary seafloor mapping conducted by the U.S. Geological Survey, discussed later in this book, would appear to confirm these basic observations made more than 250 years ago.[7]

The Geologic Story

What Stellwagen "discovered" was a submerged plateau or bank at the eastern edge of Massachusetts Bay, curving in a southeast-to-northwest direction for 18.75 miles and resembling what might have been the northward extension of Cape Cod. At its widest point to the south, about 6 miles off Race Point, Provincetown, it is 6.25 miles across. Water depths over the bank range from 65 feet to more than 300 feet on the west side, which drops off steeply. To the east, the seafloor slopes more gradually to depths of more than 600 feet.[8]

The bank was formed, along with Cape Cod and the islands of Martha's Vineyard and Nantucket, during the last major advance of continental glaciers in North America, known as the Wisconsin or Wisconsinan glaciation. The geologic story, as popularly told by Robert Oldale, geologist emeritus with the U.S. Geological Survey in Woods Hole, begins around 25,000 years ago, when what may have been a mile-high ice sheet called the Laurentide (after the St. Lawrence region of Canada) began moving southward, grinding and pushing fragments of ice and earth along with it.[9] As the glacier reached the coastal plain, which extended well beyond today's New England coastline to the edge of the continental shelf, it formed several large, tongue-like lobes. One of these was formed by a topographic depression that is now Cape Cod Bay; the other by what is now the Great South Channel to the south and east.

The Cape Cod Bay lobe was the first to begin retreating, about 18,000 years ago; leaving behind what is now the peninsula of Cape Cod and the islands of Nantucket and Martha's Vineyard. The second lobe, formed by the Great South Channel, retreated more slowly, enabling glacial debris to settle slowly from the melting ice on top of the submerged coastal plain to create the elevation now known as Stellwagen Bank.

As the ice retreated further to the north, an arm of the sea flooded the valley that is now Stellwagen Basin, while Stellwagen Bank became exposed again and probably remained above sea level for several thousand more years.

At the maximum period of glaciation, scientists estimate that the sea level fell almost 300 feet below its present level. But with the end of the ice age, the seas rose again, covering Stellwagen Bank.

Most of the sea floor of Stellwagen Bank is comprised of sand and pebbly sand that is constantly sifted and redistributed by strong currents. The shallow banks and ledges to the north, including Jeffreys Ledge and Tillies Bank, are covered with mixtures of sand and gravel, while in the deeper area of Stellwagen Basin to the west, the sea floor is made up of a mud-like mixture of sand, silt, and clay.[10]

As fascinating as the landscape of the ocean floor may be, water, or to be more specific, the movement of water, is what defines Stellwagen Bank. And just as its physical geography is a function of large-scale phenomena of the distant geologic past, the physical oceanography of the bank is primarily that of the Gulf of Maine, an area more than forty times larger.[11] Henry Bryant Bigelow, the preeminent oceanographer of his generation and the first director of the Woods Hole Oceanographic Institution, was the first to conduct a comprehensive investigation of the Gulf in the 1920s. In his seminal work *The Physical Oceanography of the Gulf of Maine* (1927), he modeled a major counterclockwise gyre that drives the ecosystem.

Coastal Currents

Generally, nutrient-rich waters fed by the cold, deep Labrador Current enter the Gulf of Maine over the Scotian Shelf, Browns Bank, and Northeast Channel, and flow counterclockwise at a rate of about 7 nautical miles per day in a southwesterly direction along the coasts of Maine and New Hampshire and into Massachusetts Bay. What is then called the Maine Coastal Current then curls eastward over the top of Cape Cod through the Race Point Channel and out to the northern edge of Georges Bank, where it forms a second clockwise gyre. From there, the currents sweep east and north toward Nova Scotia, where they divide; the major flow turns back toward the Maine coast and a smaller current moves north into the Bay of Fundy and along the coast of New Brunswick. As the Maine Coastal Current runs along the near shore of New England, it is infused with fresh water, most notably from the Merrimack River entering Massachusetts Bay at Newburyport.[12] The New England watersheds and urban areas also contribute a nasty brew of surface and atmospheric pollutants that are largely diluted, but by no means rendered harmless, by the huge volume of the bay. The cold northern waters eventually leave the Gulf of Maine through the Great South Channel south and east of Cape Cod. The complete cycle takes about three months to complete.

Because of its oceanographic dependence on the Gulf of Maine, some scientists and resource managers insist that Stellwagen Bank is not an ecosystem. By this they mean that it is not a discrete ecological unit or closed system. This perspective often complicates discussions about management alternatives and generally frustrates those who would like to see Stellwagen Bank held to a higher standard of protection. But legislative history and conventional usage have defined marine ecosystems more broadly as environments in which plants and animals interact with the chemical and physical features of that environment and display significant interdependence.

Charles "Stormy" Mayo, who has spent much of his professional life at the Provincetown Center for Coastal Studies examining the opposite ends of the food web in New England waters — zooplankton and right whales — is comfortable thinking about Stellwagen Bank as an ecosystem but quick to add that the "essence" of the system is change.

The most dynamic action is found at the edges of the bank, where strong tidal currents in the 3-meter range, augmented by wave action and the flow from the north, are deflected by the sides of the bank. The resulting vertical flow of water produces turbulent swirls called "upwellings." And what wells up and mixes with surface waters are nutrients — the decomposed remains of plants and animals — from the sea floor.

The mixing process also may be driven by internal waves created by the ebb and flow of the ocean over the bank. On the ebb tide, water is said to be flowing "downstream" into the Gulf of Maine, while on the flood tide water flows "upstream" into Massachusetts Bay. The ebb and flow is powerful enough to generate large internal waves that cause mixing even during periods of the year when the water column is stratified.[13] All this upward flow and mixing sustains large populations of phytoplankton in the upper layers of the water column, resulting in high levels of productivity that support diverse assemblages of fish species, marine mammals, seabirds, and invertebrates. While the Gulf of Maine has been the subject of considerable scientific research, scientists have only begun to understand the ecological significance of the Stellwagen Bank ecosystem.[14]

Shipwrecks

It was the hazards of navigating the Massachusetts coast that prompted Henry Stellwagen's Coast Survey of 1854 and 1855. From that early work came the charts and other aids to navigation that have saved countless lives. But the outer bars of Cape Cod and the entrance to Massachusetts Bay became no less treacherous, as the wrecks of many vessels attest.

The same underwater technology that has enhanced our understanding of the physical structure of the seafloor of Stellwagen Bank has begun to add to our appreciation of the area's historical significance. Preliminary studies have located eighteen shipwrecks on Stellwagen Bank and surrounding waters, five of which have been identified by name. The most famous is the paddle-wheel steamer *Portland*, lost during the ferocious November gale of 1898 that now bears its name. Built in Bath, Maine, in 1889, the *Portland* was used to shuttle cargo and passengers between Boston and Portland. Long (291 feet) and narrow (42 feet) with a shallow draft, she was designed for coastal steaming in moderate sea conditions.

When she left Boston at 7:00 p.m. on November 26, the *Portland* was operating as a popular "night boat" on the run to Portland. It remains a matter of speculation why the captain set out in rapidly deteriorating weather conditions, but from the wreckage found on the beaches of Cape Cod, it is reasonable to assume that the shallow-draft steamer could not maintain a heading into the wind and was blown south and eventually driven under by the mounting seas. The number of lives lost as reported in the *New York Times* at the time was estimated at 118, but the number eventually grew to about 190, making it the worst maritime disaster in New England history. The Maine Maritime Museum and others have called it New England's *Titanic*, noting that the "*Portland*'s fate was similarly entwined in defiance of the weather and the puzzling hubris of her commander."[15]

The wreck was first located by the Historic Maritime Group of New England in 1989 and photographically documented in 2002 by the National Oceanic and Atmospheric Administration (NOAA) and the University of Connecticut's National Undersea Research Center (NURC). In 2005, the site of the wreck was added to the National Register of Historic Places.

NOAA and NURC have also documented the wreckage of two Maine-built colliers, the *Frank A. Palmer* and the *Louise B. Crary*, which collided in December 1902 while hauling coal to Boston from Virginia. The *Palmer* was a 274-foot-long, four-masted schooner and is believed to have been the longest four-master ever built. The *Crary* was a 267-foot-long five-masted schooner. The sonar images of the two show the two hulls remarkably intact, locked together on the ocean floor. Both shipwrecks were added to the National Register in 2006. The list of shipwrecks also includes a number of twentieth-century fishing vessels, mostly wooden-hulled eastern-rig draggers built between the 1920s and the 1970s.

Chapter 2

A Special Place

In terms of its accessibility by small craft, Stellwagen Bank, or Middle Bank, as it was called before the Coast Survey of 1854 and is still called by some fishermen today, should be thought of as a *near-offshore* location. It has been recognized as an important fishing ground for a varied array of fisheries from the time of colonial settlement to the present day. Captain John Smith's *Description of New England*, written in 1616 to promote permanent English settlement of the area, made extensive reference to its year-round fishery, noting in some detail how merchants from Portugal, Holland, and Spain had already made fortunes off the rich cod fishery discovered by John Cabot in 1497.

To prove his point, Smith and his crew claimed to have caught sixty thousand cod in a month with hand lines. On the sketch map accompanying the account of his 1614 voyage along the Massachusetts and Maine coast, Smith drew a ship over the position of Stellwagen Bank, a cartographic convention denoting fishing grounds. A 1635 edition of the map published after his death was embellished with a drawing of a large pile of cod heads beneath the ship.[1]

Present-day Fishing

Despite the tragic decline of many stocks, most notably that of cod (see chapter 6), commercial and recreational fishing remain the most economically important human activities directly dependent on the resources of Stellwagen Bank.[2] Commercial fishing data for the period 1996 through 2005, drawn from standardized surveys and mandatory fishing vessel trip reports, show that an average of 327 vessels operating out of home ports in New England, New York, and New Jersey have been fishing the area. The vast majority (85 percent) are from home ports in Massachusetts.

The average commercial value for the period of fish and crustaceans, including the value of lobster and bluefin tuna, averaged $23 million (in 2005 dollars), based on landings of 18.4 million pounds.[3] In the context of the entire New England fishery, the total value of landings from Stellwagen Bank was actually no more than 2.8 percent of the New England total over the decade (1.9 percent excluding lobster and tuna).[4] The statistic may seem surprisingly low to some. But for smaller vessels (less than 45 feet) operating out of nearby home ports such as Gloucester, Scituate, Plymouth, and Provincetown, trips to Stellwagen Bank may be the measure of survival.

Important commercial fisheries of the area include (in descending order of landed value): American lobster, cod, yellowtail flounder, sea scallop, monk-fish (round/tails/livers), flounder (witch/gray sole), flounder (winter/black-back), Atlantic herring, flounder (American plaice/dab), and bluefin tuna. In terms of volume, mid-water trawling of Atlantic herring accounts for more than 40 percent of the total fish caught.

Comparable information on recreational fishing activity specific to Stell-wagen Bank does not exist, but data derived from party and charter boat land-ings and surveys indicates that recreational fishing in the offshore waters of Massachusetts more than doubled between 1996 and 2005, as nearshore fish-ing stocks declined during the same period.[5] For 2005, NOAA estimates that 52 party boats carrying 46,849 anglers and 115 charter boats carrying 13,012 anglers fished in the Stellwagen Bank area. Almost no reliable data is available on the number of private boats that use the area, but according to the readers of *Offshore* magazine, Stellwagen Bank has become the third-favorite fishing spot in the Northeast.[6]

Unlike the commercial fishery, the number of scheduled recreational trips is highly weather dependent, which also means that landings data varies con-siderably from year to year. However, for the 1995 to 2005 timeframe, land-ings from the offshore waters of Massachusetts (including Stellwagen Bank) totaled nearly 6 million pounds. How much of this can be attributed to Stell-wagen Bank is uncertain, but from information gleaned from vessel trip reports, it would seem that a very high percentage of the landings from char-ter and party boats working the general area came from Stellwagen Bank. The top four species landed by recreational anglers (in pounds) are cod, mackerel, bluefish, and pollock.[7]

Endangered Whale Habitat

Stellwagen Bank's complex ecosystem also provides feeding and nursery areas for five species of whales (humpback, fin, right, sei, and blue) on the federal endangered species list.[8] Of these, the most frequently sighted and favorite among whale watchers because of its dramatic surface acrobatics is the humpback whale (*Megaptera novaeangliae*).

The humpbacks that visit Stellwagen Bank are part of the North Atlantic population, estimated to be 11,570.[9] The animals spend their summers in the north feeding throughout the North Atlantic — from New England to the Canadian Maritimes to Norway, Iceland, and Greenland. Preliminary genetic analysis has not clearly identified discrete subpopulations within the North Atlantic. However, for management purposes, since 2000 NMFS has treated animals surveyed in the Gulf of Maine as a single stock. The Provincetown Center for Coastal Studies, which has been studying humpbacks in the Gulf of Maine for the past thirty years and maintains the official catalogue of individuals, estimates the Gulf of Maine stock population to be 902.[10]

The abundance of humpback whales on Stellwagen Bank is linked to the abundance of sand lance, which spawn prolifically in the sandy bottom areas of the Bank. Most years, sand lance occur on the Bank at higher levels of abundance than anywhere else in the Gulf of Maine. When sand lance are not available in great abundance or in the dense patches preferred by humpbacks, they will feed on other available schooling fish, particularly Atlantic herring, which also appear in and around the Bank (but are not associated with sand and gravelly sand) and throughout the Gulf. Humpbacks also have been reported feeding on krill in northern areas within the Gulf.

The most endangered of the large whales that visit Stellwagen Bank is the North Atlantic right whale (*Eubalaena glacialis*). With a population of only about 350 animals, their every movement along the coastal waters is a matter of great conservation concern. Within New England waters, the Great South Channel south and east of Cape Cod and Cape Cod Bay are considered critical habitats for the animals. Relatively large numbers stop to feed on dense patches of zooplankton from mid-winter to late spring before moving on to the cold waters and rich feeding grounds of the Bay of Fundy and Scotian Shelf. While Stellwagen Bank generally is not considered to be as significant a feeding area, it is definitely a part of the right whale's migratory range, and given the heavy volume of ship traffic, considered a management hot spot.

Add fin whales, sei whales, minke whales, pilot whales, and even occasional blue whales to the list, along with a rich variety of other marine mammals, sea turtles, and seabirds, and you have what one exuberant naturalist once called a "cornucopia of marine life."[11] Since the advent of whale watching in the late 1970s, millions of people have been ferried out to the Bank from a half-dozen ports from mid-April to mid-October. The direct and indirect economic value of the industry, especially on the ports of Provincetown, Plymouth, and Gloucester, has been enormous (see chapter 9).

Marine Sanctuary Nomination

In an effort to craft effective management strategies, scientists and resource managers have and will continue to examine the intricacies of the Stellwagen Bank ecosystem in relation to the greater Gulf of Maine. The process could take decades. In the meantime, from a conservation and public policy perspective, enough is known to act to protect what is left.

It was this recognition of Stellwagen Bank as a "special place" and the imminent threat of development that prompted Charles "Stormy" Mayo at the Provincetown Center for Coastal Studies and Defenders of Wildlife in Washington, D.C., to nominate it in 1982 as a national marine sanctuary under a largely ignored provision of law created during the euphoric aftermath of the first Earth Day. This was Title III of the Marine Protection, Research, and Sanctuaries Act of 1972, also known at the National Marine Sanctuaries Act.[12]

However, from 1972 to 1982, the newly created National Oceanic and Atmospheric Administration (NOAA), charged with creating a national system of marine sanctuaries that some members of Congress expected might someday rival the national park system, had designated only six sanctuaries (see chapter 3). During these early years, interest in marine sanctuaries was greatest in California and New England, where designation was considered a possible countermeasure to offshore oil and gas development. The situation only worsened during the eight years of the Reagan presidency, when the program virtually shut down. By the time Reagan left office, the only addition to the system was a quarter-square-mile coral reef in Fagatele Bay on the island of Tutuila, American Samoa.

Politically, Mayo's recommendation could not have arrived in Washington, D.C., at a worse time, although it did manage to make the cut and get onto NOAA's first site evaluation list a year later. There it remained for ten years.[13] Even then, it would take an act of Congress to give official recognition to Stellwagen Bank as a special place of national significance. Much of what follows in these pages is intended to explain the process and meaning of this action as it applies to Stellwagen Bank and the broader challenge of ocean protection.

Urban Development Pressures

As incredible as it may have seemed to some, while NOAA (within the Department of Commerce) was purportedly examining the "appropriateness" of designating Stellwagen Bank as a national marine sanctuary, the Mineral Management Service and Bureau of Mines (within the Department of the Interior) were studying the feasibility of mining the Bank for sand and gravel — more than enough sand and gravel to feed Boston's mega-public works projects only thirty miles to the west.

The first of these was the Massachusetts Water Resource Authority's (MWRA) secondary wastewater treatment facility on Deer Island and its 9-mile-long outfall pipe that daily discharges approximately 375 million gallons of treated effluent from the plant to a point just west of Stellwagen Bank. Construction of the facility was the outcome of a successful lawsuit brought by the Boston-based Conservation Law Foundation (CLF) in 1983 to clean up Boston Harbor, purported to be the most polluted urban harbor in the United States. (George H. W. Bush used this to great advantage in his presidential campaign against Massachusetts Governor Michael Dukakis.) More than anything in the region, the project symbolized an awakening to the fact Massachusetts is the *Bay State*; that much of its history, economy, and splendor has had to do with the marine environment.

While the effects of the outfall pipe on the marine environment were a concern during the planning stages and will continue to be monitored closely for any adverse long-term environmental effects, it was a monumental undertaking whose time had come. Projected at one point to cost as much as $6 billion, the project came in at $3.9 billion, due primarily to the watchful eye of U.S. First District Court Judge David Mazzone, who had ordered a full cleanup of the harbor in 1985 in response to the CLF lawsuit. Throughout the construction of the treatment plant and outfall pipe, Judge Mazzone required detailed progress reports and prohibited unions from striking. He was present for the opening ceremony on September 6, 2000, and was given the honor of turning the valve that opened the 25-foot-diameter outfall pipe. Within a matter of months, the cleanup of Boston Harbor was well underway, and to date there has been no evidence that the water quality of Massachusetts Bay (including Stellwagen Bank) has been degraded significantly.

Then there was the Big Dig. Officially known as the Central Artery/Third Harbor Tunnel Project, its primary purpose was to bury the aging and monstrous elevated swath of Interstate 93 that had separated the heart of the city from the waterfront since the late 1950s. Construction began in 1992 and ended at the end of 2007 at an estimated final cost of $14.8 billion — more than six times its original projected cost. The Big Dig was a nightmare for Bostonians and interstate travelers, but it has thus far made travel through the city faster and safer. The land previously occupied by the Central Artery is now largely open space, and for the first time in a half-century the heart of the city is reconnected to its spectacular waterfront.

The successful completion of these two mega-projects has been like a modern-day shot heard round the world. Boston is alive and well and once again facing the sea. The environmental bonus is that Stellwagen Bank did not have to be sacrificed in the process — at least not for these two projects.

Studies conducted in the 1970s and 1980s estimated that the volume of sand and gravel on or adjacent to Stellwagen Bank was 114.7 million cubic yards. Most of this is in less than 130 feet of water, which would have made it easily "recoverable" by available mining technology. According to the Mineral Management Service, the most likely method of mining would have been a form of excavation utilizing anchored suction dredges.

The widespread perception in Massachusetts, especially during the Reagan administration, was that anything that could be scraped, excavated, or drilled for in federal waters was available. Representative Gerry Studds, whose district included fishing communities along the South Shore directly west of Stellwagen Bank, was incredulous. Elected to Congress in 1973, Studds was a key member and for a short period in the 1990s chair of the House Merchant Marine and Fisheries Committee. From this position of considerable authority, he was a co-author or key sponsor of virtually every congressional statute or amendment affecting the marine environment until his retirement in 1997.

By the time Interior's interest in leasing sand and gravel on Stellwagen Bank became known, Studds had already been pressing for federal recognition of Stellwagen Bank for five years. That the federal government "would even consider the possibility of sand and gravel mining in a highly productive marine ecosystem is nothing short of ludicrous," he told his colleagues.

"Stellwagen Bank is sand and gravel — mine it, and you destroy the very reason for establishing this sanctuary in the first place. . . . This ridiculous debate
must be stopped here and now.[14]

Eighth Wonder of the World

While large-scale sand and gravel mining was a more realistic threat to the
ecological integrity of Stellwagen Bank, it took a private developer with a
loony imagination and a strong dose of balderdash to capture public attention. His name was Richard Gugel, a self-promoter with a scheme to make
millions constructing artificial islands in federal waters. They were to be what
he unabashedly called the "Eighth Wonder of the World."

Gugel's Taj Mahal Artificial Islands, designed for an unspecified location off the coast of New York or New Jersey, was his first inspiration. He
approached the Army Corps of Engineers' New York District with the idea
in 1983 but got nowhere.

He then turned his attention to Stellwagen Bank and came up with a plan
to build a resort casino on what he called Gugel's Arabian Nights Artificial
Islands. The plan, submitted to the Army Corps of Engineers' New England
District in 1988 for review under the Rivers and Harbors Act, called for construction of a hotel, casino, restaurants, apartments, a hospital, heliport, and
marina all capable of accommodating one hundred thousand people. All of
this was to be built on a 1,000-foot-wide octagonal steel platform supported
by sixteen piles driven to bedrock. It was to be located at latitude 42°23′ north,
longitude 70°23′ west, 30 miles east of Boston, near what is known as the
Northwest Corner.

A sketch of the project vaguely resembles the authentic Taj Mahal with
its central white-domed mausoleum surrounded by four minarets, except
in the Gugel version the central tower would have housed a rotating night
club, hotel, casino, and convention center. The infrastructure for the platform,
including a diesel-fueled electric power plant, garbage disposal facilities, and
sewage treatment, were to be located below the main level, which was to be
60 feet above the water at mean high tide.

By 1990, Gugel's vision had grown to include two additional platforms, all
connected by gangways. The revised plan shifted the project further to the
north and west off the Bank itself. Gugel's Arabian Nights drew nationwide
media attention both for its audacity and for the fact that Gugel, who some

believe had absolutely no financial backing, seemed to be thumbing his nose at Massachusetts for its opposition to casino gambling.[15] He also seems to have believed that he could get away with almost anything in federal waters, a view shared by many at the time.

Gugel claims never to have been aware of the ecological and historical importance of Stellwagen Bank. In a letter written to NOAA in 1991, Gugel accused Senator John Kerry of introducing legislation that ultimately declared Stellwagen Bank as a national marine sanctuary for the sole purpose of stopping his project.[16] In the same letter, he claimed not to have been aware of the efforts of the Stellwagen Bank Coalition to create a sanctuary. Comprised of more than sixty environmental, education, fishing, and research organizations, the coalition had lobbied effectively for five years for some form of lasting protection (see appendix F for a complete list of coalition members).

In the end, Gugel's artificial islands had much the same galvanizing effect as Walt Disney's proposal in the 1960s to build a gigantic ski resort in California's Mineral King Valley adjacent to Sequoia National Park. In the case of Mineral King Valley, Congress brought an end to what the Sierra Club and others portrayed as an attempted commercialization of a national treasure and annexed it to Sequoia National Park in 1978.

In the case of Stellwagen Bank, Congress brought an end to interagency wrangling and the speculations of private interests in 1992 by designating Stellwagen Bank as a national marine sanctuary. But as the record shows, the wrangling and debate over the privatization of public resources continue to this day.

Chapter 3

Designation

By 1988, proponents of marine sanctuary status for Stellwagen Bank were growing impatient with the politics and process of designation. But they were not alone. Since the passage of the National Marine Sanctuaries Act (NMSA) in 1972, only five sanctuaries had been established.[1] Early proponents of marine sanctuaries in Washington, D.C., such as the Center for Marine Conservation and Coastal States Organization, struggled just to keep the program alive.

The Reagan administration's crusade against environmental regulation, science, and planning made infant programs like marine sanctuaries, coastal zone management, and Sea Grant easy targets for budget cuts and bureaucratic subterfuge. The word soon got around that anyone trying to advance his or her career in government in these areas should seek other employment. As draconian as the Reagan administration's environmental policies were, the statutes survived and representatives from coastal states managed to eke out basic levels of funding to keep the programs afloat.

Along with many nominations, Stellwagen Bank had languished on NOAA's Site Evaluation List (SEL) since 1983. There is little doubt that the Reagan administration's attempts to scuttle the sanctuaries program through the budget and appointments processes had a lot to do with this. But the national marine sanctuaries program, now thirty-five years old, also has suffered greatly by never having a well-defined mission or constituency. As a consequence, political support has been inconsistent. Further complicating matters has been the low priority it has received by its parent agency, the National Oceanic and Atmospheric Administration (NOAA), the presumed "oceans agency," which arguably is inappropriately administered by the Department of Commerce.

The principal difficulty facing Stellwagen Bank and other candidate sites was the statutory provision that placed the designation process in the hands of the secretary of commerce (meaning NOAA), with somewhat vague selection criteria and no performance deadlines. This process stood in stark contrast with the more customary practice of congressional designation of national parks, wildlife refuges, seashores, and wilderness areas. As long as authority to designate national marine sanctuaries remained a discretionary administrative process, administrative infighting and White House interference would continue.

The Amendments of 1988

Congress partially cleared the logjam in 1988 when it amended the NMSA in a number of significant ways. First, it required the secretary of commerce to designate four sites: Cordell Bank off the coast of central California, Flower Garden Banks in the Gulf of Mexico, Monterey Bay (California), and the Washington Outer Banks. Second, the secretary was required to issue prospectuses and feasibility studies for a number of areas that had been languishing for years. Among these was Stellwagen Bank.

The 1988 amendments further required that the prospectus for Stellwagen Bank be submitted to Congress no later than September 30, 1990. The deadline forced NOAA to move Stellwagen from its evaluation list to its active candidate list and to conduct a series of public scoping meetings in 1989. Following the scoping meetings, NOAA prepared a draft environmental impact statement and management plan (DEIS/MP), issued for further public comment on February 8, 1991.

To describe congressional proponents of ocean protection as being anything less than ripping mad in 1990 would be an understatement. Not only had NOAA continued to plod along, but it invented policies it used for opposing or further delaying designation of new sanctuaries. In Massachusetts Bay, NOAA claimed it was not federal policy to include a federal dredge dump site within the boundaries of a marine sanctuary, as the Commonwealth of Massachusetts, fishermen, and environmentalists had advocated.[2] In California, it came up with a new reason for not designating Monterey Bay, claiming the designation of the Channel Islands in 1980 during the Carter administration had fulfilled the region's quota. This idea of establishing regional balance or representation within the system had never been part of the NMSA, but is an issue that continues to burden the program.

Among congressional proponents of marine protection and the general public, there has never been much doubt that priority should be given to those areas where there are clear threats to the marine environment. Representative Leon Panetta, the leading congressional proponent for Monterey Bay, was outraged. Panetta, who would go on to become Bill Clinton's chief of staff and chairman of the Pew Oceans Commission, would join Gerry Studds, whose Stellwagen proposal also seemed dead in the water, in pressing for immediate congressional designation.

For Senator John Kerry, who had written Stellwagen Bank into the 1988 amendments, the threat of sand and gravel mining was very real. He concluded that congressional designation was the only way to extend protection to Stellwagen Bank and to move the sanctuary program forward. His initiative in the Senate quickly gained support on both coasts, especially from Ernest Hollings (D-S.C.), a longtime supporter of the sanctuaries program, and Alan Cranston, the leading Senate opponent of near-shore oil exploration and development since the 1969 eruption of an oil platform in the Santa Barbara Channel.

The Oceans Act of 1992

Prior to NOAA's issuance of the final environmental impact statement and management plan (FEIS/MP) in July 1993, Congress passed the Oceans Act of 1992, containing the National Marine Sanctuaries Program Amendments Act of 1992.[3] The act established the Hawaiian Islands Humpback Whale, Monterey Bay, and Stellwagen Bank National Marine Sanctuaries. Stellwagen had finally made it.

The immediate effect of the designation was that the following activities were prohibited:

1. Discharging or depositing, from within the boundaries of the sanctuary, any material or other matter except: (i) fish, fish wastes, chumming materials, or bait used in or resulting from traditional fishing operations in the Sanctuary; (ii) biodegradable effluent incidental to vessel use and generated by marine sanitation devices approved in accordance with Section 312 of the Federal Water Pollution Control Act as amended, (FWPCA), 33 U.S.C. 1322 et seq.; (iii) water generated by routine vessel operations (e.g., cooling water, deck wash down, and graywater as defined by Section 312 of the FWPCA), excluding oily wastes from bilge pumping; or (iv) engine exhaust.

2. Discharging or depositing, from beyond the boundary of the sanctuary,

any material or other matter, except those listed above, that subsequently enters the sanctuary and injures a sanctuary resource or quality.

3. Exploring for, developing, or producing industrial materials (including clay, stone, sand, gravel, metalliferous ore, and non-metalliferous ore) in the sanctuary.

4. Drilling into, dredging, or otherwise altering the seabed of the sanctuary; or constructing, placing, or abandoning any structure or material or other matter on the seabed of the sanctuary, except as an incidental result of: (i) anchoring vessels; (ii) traditional fishing operations; or (iii) installation of navigational aids.

5. Moving, removing, or injuring, or attempting to move, remove, or injure, a sanctuary historical resource. This prohibition does not apply to moving, removing, or injury resulting incidentally from traditional fishing operations.

6. Taking any marine reptile, marine mammal, or seabird in or above the sanctuary, except as permitted by regulations, as amended, promulgated under the Marine Mammal Protection Act (MMPA), as amended, 16 U.S.C. 1361 et seq.; the Endangered Species Act (ESA), as amended, 16 U.S.C. 1531 et seq.; and the Migratory Bird Treaty Act (MBTA), as amended, 16 U.S.C. 703 et seq.

7. Lightering in the sanctuary.

8. Possessing within the sanctuary (regardless of where taken, moved, or removed from), except as necessary for valid law-enforcement purposes, any historical resource, or any marine mammal, marine reptile, or seabird taken in violation of regulations, as amended, promulgated under the MMPA, ESA, or MBTA.

9. Interfering with, obstructing, delaying, or preventing an investigation, search, seizure, or disposition of seized property in connection with enforcement of the act or any regulation or permit issued under the act.[4]

Fishing within the Sanctuary

One of the primary objectives of those advocating for sanctuary designation of Stellwagen Bank always had been protection of the fishing ground. Prohibiting sand and gravel mining, the single greatest threat at the time, therefore, was a great victory. But for the fishing industry, language in the designation document specifically allowing fishing was considered added insurance.[5]

What the 1993 designation document and management plan made abundantly clear is that fisheries management remains the primary (though not the exclusive) responsibility of the National Marine Fisheries Service (NMFS) working in collaboration with the New England Fishery Management Council (NEFMC), as authorized by the Magnuson Fishery Conservation and Management Act (16 U.S. Code §§1801 *et seq.*). Section 304(a)(5) of the NMSA established this line of authority, stating that "the draft regulations prepared by the Council, or a Council determination that regulations are not necessary . . . shall be accepted and issued as proposed regulations by the Secretary [of Commerce] unless the Secretary finds that the Council's action fails to fulfill the purposes and policies [of the Act] and the goals and objectives of the proposed designation." Under this scenario, the secretary of commerce is authorized to issue new fishing regulations specific to the sanctuary. Still, during the comment period for the Stellwagen Bank proposal, the council and several commercial fishermen's organizations insisted that regulations on fisheries in the sanctuary should remain entirely the responsibility of NMFS and the New England Fishery Management Council. The National Ocean Service (NOS) within NOAA, which administers the sanctuaries program, responded in the final environmental impact statement on the Stellwagen Bank designation by stating:

> NOAA/NOS has determined that while the regulatory structure for management of fisheries is adequate, current implementation of that structure is not fully attaining the objectives mandated under MFCMA. The NEFMC and NMFS are currently responding to a Court order to revise the FMP's for groundfish species, so as to design a rebuilding program for those stocks.
>
> NOAA/NOS believes this is an appropriate mechanism to address the current problems related to groundfish stocks. In addition, Congress is developing legislation to address this problem. Therefore, NOAA/NOS is neither regulating fishing nor listing fishing as an activity subject to a sanctuary regulation. NOAA/NOS intends to work closely with the NEFMC and NMFS to establish, via the sanctuary, a broad forum representing multiple sources of possible assistance to the NEFMC and NMFS in the attainment of mutual objectives; and will also work with those entities on the impacts of fishing upon other sanctuary resources and other sanctuary users.[6]

What the council claimed was a contradiction between Magnuson and the Sanctuaries Act was in fact a solution to a regulatory gap perceived by some of the principal architects of both laws; most notably Gerry Studds, who in 1993 assumed the chairmanship of the House Merchant Marine and Fisheries Committee.

There was more than a hint in the final environmental impact statement and management plan that overfishing and some degree of habitat disturbance might be occurring within the sanctuary, thereby threatening the long-term viability of fisheries as a resource within the sanctuary. Today, fifteen years after the designation, what was once a hint of things to come has become a reality. In the not-too-distant future, scientists will have enough information to guide what will become a true test of the Solomon-like coordination that lawmakers envisioned would someday be required to integrate public policy.

Dispute over Boundaries

Notwithstanding eloquent statements about such things as resource protection, sustainability, intergovernmental coordination, and the public interest, the creation of new national forests, parks, and wildlife refuges is rarely harmonious. It has not been much different with national marine sanctuaries.

In the case of Stellwagen Bank, the boundary lines debated in the early 1990s were essentially battle lines drawn by governmental and nongovernmental interests in a protracted struggle that continues to this day. Some scholars have attributed the struggle to the "growing pains" of a still relatively young and chronically underfunded federal agency. Those more critical of the process, which in the case of Stellwagen has been underway for more than fifteen years, believe that the very existence of the sanctuary is still a matter of negotiation. This brings chills to those who earnestly believe that the sanctuary needs greater protection and hope to those opposed to any further governmental interference in their use of the area.

The boundary first proposed by NOAA in 1991 encompassed approximately 521 square miles of federal waters, including Stellwagen Bank and a buffer area of about 5 miles in all directions.[7] The area included some of the hot spots for whale watching and some of the areas that had been fished historically. The southeastern corner was adjacent to state waters designated as the Cape Cod Ocean Sanctuary, while the southern border coincided with the seaward limit of the state's Cape Cod Bay Ocean Sanctuary.[8] The western boundary line included portions of Stellwagen Basin and deliberately avoided the Massachusetts Bay Disposal Site (MBDS). By most accounts, it was a modest proposal focused primarily on Stellwagen Bank.

The sanctuary program's rationale for not including the disposal site, which at the time was being relocated a mile or two to the west, was two-fold. First, the planners stated that "inclusion of all or part of the MBDS would conflict with the general NOAA policy against ocean disposal activities in marine sanctuaries." Secondly, "Encompassing the MBDS within the sanctuary is not necessary to protect sanctuary resources or qualities, because, pursuant to their own programs, [the Environmental Protection Agency] and [Corps of Engineers] ocean disposal activities must avoid harm to sanctuary resources."[9]

The principal advocate for a considerably smaller sanctuary was the New England Fisheries Management Council. By a majority vote of its membership, the council endorsed a boundary alternative floated by NOAA and labeled as Boundary Alternative #4. Nearly half the size (436 square miles) of the sanctuary eventually created by Congress, it encompassed the entirety of Stellwagen Bank. The northern and southern boundaries did not coincide with the state's ocean sanctuaries and the eastern boundary was tight up against the edge of the Bank. The western boundary, on the other hand, included more of Stellwagen Basin and the MBDS.

In its 1991 comments on the draft environmental impact statement, the council was critical of plans for the sanctuary without being opposed to its designation, an obvious strategic move given the strong support the proposal had within the same congressional committees that oversaw fisheries management. Council chairman Robert Jones stated forcefully that New England's commercial fishermen wanted no regulatory interference from the sanctuary and remained suspicious that the sanctuary program eventually would undermine the "exclusive authority" over fisheries management conferred upon the council by the Magnuson Act.[10]

Jones went on to state that the smaller sanctuary represented by Boundary Alternative #4 had the support of New England fishermen and that including the MBDS in the sanctuary "will allow closer monitoring, regulation, and possible remediation of an area that could pose significant threats to fish habitat."

Another group calling itself the Stellwagen Bank Commercial Fisheries Cooperative echoed the New England Fisheries Management Council's concerns over the operation of the MBDS, stating that "irregardless of where the western boundary is drawn, water and habitat quality of Stellwagen Basin will be affected by inappropriate uses of the MBDS or inadequate treatment of effluent from the Boston Harbor Outfall Pipe."[11]

While many individual fishermen and fishermen's associations had expressed concerns about the potential impact of oil and gas exploration and sand and gravel mining, the council's chilly endorsement of a small sanctuary quickly led some to conclude that, given the choice, the council would have preferred no sanctuary at all.

Advocates of a larger sanctuary were numerous and included a coalition of environmental, education, and research groups, whale-watching companies, and a smattering of commercial and recreational fishermen calling itself the Stellwagen Bank Coalition.[12] The coalition supported Boundary Alternative #3, which encompassed 927 square miles.[13] In its written comments, it argued that the "national significance and sensitivity of the Stellwagen Bank region clearly demand that it be afforded the strongest possible protection through the largest feasible boundary."[14] The coalition disputed NOAA's contention that its preferred alternative included the entirety of the important local habitats for fishery and marine mammal resources, noting that the movement of these animals varies seasonally and from year to year. Boundary Alternative #3 included additional habitats east of Stellwagen Bank, Tillies Bank, and the southern portion of Jeffreys Ledge.

The northwestern border of Alternative #3 coincided with state waters designated as the North Shore Ocean Sanctuary, while the southeastern corner was adjacent to state waters designated as the Cape Cod Ocean Sanctuary. Finally, the southern border coincided with the seaward limit of the state's Cape Cod Bay Ocean Sanctuary. The object of butting the Stellwagen sanctuary up against the three state ocean sanctuaries was to establish a basis for cooperative ocean management between NOAA and the Commonwealth.

Boundary Alternative #3 shifted the western boundary of the sanctuary even further toward shore than the Fisheries Management Council's proposal, so as to include more of Stellwagen Basin and all of the MBDS. In a rare instance of agreement, the coalition and the council found themselves advocating for more monitoring of activities at the disposal site and another layer of protection.

Disagreement over the MBDS revealed a number of issues that would haunt the planning and management process for years to come. The first of these was the relevance of consensus. Early on, participants in the discussion, annoyingly called "stakeholders," were led to believe that the national marine sanctuary program was built around "consensus decisionmaking," a process much talked about but little understood. On issues of minor significance, it enabled diverse interests to drift slowly toward the center without appearing to have given up much ground. But on the *big* issues (and the MBDS was one of the first to qualify), one of two things happens. Either no decisive action is taken (which may explain why it has taken NOAA fifteen years to update its 1993 management plan) or NOAA relies on the ambiguities of the Sanctuaries Act to shift positions. For NOAA to have insisted that a disposal site was incompatible with the purposes of a sanctuary, while taking little or no action on other incompatible or destructive uses was and continues to be perplexing.

Virtually every environmental and fishing organization in the region thought the disposal site should be included within the boundaries of the sanctuary, as did the Commonwealth of Massachusetts and City of Boston.[15] The underlying regulatory issue was whether existing federal regulatory authority, principally the Ocean Dumping Act (Title I of the Marine Protection, Research, and Sanctuaries Act MPRSA), was sufficient to protect the sanctuary. Under the act, disposal of dredge materials is regulated by the Army Corps of Engineers, while all other disposal activities are regulated by the Environmental Protection Agency. Both are required not to permit activities that endanger "the marine environment" and "ecological systems," but that same prescription applies to all ocean areas. How then was sanctuary designation going to make a difference? Time and again throughout the planning process, this seems to have been the lingering question.

Recognizing that NOAA was again about to become paralyzed by interagency controversy, Gerry Studds and John Kerry pressed their colleagues for swift action. Even before NOAA had completed its lethargic NEPA review, Congress stepped in and passed the Oceans Act of 1992, designating the Stellwagen Bank National Marine Sanctuary and establishing its boundary.[16] President George H. W. Bush signed the bill into law on November 4, 1992.[17]

The final boundary, which remains in effect, delineated a rectangular-shaped area totaling approximately 842 square miles, 321 square miles larger than NOAA had recommended.[18] It resembles Boundary Alternative #3 with its sea-monster bites taken off the northwest and southeast corners where the state ocean sanctuaries adjoin, but the western boundary was shifted to the east, primarily to avoid the MBDS.

The congressionally mandated boundary is likely to stand for the near future, but as researchers learn more about important habitats, boundary adjustments seem inevitable. Indeed, the relocation in 2007 of the Boston shipping lanes, discussed in chapter 7, could be considered an internal boundary, as would any form of ocean zoning that NOAA might implement to further its stewardship objectives.

Chapter 4

If Not Wilderness, What?

The growing demand for natural resources on Stellwagen Bank in the 1980s was only a sampling of the problems of growth that built rapidly after World War II. In his highly popular book, *The Quiet Crisis*, Stewart Udall, who served as Secretary of the Interior under Presidents Kennedy and Johnson, alerted the nation to the need for swift action. "Our accomplishments in minerals and energy, in electronics and aircraft, in autos and agriculture have lifted us to new heights of affluence," he wrote, "but in the process we have lost ground in the attempt to provide a habitat that will, each day, renew the meaning of the human enterprise. . . . It is the seven seas themselves, the one remaining largely unspoiled, untapped resource, which now represent the largest remaining frontier of conservation on this earth. . . . Yet, save for a few farsighted treaties, we have no plan of management for these common resources."[1]

While the seeds of the modern environmental movement had been sown and been well cultivated by the mid-1950s, the 1960s marked the beginning. In less than a decade, public and governmental response to the quiet crisis would be in full swing.

In 1961, Kennedy signed into law a bill he had championed in the U.S. Senate establishing the Cape Cod National Seashore. In his signing remarks, he spoke of the Cape Cod National Seashore becoming but one of a great national system of seashores that he hoped would be protected.[2]

Three years later, Lyndon Johnson signed the Wilderness Act, establishing a national wilderness preservation system that now includes 662 areas comprised of more than 105 million acres of federal land.[3] The Wilderness Act was the outcome of eight years of feverish campaigning by conservationists (the term "environmentalist" would not come into general use for several more years) with a decidedly preservationist bent.[4]

In his special message to Congress on natural beauty in 1965, Johnson spoke broadly about the need for what he called a "new conservation," the object of which should be "not just man's welfare but the dignity of man's spirit."[5] While the focus of the Wilderness Act was entirely terrestrial, soon many would come to see the spiritual, educational, and scientific value of marine wilderness areas.

In 1966, Johnson sought the advice of his Science Advisory Committee on the issue of ocean management raised by Udall and others. The committee's Panel on Oceanography, chaired by Gordon J. F. MacDonald, chairman of UCLA's Institute of Geophysics and Planetary Sciences, found that the government's involvement in the field of oceanography had, in the words of one observer, "evolved into an anarchy of some twenty agencies."[6] The meeting ground at the time was the Interagency Committee on Oceanography, an ad hoc agency within the Executive Office invisible to the general public and generally unaccountable to Congress. The remedy seemed obvious: Create a new agency. The panel advised combining the oceanographic activities of the Environmental Science Services Administration, Geological Survey, Bureaus of Commercial Fisheries and Mines, and Coast Guard. As the title of its report, *Effective Use of the Sea,* made clear, the primary function of the proposed new agency would be to coordinate the nation's exploration and uses of the sea.[7] The panel, however, was not blind to the need to protect and even preserve some areas for research, education, and purely ecological purposes when it also recommended "the establishment of a system of marine wilderness preserves" based on the principles of the Wilderness Act of 1964. The reasons the panel gave for creating such preserves included provision of ecological baselines against which to compare modified areas; preservation of major types of unmodified habitats for research and education in marine sciences; and provision of continuing opportunities for marine wildernes recreation.[8]

Congress immediately picked up on the President's initiative and the thoughts of the Science Advisory Committee about government reorganization by creating the Commission on Marine Science, Engineering, and Resources to examine ways of coordinating and implementing national ocean programs. It became known as the Stratton Commission after its chairman, Julius Stratton, chairman of the Ford Foundation. As many hoped for, the commission took a broad, multidisciplinary approach and in 1969 produced a report entitled *Our Nation and the Sea: A Plan for National Action* that served as a blueprint for ocean policy for many years.[9]

Creation of NOAA

Among the Stratton Commission's many recommendations, the two that were acted upon almost instantly were the establishment of a national program to assist states in managing their coastal zones and the creation of a single agency to coordinate and administer ocean programs. The first of these led to passage of the Coastal Zone Management Act of 1972; the second, in a roundabout fashion, to the creation of NOAA.

The Stratton Commission's recommendation for an oceans agency was modeled after the civilian National Aeronautics and Space Administration (NASA). The basic concept underlying NASA was to elevate the importance of space exploration for scientific and commercial purposes by removing it from the military bureaucracy of the Pentagon. The Stratton Commission called for transferring a number of functions from the Interior and Commerce departments to the new entity and giving it independence, thereby sharpening its focus.

The same year the Stratton Commission report was published, President Nixon turned to Roy Ash, chairman of his Advisory Council on Executive Organization, for advice on whether all federal environmental activities should be unified within one agency.[10] Ash's initial preference was for a single department. James Whitaker, who coordinated White House environment and natural resources policy from 1969 to 1972, recalls that the plan was to replace the Department of the Interior with a new Department of Environment and Natural Resources.[11] Had this plan been adopted, some, if not all, of the oceans programs of the federal government might have fallen to the new cabinet-level department. The plan was met with instant resistance, recalls Whitaker. "We had big fights [over] the cabinet office. You should see a cabinet officer when he's told you're going to take a piece of his department away."

Sensing the President's desire to act quickly, Ash soon changed his mind and in a memorandum to the President dated April of 1970, he came up with a reorganization plan that assigned all the anti-pollution regulatory programs to a single new agency. Meanwhile, Commerce Secretary Maurice Stans was resisting the Stratton Commission's recommendation to shift the Environmental Science Services Administration (ESSA) and its ten thousand employees from Commerce to either a new independent agency or an agency within Interior.

Concerned that a proposal to create one or more new cabinet-level departments might bog down in Congress, Nixon exercised his authority "to promote the better execution of the laws, the more effective management of
the executive branch of its agencies and functions, and the expeditious
administration of the public business" by reshuffling existing environmental programs.[12] In a message to Congress dated July 9, 1970, he unveiled two
reorganization plans.[13] The first established the sub-cabinet-level Environmental Protection Agency (EPA), comprised of functions transferred from
the Departments of the Interior; Health, Education and Welfare; and Agriculture. The second established the National Oceanic and Atmospheric
Administration (NOAA) within the Department of Commerce, comprised
of functions transferred from the Departments of the Interior and Defense
and the National Science Foundation. Under existing reorganization authority at the time, Nixon could create a sub-cabinet-level agency or administration without an act of Congress. In an interview granted many years later,
Whitaker said, "This is how we got EPA and how we got NOAA. The two of
them. Bang, Bang."[14]

One proposal had been to establish NOAA within Interior rather than
Commerce, a move that conceivably would have given the agency more of
a preservation perspective. It has long been believed by government insid-
ers that if any serious consideration was ever given to placing NOAA within
Interior, it quickly evaporated when Interior Secretary Walter Hickel publicly
criticized the Nixon administration's Vietnam War policy after the shooting
of college students at Kent State University. Hickel was fired on Thanksgiving
Eve of 1970 and replaced by former Republican National Committee chairman and four-term Maryland congressman Rogers Morton. By year's end,
the EPA and NOAA were in business.

Despite all the blue-ribbon commission reports and Nixon's reorganization of the federal bureaucracy, within the anarchy of agencies that had been
dealing with the marine environment, preservation was still not a priority.

The Santa Barbara Oil Spill

It would take a singular dramatic event and political action before attitudes
and public policies would begin to change. The event was the blowout, on January 28, 1969, of a Union Oil platform in the Santa Barbara Channel 6 miles
off the coast of Summerland, resulting in the release over a period of eleven

days of 3 million gallons of crude oil. The spill formed an 800-square-mile tarry slick that winds and tides spread out over 35 miles of coastline. There was no loss of human life but the death toll for wildlife included more than thirty-five hundred seabirds.

The blowout was like a shot heard round the nation. The blame was directed largely at Interior for conducting a highly permissive and poorly regulated leasing program. On the West Coast, Senator Alan Cranston immediately introduced legislation to halt all oil and gas drilling in the Santa Barbara Channel, while on the East Coast, Representative Hastings Keith renewed his calls for some form of wilderness designation of Georges Bank.

Investigations of the Santa Barbara blowout largely substantiated claims of lax management. Less than three months after the accident, Interior Secretary Hickel announced the establishment of a 55,000-acre Santa Barbara Channel Ecological Preserve where no oil and gas leasing would be permitted.

If the creation of the preserve was an attempt to appease, it failed. The Santa Barbara oil spill instantly became a nationwide symbol for environmental protest. In fact, the idea of a nationwide teach-in on the environment that led to the first Earth Day only months later on April 22, 1970, first came to Wisconsin Senator Gaylord Nelson while he was returning from an inspection of the Santa Barbara oil spill. He called it a "horrible scene" and joined Cranston and others in the Senate in calling for suspension of oil leasing adjacent to any California state waters designated as sanctuaries.

But Interior held fast and opposed any legislative effort to undermine its authority under the Outer Continental Shelf Lands Act (OCSLA) on the grounds that the act calls for multiple use of the seabed and provides the government with sufficient authority to protect the environment.[15] Not everyone in successive administrations or Congress would agree with this assessment, but with few exceptions, for the next twenty years Interior would successfully defeat or table numerous proposals for no-lease zones, ocean preserves, and sanctuaries.

Definitions

What is a national marine sanctuary? More to the point of this inquiry, what is the Gerry E. Studds Stellwagen Bank National Marine Sanctuary? The questions seem simple enough, but the answers are not. Merely asking the questions tends to evoke confusion and controversy.

For starters, both questions use the word "sanctuary," which is rich in meaning. Of course, one definition of sanctuary is a consecrated place or place of worship. For the early transcendentalists of New England, natural areas provided settings for discovering the spiritual meaning of life. And while setting aside natural areas can be justified for empirically sound reasons such as ensuring biodiversity, equally valid intuitive and spiritual reasons often exist for doing so.

Perhaps a more relevant definition for purposes of this discussion is that of a place of refuge and protection. Applying this definition, national marine sanctuaries could be thought of as the marine equivalents of national wildlife refuges, which exist primarily to safeguard wildlife populations. The well-established National Wildlife Refuge System currently is comprised of 547 areas totaling approximately 95 million acres.[16] Within 317 refuges, hunting, trapping, and fishing are permitted *when they are compatible with the purposes for which the refuge was established* and acquired. Compatibility is determined through a complex process of scientific study and public involvement. Other refuges are managed to protect endangered species and many provide unique opportunities for scientific research.

Yet another definition that circulated in the minds of early proponents of the national marine sanctuary system was that of a wilderness area. Using this definition, the question of what constitutes a marine sanctuary would be clear and unambiguous. Under the Wilderness Act of 1964 wilderness is defined as follows:

A wilderness, in contrast with those areas where man and his works dominate the landscape, is hereby recognized as an area where the earth and its community of life are untrammeled by man, where man himself is a visitor who does not remain. An area of wilderness is further defined to mean in this Act an area of undeveloped Federal land retaining its primeval character and influence, without permanent improvements or human habitation, which is protected and managed so as to preserve its natural conditions and which (1) generally appears to have been affected primarily by the forces of nature, with the imprint of man's work substantially unnoticeable; (2) has outstanding opportunities for solitude or a primitive and unconfined type of recreation; (3) has at least five thousand acres of land or is of sufficient size as to make practicable its preservation and use in an unimpaired condition; and (4) may also contain ecological, geological, or other features of scientific, educational, scenic, or historical value.[17]

While the ideas incorporated in the national wildlife refuge and wilderness systems may apply to marine sanctuaries, a close reading of the National Marine Sanctuaries Act and understanding of its legislative history describes a planning process for a finite number of "special" areas that conceivably might be managed and to some degree protected in a variety of ways. Viewed from this perspective, a national marine sanctuary ultimately is defined by its management plan, and the uses allowed within a sanctuary can be only those that are determined to be compatible with the purposes for which the sanctuary was first designated.

For Stellwagen Bank, the immediate challenge will be to adopt and implement a management plan that fulfills this basic charge. The difficulty will be largely in overcoming a lack of leadership at the highest levels that has plagued the national marine sanctuaries program almost since its inception.

Legislative History

In the late 1960s, congressional interest in some form of ocean preservation was driven largely by public concerns about oil and gas exploration and development along the California coast and on the Georges Bank fishing grounds off the coast of Massachusetts.[18] Representatives Phil Burton (D-Ca.), George Brown (D-Ca.), and Hastings Keith, (D.-Mass.), and Senator Alan Cranston (D-Ca.), introduced one bill after another aimed at limiting Interior's authority over the OCS and creating a system of marine wilderness preserves. But in hearings in both houses, the ideas were met with stiff opposition from industry and Interior. If any thought ever existed that NOAA might be more receptive to preservation had it been folded into Interior, no evidence showed to support it. Interior officials repeatedly argued that ample authority existed under the OCSLA to protect the marine environment.

Congressional interest in the marine environment, however, was not limited to the threat of oil spills. Everything from municipal garbage to industrial wastes was being barged out to sea for dumping. Images of ocean pollution were appearing on the front pages of newspapers and the evening television news. Mercury poisoning of fish already had become a worldwide problem. Even before the ink had dried on the reorganization plan that set up the Environmental Protection Agency, President Nixon turned to his newly created Council on Environmental Quality (CEQ) chaired by Russell Train, former president of the Conservation Foundation, for a solution.[19] CEQ's report

on ocean dumping quickly led to passage in 1972 of a multipurpose piece of
ocean legislation called the Marine Protection, Research, and Sanctuaries Act
(MPRSA).[20]

Title I of the act, which became known as the Ocean Dumping Act, authorized the EPA to regulate ocean dumping of industrial wastes, sewage sludge,
and other wastes through a permit program. Subsequent amendments to
Title I eventually led to a complete prohibition of dumping of sewage sludge,
industrial wastes, and medical wastes at sea. The act also authorized the secretary of the Army to issue permits for the disposal of dredge spoil material at
suitable locations identified by the EPA.

Title II authorized the secretary of commerce to study "the possible long-
range effects of pollution, overfishing, and man-induced changes of ocean
ecosystems." The task would be assigned to the newly created agency, NOAA,
while the EPA was authorized to conduct research on alternatives to ocean
dumping.

Finally, Title III, now known as the National Marine Sanctuaries Act
(NMSA), authorized the secretary of commerce "to identify and designate
as national marine sanctuaries areas of special national significance and to
manage these areas as the National Marine Sanctuary System" (for the complete text of the act, see appendix B).[21] Again, NOAA would be assigned to
the task.

Although the CEQ had called for "protecting those portions of the marine
environment which are biologically most important" and creating "marine
research preserves to protect representative marine ecosystems and to serve
as ecological reference points" (an idea floated earlier by President Johnson's
Science Advisory Council), it appears that Train may have thought this task
should fall to EPA. Interior meanwhile remained firmly opposed to any type
of sanctuary program.

The sanctuaries (not reserves or preserves) language supported by Hastings Keith and others was introduced during the House markup of the bill
by the chair of the House Oceanography Subcommittee of the Merchant
Marine and Fisheries Committee Alton Lennon (D-N.C.). Sanctuaries were
described in broad terms and no prohibitions were made on industrial development of any kind. The language was a far cry from the unambiguous and
poetic lines of the Wilderness Act.

By the time the Marine Protection, Research, and Sanctuaries Act came
up for a floor vote in the House, the sanctuaries provisions of Title III had

been reduced to an innocuous planning process. Even in this weakened form, sanctuaries still were considered by some in the administration and Congress to be a threat to energy development. Among them was the powerful chairman of the Interior Committee, Wayne Aspinall (D-Colo.), who tried deleting Title III entirely with a last-minute floor amendment. In the end, Title III successfully rode the coat tails of the ocean-dumping titles of the act and passed in the House on September 9, 1971, by a vote of 300 to 4.

In the Senate, the sanctuaries program had virtually no friends. The Subcommittee on Oceans and Atmosphere, chaired by Ernest Hollings (D-S.C.), deleted Title III during its markup, and the bill passed 73 to 0. Ironically, Hollings eventually would become a staunch supporter of the national marine sanctuary program. With the sanctuaries program in the House version of the bill but not in the Senate version, it was left to the House–Senate conference committee to reconcile the two bills. As often happens when there is a congressional standoff over one element of a piece of legislation, the debate jumps quantum-like to another element entirely. In this case, it was a jurisdictional squabble between the EPA and Army Corps over the dumping of dredge spoils that diverted attention from the marine sanctuaries provisions of the act. Some months later, the Marine Protection, Research, and Sanctuaries Act emerged from the conference committee more or less in the form it had come out of the House — with Title III. President Nixon signed the bill into law on October 23, 1972.

An Amalgam of Ideas

Lawmakers, administrators, and the general public have been quarreling over the purpose of the National Marine Sanctuaries Act ever since. As William Chandler and Hannah Gillelan of the Marine Conservation Biology Institute noted in their detailed legislative history of the act, what finally emerged from Congress in 1972 was an "amalgam of ideas" and an implementation plan that subordinated substance to process.[22] And to make matters worse, until 1992, when Congress stepped in and designated four sanctuaries, including Stellwagen Bank, the act delegated the entire task of designating sanctuaries to an agency with little experience in public lands management and what many believe is a bias toward resource use.

It should come as no surprise, therefore, that to date only thirteen national marine sanctuaries encompassing less than one-half of one percent of U.S.

waters have been created. And since 2000, there has been a congressional moratorium on the creation of any more.

But for a few visionaries like Massachusetts' Hastings Keith, what Chandler and Gillelan found was that the National Marine Sanctuaries Act was never intended as a landmark piece of ocean preservation legislation. As an organic statute, it needs to be thought of more as a management tool that *presumes* multiple use of the sea. However — and this is when the interaction of public policy and science becomes interesting — the presumption of multiple use may not in all instances fulfill the requirement of the law "to maintain the natural biological communities in the national marine sanctuaries and to protect, and where appropriate, restore and enhance natural habitats, populations, and ecological processes."[23] Through the management planning process, a sanctuary might find it necessary to regulate or even prohibit activities not considered to pose a problem at the time of designation. In the case of national parks, forests, and wildlife refuges, Congress responded to public demand for greater protection of selected areas by passing the Wilderness Act of 1964. In time, a similar process might be applied to national marine sanctuaries or larger and more comprehensive system of marine areas.

PART II

AN INAUSPICIOUS BEGINNING

1992–2007

Chapter 5

An Ocean Runs Through It

In 2001, the National Marine Sanctuary Program (NMSP) developed a monitoring program to assess the condition of its thirteen sanctuaries. While the program acknowledges that "each area has its own concerns and requirements for environmental monitoring," it argues that the "the ecosystem structure and function of all these areas have similarities and are influenced by common factors that interact in comparable ways."[1] Based on this general assumption, NMSP asked each sanctuary a series of questions about water quality, habitat, fishes and marine mammals, and marine archaeological resources derived from the program's overall mission.

State of the Sanctuary

For the Stellwagen Bank sanctuary, the evaluation process began in 2006. To answer the questions, sanctuary staff conferred among themselves and consulted with outside experts. The compilation of their responses was then peer reviewed, published, and quietly released in April 2007 as NOAA's 2007 Condition Report.[2] Taking into account that opinions may vary on the relative importance of the resources under investigation and that measurements of change may vary both in accuracy and degree of significance, the report nevertheless provides resource managers, lawmakers, and the general public with a useful snapshot of the sanctuary.

And the picture is? Not good. Not even not "good," but "fair-to-poor." Of the seventeen questions relating to water quality, habitat, living resources, and maritime archaeological resources, current conditions for Stellwagen Bank were rated "good" only three times, "good-to-fair" four times, "fair" three times, "fair-to-poor" six times, and "poor" once. That amounts to a grade of C− or D+. The questions and answers (summarized) were as follows:

1. Are specific or multiple stressors, including changing oceanographic and atmospheric conditions, affecting water quality? **Status:** good/fair. **Basis for judgment:** Numerous contaminants at low levels.

2. What is the eutrophic condition of sanctuary waters? **Status:** good. **Basis for judgment:** Ongoing monitoring.

3. Do sanctuary waters pose risks to human health? **Status:** good. **Basis for judgment:** Ongoing monitoring.

4. What are the levels of human activities that may influence [water quality]? **Status:** good/fair. **Basis for judgment:** Boston outfall and vessel discharges.

5. What are the abundance and distribution of major habitat types? **Status:** Fair. **Basis for judgment:** Alteration of microhabitat due to bottom dragging and dredging.

6. What is the condition of biologically structured habitats? **Status:** fair/poor. **Basis for judgment:** Fishing gear impacts.

7. What are the contaminant concentrations in sanctuary habitats? **Status:** good/fair. **Basis for judgment:** Limited monitoring results.

8. What are the levels of human activities that may influence habitat quality? **Status:** fair/poor and declining. **Basis for judgment:** Fishing gear impacts and shipping.

9. What is the status of biodiversity? **Status:** fair/poor. **Basis for judgment:** Long-term changes in fish diversity, but improving.

10. What is the status of environmentally sustainable fishing? **Status:** fair/poor. **Basis for judgment:** Scientific assessments of regional and local groundfish populations.

11. What is the status of nonindigenous species? **Status:** good/fair, but declining. **Basis for judgment:** Recent invasives discovered.

12. What is the status of key species? **Status:** fair/poor. **Basis for judgment:** Cod (keystone species) and sand lance (key species).

13. What is the condition or health of key species? **Status:** fair. **Basis for judgment:** Ship strikes and entanglement of whales.

14. What are the levels of human activities that may influence living resource quality? **Status:** fair/poor. **Basis for judgment:** Stable levels of activity.

15. What is the integrity of known maritime archaeological resources? **Status:** fair but declining. **Basis for judgment:** Fishing gear impacts.

16. Do known maritime archaeological resources pose an environmental hazard? **Status:** good. **Basis for judgment:** Lack of hazardous cargoes.

17. What are the levels of human activities that may influence maritime archaeological resource quality? **Status:** poor and declining. **Basis for judgment:** Fishing gear impacts.[3]

For many close to the machinations and politics of sanctuary planning and management, the very un-sanctuary-like report card came as no surprise. Among those who had expected designation of this "special place" called Stellwagen Bank to lead to innovative ways of protecting the marine environment, the sanctuary has been a major disappointment. The multiple-use management principles underlying both the National Marine Sanctuaries Act and the designation of Stellwagen Bank have buttressed a laissez-faire approach to most commercial activities within the sanctuary. With the exception of the highly publicized discovery of three historic shipwrecks, the steamship *Portland* and the schooners *Frank A. Palmer* and *Louise B. Crary*, the sanctuary has attracted little public attention.

Until the issuance of the Condition Report, the general public had little idea of what was happening in this still relatively new, if not novel, federally protected area. The *Boston Globe*'s coverage of the Condition Report, for which there was little follow-up, nevertheless sounded an alarm. Its headline read, "Humans a threat to ocean preserve — Stellwagen Bank deemed at Risk," and it placed much of the blame on the sanctuary program itself. "Instead of creating an underwater park," the *Globe* quoted critics as saying, "its protectors have allowed the bank to become an industrial zone, where heavy fishing nets scrape the sea bottom to disrupt habitat for fish that are struggling to recover from overfishing. The nets can also tear apart historic shipwrecks resting on the sea bottom. Whales that feed in Stellwagen are in danger of becoming struck by tankers and other large ships that pass through its waters or of being harassed by some of the more than 1 million whale watchers who visit each year."[4]

Senator John Kerry told the *Globe* that "these latest findings are unacceptable. We must take action now in order to address the problems in the sanctuary, so we can get back on the path toward preserving the marine and ecology health of Massachusetts Bay."[5] Outraged as he may have been, the senator did not offer any suggestions about how NOAA might get "back on the path."

In one respect, the sanctuary's self-evaluation may have been extreme in that it overlooked what might have been the state of the sanctuary had Congress not prohibited sand and gravel mining and drilling in 1992 when the sanctuary was designated. In other words, conditions could be worse.

The Condition Report begins with the guarded assessment that "most water quality parameters at Stellwagen Bank appear to suggest relatively good conditions." "Appear" and "suggest" are qualifiers that essentially mean that considerably more monitoring and research are needed. The report continues:

> Habitat quality, on the other hand, has deteriorated over many years, primarily as a result of long-term use of bottom dragging gear to catch fish. . . . Living resource conditions have followed trends similar to those of habitats, and are generally considered to be in fair or fair-to-poor condition. And while the abundance and diversity of bottom dwelling communities may improve with fishing regulations, surface dwelling marine mammals are at considerable risk from strikes by increasing vessel traffic in New England, from entanglement from lines attached to fishing gear, and noise disturbance from increasing vessel traffic. The principal threat to maritime archaeological resources in the sanctuary comes from contact by bottom dragging gear.[6]

Chapters 6 through 9 will examine some of the key findings of the Condition Report relating to habitat, biodiversity, and marine mammals in more detail. The balance of this chapter examines the various influences on the water quality of the sanctuary.

The Boston Outfall

Foremost on the minds of many researchers and downstream citizens during the planning and design phases of the Boston Harbor cleanup during the 1990s was the possibility of increased eutrophication and contaminant loading, resulting from the daily discharge of approximately 360 million gallons of treated wastewater into Massachusetts Bay 12 miles west of the sanctuary. Legal and political challenges to the actual location of the Boston Outfall were dismissed largely based on computer models used to simulate effluent transport and dilution.

Since the outfall became operational on September 6, 2000, water-quality studies conducted as a condition of the EPA discharge permit issued to the Massachusetts Water Resources Authority (MWRA) consistently have shown that the effluent is diluted quickly, as predicted. The MWRA monitoring program is ongoing and periodically reviewed by an independent team of scientists and public interest groups. Meanwhile, the cleanup of Boston Harbor has been nothing less than miraculous.

One scientist in the region who continues to reserve judgment on the matter is Charles "Stormy" Mayo at the Provincetown Center for Coastal Studies (PCCS). He has been studying the resource base of Cape Cod and Massachusetts Bays and foraging behavior of right whales for more than a quarter of a century. And for several years with partial funding from the Massachusetts Environmental Trust, whose revenues are generated in part from the sale of automobile license plates depicting a breaching right whale, Mayo and his team examined the effects of the outfall on the abundance and distribution of zooplankton, specifically the crustaceans known as copepods, which are the major food source of right whales.

After four years of study, the PCCS researchers reported that they had found no clear changes. But Mayo is quick to add that "that may just be because our time series was so short that we could not 'see' the effect of the outfall when measuring the variations in zooplankton cluttered by inter-annual, and other natural, variability."[7]

"My take," continues Mayo, "is that the outfall then and now has an effect. How can it not? We just might be shocked at what has happened here with respect to zooplankton and phytoplankton, but we cannot pin such influences down because of the immense changes that naturally occur in the background. This is an immense problem when you think of it, because it opens the door to the kind of gradualism in the despoiling of the coastal environment that we have seen: Any one influence cannot be documented, but the addition of all of them is huge."

Regional Influences

This nagging and common-sense concern about the small but cumulative effects of discharging large volumes of fresh water and effluent into the bay was clearly on the minds of the MWRA in the fall of 2000 just as the outfall began operation, as abnormally high levels of chlorophyll were being reported at MWRA's monitoring stations in the bay. Satellite imagery quickly confirmed the existence of a region-wide algal bloom of the common nuisance phytoplankton *Phaeocystis* extending from the Bay of Fundy to New Jersey. The fact that the bloom was regional clearly eliminated any causal link to the outfall. But was an outfall effect within the bay being lost in the enormity of the bloom?

Over and over, we are reminded that the Stellwagen Bank National Marine Sanctuary is a relatively small area representing only 2 percent of the Gulf of Maine.[8] Much within the sanctuary is affected and almost everything is explained by first understanding that an ocean runs throughout it. The water quality of the sanctuary, good or bad, is essentially the water quality of the off-shore waters of the Gulf.

The "normal" nutrient cycle throughout Massachusetts and Cape Cod bays begins in the spring, with rising water temperatures and increasing sunlight supporting a rapid growth of plankton taking up nutrients that are swept up to the surface by upwellings and winter storms. Spring blooms of phytoplankton turn the bays a dark green color, a phenomenon any school-child on a whale watch instantly comments upon when any large whale with white markings rises to the surface. As the season wears on and temperatures continue to rise, a thermocline or boundary is formed between the warmer, lighter surface waters and colder, heavier subsurface waters. By summertime, the water column is fully stratified and except during major storms mixing slows down. As temperatures drop and light diminishes in the fall, phyto-plankton photosynthesis slows down and eventually stops. The phytoplank-ton then die and sink to the bottom, where they break down into inorganic nutrients that will be recycled to the surface as the water column overturns throughout the late fall and winter.

Just as the weather is difficult to predict, the nutrient cycle in Massachu-setts and Cape Cod Bays is never text-book perfect. When things are seem-ingly out of whack, more often than not they rearrange themselves and create what Mayo has called a "condition of dynamic equilibrium in which contin-ual change is the essence of a system that only appears changeless."[9]

Phaeocystis blooms occur frequently during this "normal" seasonal cycle of the Massachusetts and Cape Cod bays. In moderation, there is not much to worry about. But an explosive spring bloom that sucks up nutrients like a huge vacuum cleaner upsets the food web. Given all the natural variabil-ity of the system, scientists are hard-pressed to explain the structure of the food web in fine detail. Nevertheless, *Phaeocystis* is considered a nuisance alga because it is capable of messing up the system.

A fall bloom like the one in 2000 is uncommon and potentially even more troublesome, as it is the time of year when right whales begin arriving. By out-competing other species of phytoplankton that are better sources of food for zooplankton upon which right whales depend, an overabundance of *Phaeo-cystis* could have a negative impact on the whales' foraging requirements.

In any event, by the winter and spring of 2001, chlorophyll levels had declined to levels lower than in the previous two years. The bloom had had no observable effect on conditions within the sanctuary or on right whale abundance or distribution. MWRA was relieved to conclude that no evidence linked the bloom to the Boston Outfall.[10] Scientists remained unsure how to explain the fall bloom of 2000 and could only deduce that it had something to do with an area-wide fluctuation in nutrient levels.

Red Tides

Nutrient enrichment is especially worrisome because it is a factor in the development of harmful algal blooms (HABs), often referred to as "red tides" because of the pigmentation of certain species of algae. However, not all blooms are red or reddish-brown and not all red tides are harmful, so scientists prefer the term HAB. In fact, most species of algae or phytoplankton are not harmful and their importance to the marine ecosystem is beyond measure. Capable of taking up tremendous amounts of carbon and nutrients, they comprise the base of the food web.

A few dozen species of algae, however, produce minute amounts of neurotoxins that when concentrated and ingested can cause die-offs of shellfish, fish, seabirds, and marine mammals. Humans who eat contaminated fish or shellfish can experience neurological damage or die as well.

Alarms went off throughout the Gulf of Maine in the spring of 2005 when a major HAB event involving the toxic dinoflagellate *Alexandrium* occurred. By late spring, it had forced the closure of shellfish beds from the Bay of Fundy to Narragansett Bay. The loss to the New England seafood industry was estimated to be in the range of $50 million.

The bloom was first reported by Don Anderson, director of the Coastal Ocean Institute at the Woods Hole Oceanographic Institution and one of the world's leading authorities on marine biotoxins and HABs. He and his team have created a regional observation and modeling program for the Gulf of Maine (including Stellwagen Bank) and adjacent shelf waters. These days, the focus of his research has shifted away from the blooms themselves, which can occur almost too rapidly to observe, to *Alexandrium* cysts. By locating major cyst beds and learning more about what triggers a bloom, Anderson hopes to be able to forecast algal blooms and provide resource managers with an early warning system.

Subsequent to the 2005 event, which began in the water column above previously known cyst beds along the southern coast of Maine, Anderson found a high concentration of *Alexandrium* cysts in the sediments of the sanctuary. This has led to speculation about future blooms in the sanctuary and what impact they might have on living marine resources. There has even been some speculation that such blooms might be enhanced or accelerated by effluent from the Boston Outfall. The 2005 event was too large for Anderson and his team to have teased out of the data a discrete "outfall effect" but the possibility has not been ruled out.

Chemical Contaminants

Yet another influence on both water quality and habitat is the resuspension and redistribution of chemical contaminants historically dumped in Boston Harbor and at the Massachusetts Bay Disposal Site located just west of the sanctuary. Here the news is good. A regional study recently conducted as part of the NOAA National Status and Trends Bioeffects and Benthic Surveillance Programs contrasted 2004 data with historical data from the MWRA on concentrations of selected metals (cadmium and lead) and organics (PCBs and DDT). The areas sampled included Boston Harbor, Massachusetts Bay, Cape Cod Bay, the area between the two bays, and Stellwagen Bank. Contaminant concentrations in the sanctuary were found to be the lowest and conditions appeared to be stable.[11]

But "stable" is a relative term. The contaminants initially dissolved in seawater and efficiently absorbed by the kinds of fine-grained particles found in the silts and muddy bottoms of the sanctuary can be easily resuspended by winter storms and winds from the northeast. Michael Bothner, a geochemical oceanographer with the U.S. Geological Survey (USGS) in Woods Hole, and his colleagues at USGS describe the sediments as "a lingering source of contamination."[12]

Bothner is at the center of a multidisciplinary research effort to assess the fate of contaminants in the coastal waters of the region. The critical element of this research has been sea-floor mapping of western Massachusetts Bay and the sanctuary. The maps are based on high-resolution, multi-beam, echo-sounding surveys that show the distribution of bottom sediment in relation to topography. When combined with computer models that simulate the effects of wind, currents, and tides, the USGS research program is able to monitor sediment transport.[13]

The redistribution of sediments can be both beneficial and detrimental, as geochemical studies of oxygen, radioactive isotopes, and metal have shown. In instances where contaminants are mixed rapidly, they can be diluted and transported out of an area by currents and tides. Or the sediments may be redeposited only centimeters away. This can occur, explains Bothner, in the case of certain benthic organisms, such as worms, feeding and defecating in the sediments (a process known as bioturbation), diluting the contaminants in the process. However, "for contaminants that are dangerous at even low concentrations, the downward mixing [from bioturbation] could be an environmental detriment because it transports the contaminants below the zone of normal resuspension and subsequent transport away from the near-shore environment."[14]

Effluent Dumping

The NOAA Condition Report also briefly examined a number of trends that may warrant management attention in the near future. The one most often discussed among sanctuary defenders is the growing number of cruise ships that pass through the sanctuary. These huge floating cities currently are allowed to discharge biodegradable effluent. Although the environmental impact of this practice has not been researched, most observers feel the sheer volume of the discharge violates the intent of the Clean Water and National Marine Sanctuaries Acts. Ongoing effluent dumping from smaller commercial, recreational, research, and educational vessels, including the entire whale-watching fleet, also raises issues of stewardship responsibilities.

What is significant about all of these potentially negative impacts on the water quality of the sanctuary is their regional scale, reinforcing the spatial and temporal realities of the sanctuary being part of the larger Gulf of Maine ecosystem and that its water quality for the most part is not something the sanctuary itself can manage.

The ultimate protection of the sanctuary's water quality will depend on larger and more comprehensive monitoring programs, such as those being conducted by Anderson, the MWRA, and a program still under development by the University of Maine called GoMOOS, short for the Gulf of Maine Ocean Observing System. At the same time, if water quality is the single most critical aspect of the sanctuary, the sanctuary ought to have its own monitoring capacity, something that has been a budgetary issue for years.

Chapter 6

Business as Usual

While some in Congress may have envisioned national marine sanctuaries as the marine equivalents of parks, refuges, or wilderness areas, early proponents of Stellwagen Bank becoming a sanctuary were almost unanimous in their belief that recreational and commercial fishing, including fishing for shellfish and invertebrates, were compatible uses — at least in principle.[1] The original designation bills introduced by Gerry Studds and John Kerry clearly were targeted at prohibiting sand and gravel mining and other industrial activities — in part to protect fishing activity. It is equally clear from their strident records on sustainable fisheries that by allowing fishing activity to continue, they were not condoning fishing practices that would deteriorate the marine environment and ultimately undermine the future of the industry.[2]

To allay the concerns of fishing interests that sanctuary designation might lead to stringent gear restrictions, the final regulations issued by NOAA not only listed fishing as an allowed activity but exempted what it termed "traditional fishing" methods from the prohibition against "dredging or otherwise altering the seabed of the Sanctuary." Traditional fishing was vaguely defined as "commercial or recreational fishing methods which have been conducted in the past." By "past" NOAA was not referring to colonial times or for that matter to the first half of the twentieth century. The intent quite clearly was to allow the continued use of bottom trawls that in the post–World War II era became the tools of the industry for catching cod, haddock, flounder, and other groundfish.

By exempting "traditional fishing" from the prohibition within the sanctuary against significant alteration of the seabed, NOAA set a semantic and regulatory trap that inevitably would spring on both the sanctuary program and the fishing industry. At that point, fishing by such methods would be determined to be in violation (and arguably already has violated) one of the central purposes of the National Marine Sanctuaries Act: namely, "to maintain the natural biological communities in the national marine sanctuaries, and to protect, and, where appropriate, restore and enhance natural habitats, populations, and ecological processes."[3]

The most commonly used trawl in New England, accounting for more than 50 percent of the gear types used on Stellwagen Bank, is the otter trawl. The otter trawl consists of a large conical net that is towed along the seafloor to catch bottom-dwelling fish such as cod, haddock, flounder, pollock, redfish, and other groundfish species. The mouth of the net is held open vertically by a series of floats and weights, while heavy "otter boards" or trawl doors often equipped with a steel sole for good contact with the seafloor control the horizontal opening.

Impacts of Fishing Gear

The trawls are designed to scrape the seafloor and stir up sediments that startle their prey into the net. In the process, the trawls also dislodge and crush tons of plants and animals such as sponges, hydroids, urchins, sea squirts, and level sedimentary structures such as sand waves and depressions that provide refuge for young fish. No less of an authority than the noted undersea explorer Sylvia Earle, who served briefly as NOAA's chief scientist, has described trawling to be "so obviously destructive it's a no-brainer."[4]

In 2002, the Ocean Studies Board of the National Research Council, based on an extensive review of scientific literature concluded the following:

> Trawling and dredging can reduce habitat complexity by removing or damaging the biological and physical structures of the seafloor. The extent of the initial effects and the rate of recovery depend on the habitat stability. The more stable biogenic (i.e., of biological origin), gravel, and mud habitats experience the greatest changes and have the slowest recovery rates. In contrast, less consolidated coarse sediments in areas of high natural disturbance show fewer initial effects. Because those habitats tend to be populated by opportunistic species that recolonize more rapidly, recovery is faster as well. Significant alterations to habitat can cause changes in the associated biological communities, potentially altering the composition and productivity of fish communities that depend on seafloor habitats for food and refuge.[5]

During the early 1990s, as fish stocks continued to plummet and just as the sanctuary came into existence, the concerns of scientists and managers alike finally were reflected in public policy. The 1996 amendments to the Magnuson-Stevens Act required regional fishery management councils to identify essential fish habitats (EFHs), address the effects of fishing on those areas, and takes steps to encourage habitat conservation and enhancement.

While the impact of fishing gear on fish populations should remain a fisheries management and regulatory concern, the responsibilities and concerns of the sanctuary's managers extend to the entire biogenic and sedimentary structure of the seafloor. Peter Auster, science director of NOAA's National Undersea Research Center at the University of Connecticut at Avery Point, has been studying the seafloor of the sanctuary for the past dozen years and has documented dramatic alteration of the physical structure or complexity of benthic habitats. In his various writings and presentations, Auster repeatedly argues that the metrics for determining ecological integrity are not limited to commercial fisheries.

> Impacts of fishing gear have to be understood not simply in terms of fishing gear, have to be understood not simply in terms of removal of targeted species, but also in terms of their impact on ecosystem productivity. Productivity has a strict biological definition but, in a broader ecosystem-based management sense, it includes human values and a vision of what the fishery should produce and what degree of biodiversity should be maintained in the system.[6]

Otter trawls are not the only mobile gear altering the physical structure of the sanctuary. With the help of side-scan sonar and high-resolution photography obtained from small remotely operated and manned submarines, Auster and his colleagues have documented the impact of scallop dredge gear on sand waves and ripples and the smoothing of shell beds. Scallopers are quick to protest that strong storms from the northeast are the primary cause of bottom disturbance, but Auster replies that these disturbances "do not occur every year. By contrast, mobile fishing gear is deployed on the bank on a nearly daily basis."

There is little reasonable doubt at this time that the benthic habitat of Stellwagen Bank has been altered significantly. The ongoing debate is over how much alteration is acceptable. No fish or invertebrate species have gone extinct. For some scientists, managers, and fishermen—even though patterns of dominance have changed—mere avoidance of extinction may be an acceptable standard.

For others like Auster, this approach to management—living on the edge of extinction, so to speak—can only lead to what biologist Garrett Hardin in 1968 metaphorically called the tragedy of the commons.[7] Referring to a rational herdsman sharing a common pasture—though he might just as well have described the actions of a rational fisherman—the scenario goes as follows:

> The only sensible course is to add another animal to his herd. And another; and another. . . . But this is the conclusion reached by each and every rational herdsman sharing a commons. Therein is the tragedy. Each man is locked into a system that compels him to increase his herd without limit—in a world that is limited. Ruin is the destination toward which all men rush, each pursuing his own best interest in a society that believes in the freedom of the commons. Freedom in a commons brings ruin to all. . . .
>
> Likewise, the oceans of the world continue to suffer from the survival of the philosophy of the commons. Maritime nations still respond automatically to the shibboleth of the "freedom of the seas." Professing to believe in "the inexhaustible resources of the oceans," they bring species after species of fish and whales closer to extinction.[8]

While the NOAA Condition Report rates habitat quality within the sanctuary as only fair or fair-to-poor, Craig MacDonald, the sanctuary's superintendent since 2001, is still holding out for more definitive science before taking action against trawling and dredging. That might come soon enough as the findings of a long-term study called the Seafloor Habitat Recovery and Monitoring Project (SHRMP) are analyzed.

SHRMP is an ongoing collaboration between the sanctuary and the Pfleger Institute of Environmental Research involving the use of autonomous underwater vehicles (AUVs) and video drift cameras. The project was initiated in 1998 following the New England Fisheries Management Council's creation of the Western Gulf of Maine Closure Area (WGoMCA) as an EFH in response to the Sustainable Fisheries Act. The area includes a triangular section of the sanctuary along its eastern boundary that encompasses 22 percent of the total area of the sanctuary. It is a marine scientist's dream come true, affording a unique opportunity to observe the recovery of an area previously actively fished for cod, haddock, flatfish, and other groundfish. The research team has also set up a series of paired stations that enable them to compare habitat conditions in the sanctuary both within and outside the closed area.

The damaging effects of trawls are not limited to ocean habitats but include potential and actual disturbance of numerous historic resources, notably several recently discovered shipwrecks. The *Paul Palmer*, a five-masted schooner that caught fire and sank off Highland Light in 1913, has been "heavily degraded" by trawling activity, according to the sanctuary's staff. Some of the historic eastern-rig dragger wrecks located by the sanctuary also have been damaged by the nets and trawl doors of modern trawlers.

It is illegal to move, remove, or injure historic resources within the sanctuary, a prohibition that certainly would apply to shipwrecks now listed on the National Register of Historic Places. But, as with many sanctuary regulations, there is the NOAA equivalent of Catch 22: the "traditional fishing" exemption.

The Hibernia Transatlantic Project

The Seafloor Habitat Recovery and Monitoring Project (SHRMP) also has been expanded to monitor habitat recovery from the Hibernia Transatlantic Project, a transatlantic fiber-optic cable across the sanctuary, laid by the company 360networks, inc. (formerly Worldwide Fiber), a Canadian firm based in Vancouver.[9] Although drilling into, dredging, or otherwise altering the seabed of the sanctuary is prohibited, NOAA has discretionary authority to approve otherwise prohibited activities that are determined to have "only negligible short-term adverse effects on Sanctuary resources."[10]

Lacking specific regulations applicable to the Hibernia Transatlantic Project, in 2000 NOAA rushed through revised regulations specific to underwater cables and within months signed off on a permit issued by the Army Corps of Engineers for the laying of a cable from Boston to Ireland traversing 12 miles of the sanctuary along its northern border. NOAA's environmental assessment concluded that "the temporary disturbance of sediments caused by installation of the cable should have no significant effect on water quality and should have no harm to marine biota from increased levels of toxicants."[11]

The environmental assessment considered a northern alternative that would have avoided the sanctuary altogether, but it would have required going around Jeffreys Ledge and laying 64 miles of additional cable, of which about 1 mile would have been on top of bedrock and exposed. In the final analysis, NOAA approved the less-costly alternative on the grounds that it would cause only "temporary disturbance" to the sanctuary. Side-scan sonar images collected in 2006, however, show the trench produced during the cable burial is still visible along most of its path through the sanctuary. About 32 feet of cable is exposed.

While the impact of the cable is probably less than that made by a scallop dragger in a single day, the case illustrates a propensity among NOAA administrators to practice multiple-use management at the risk of undermining the primary goal of the sanctuary program: to protect resources for future generations. The situation is not unlike those facing other federal land management agencies every year, but unlike the Forest Service, Fish and Wildlife Service, or National Park Service, the sanctuary has not been able to figure out a publicly transparent way of determining what activities are compatible with its basic mission. Are there areas within the Stellwagen Bank National Marine Sanctuary that ought to be treated as wilderness areas or no-take zones?

In the case of the fiber optic cable, the applicant's preferred alternative was to cross the sanctuary. It was the least-costly and the shortest route between two points. But a longer and presumably more costly northern alternative that avoided the sanctuary was determined by NOAA to be technically feasible. Why then was it not NOAA's preferred alternative? Where were the Keep Out signs?

The Magnuson-Stevens Act

Nothing better illustrates the differences between the administration of the National Marine Sanctuaries Act and the Magnuson-Stevens Fishery Conservation and Management Act than the current status and trends regarding biodiversity, extracted species, and key species within the boundaries of the Stellwagen Bank National Marine Sanctuary.

The National Marine Sanctuaries Act is site-specific. The Magnuson-Stevens Act is regional in scope. Both are administered by NOAA, albeit by separate agencies, although the official word from headquarters is that there is only one NOAA policy in the Gulf of Maine. Translated, this means that the two acts are intended to complement one another. But on any given day, the topics of primary concern, even the language used at the regional offices of the National Marine Fisheries Service (NMFS, aka NOAA Fisheries Service) and the Stellwagen Bank National Marine Sanctuary (SBNMS) are likely to be quite different.[12] It is a classic example of scientific and bureaucratic cross-speak. The fisheries scientists and managers are focused on population dynamics in a desperate effort to restore depleted New England fisheries. The sanctuary scientists and managers, on the other hand, are focused on biodiversity.

The Magnuson Act (later amended and now called the Magnuson-Stevens Act) was passed in 1976, four years after the Sanctuaries Act, and is the primary law dealing with fishing in federal waters, which are defined as extending seaward 200 miles from the edge of state waters (generally 3 miles offshore). Following a 1983 proclamation by President Reagan, this area became known as the Exclusive Economic Zone (EEZ). Foreign fishing, which by the 1970s accounted for nearly 75 percent of the fish caught off the U.S. coastline, was prohibited within the EEZ except by international agreement.

At the same time, Magnuson-Stevens established a system of fisheries management and conservation built on the principle of consensus that is administered by eight regional fishery management councils. For the Gulf of Maine (including Stellwagen Bank), Georges Bank, and southern New England, management authority rests primarily with the New England Fishery Management Council and overlaps with the Mid-Atlantic Council for some species.

Each management council is charged with preparing management plans and regulations for the fisheries under its jurisdiction. The plans and proposed regulations are subject to approval by the secretary of the Department of Commerce. If approved, NMFS then must issue regulations to implement the plan. The process has been criticized widely for being slow and cumbersome and dominated by industry interests.

To date, the New England Fishery Management Council has developed nine management plans for Northeast multi-species groundfish (including cod, haddock, and flounder), scallop, monkfish, herring, small-mesh multi-species (including whiting and two stocks of hake), red crab, and the Northeast skate complex. Two additional plans for monkfish and spiny dogfish have been prepared jointly with the Mid-Atlantic Council.

The key management principle guiding the council's work is optimum yield, which is defined as "the amount of fish which will provide the greatest overall benefit to the Nation particularly with respect to food production and recreational opportunity, and taking into account the protection of marine ecosystems."[13] Under the best of circumstances, pursuit of optimum yield requires a delicate balance of economic, social, and ecological factors. The best of circumstances likely would include a management regime guided by a wealth of science, enlightened self-interests, an equitable allocation of fishing rights, and a superabundance of fish. Under more realistic conditions — which presently include insufficient science, depleted fishing stocks, collective denial of the severity of the crisis, and many fishermen struggling to make a living — the balance scales are almost always tilted away from ecological factors.

Once the foreign fleets moved out, the U.S. fleets grew rapidly with encouragement and financial assistance in the form of loan guarantees and tax incentives from the federal government. By 1991, fifteen years after the passage of the Magnuson Act, overfishing, for which the foreigners had been blamed, had become an alarming domestic crisis. In the first ten years, groundfish stocks plummeted by 65 percent. By 1989, cod, haddock, and yellowtail flounder were declared to be so overfished that even some fishermen began turning to lawmakers for legislative relief.

The Groundfish Crisis Continues

Gerry Studds, who had been a central figure in the drafting and passage of both the Sanctuaries Act and Magnuson-Stevens Act, responded with the Groundfish Restoration Act, aimed at setting severe restriction on the industry. Mark Forest, an aide to Studds at the time and currently chief of staff for Representative William Delahunt (D-Mass.) who succeeded Studds, recalled recently how Studds was "amazed that the industry was in denial for so long." "The Provincetown fleet had shrunk from about sixty or seventy boats in 1980 to half as many in the early nineties and most of them were trying to get out of the business. The New Bedford Fleet was able to hang in but you could still see the trend from the early eighties — everything was going in the wrong direction."[14] Studds, who had long been considered one of the fishing industry's best friends in Congress, took a lot of heat for introducing the bill but refused to back off, certain that the long-term economic interests of his constituents depended on creating a sustainable fishery, which in the short run meant making huge sacrifices. But the fleets were still in denial, opposition built rapidly, and the bill never made it out of committee.

As if the pending outcome had not been obvious to anyone who cared to examine the issue, only a year later the once-bountiful Canadian cod fishery was declared to be on the brink of extinction, forcing the government to impose a moratorium in 1992 — the same year the sanctuary was created. Since that time, the Canadian cod fishery has not rebounded and most experts now believe it may never recover.

In 1991, just as the Canadian crisis came to a head and interest in creating marine sanctuaries was building on the East and West coasts, the Conservation Law Foundation filed an historic lawsuit against NMFS, alleging that the agency had approved a management plan submitted by the New England Fisheries Management Council that did little to protect New England groundfish from overfishing. In a settlement, NMFS was required to come up with a new plan aimed at cutting mortality by 50 percent over five years. The settlement led to stricter regulations and unprecedented closures of fisheries, but the regulations were again slow to emerge and proved to be too little too late. Most groundfish stocks continued to plummet.

The Sustainable Fisheries Act

During reauthorization of the Magnuson-Stevens Act in 1996, Congress turned the valves another turn or two tighter with passage of the Sustainable Fisheries Act. The law specifically required that overfishing be regulated and that overfished stocks be rebuilt. And for those who did not understand the earlier intent of Magnuson-Stevens, the Sustainable Fisheries Act left no doubt as to what constituted overfishing or optimum yield, and, most importantly, it directed NMFS to begin protecting essential fish habitats for spawning, breeding, feeding, or growth to maturity.

"The original act conceived that the fishing industry would have a vested interest to protect the resource," says Forest. This helps explain the reliance on consensus decisionmaking within the regional councils; something Studds later would admit had been a mistake.[15] The Sustainable Fisheries Act did nothing to wrest control of the planning process from the councils, but by mandating a halt to overfishing recovery, it created a default position for NMFS to fall back on if the plans prepared by the councils were inadequate.

Following passage of the Sustainable Fisheries Act, the New England Fisheries Management Council spent two years wrangling over how to amend its multi-species management plan before stricter regulations were set in place. Still, the stock of New England groundfish continued to decline.

In 2001, the Conservation Law Foundation again concluded that the rebuilding plans were inadequate and sued NMFS for allegedly violating the overfishing, stock rebuilding, and bycatch provisions of Magnuson-Stevens, as amended by the Sustainable Fisheries Act.[16] A year later, the U.S. District Court for the District of Columbia upheld the allegations. The lawsuit led to another settlement, the development of an amended management plan known as Amendment 13, and even tighter regulations that theoretically comply with the Sustainable Fisheries Act. Amendment 13 did not take effect until May 2004. In the interim, Georges Bank cod had declined by another 25 percent.[17]

It is too early to tell if Amendment 13 is working. The council is already teasing recent data showing juvenile cod populations trending slowly upward and reports have been published indicating that haddock and yellowtail flounder populations are rebounding. The goal of Amendment 13, if faithfully implemented, is sustainability, but past practice and the politics of fisheries management continue to point toward a state of commercial extinction.[18]

Managing Biological Communities

While the legal responsibility for fisheries management rests with the New England Fisheries Management Council and NMFS, the sanctuary has broad responsibility for resource protection, including the restoration and maintenance of biological communities and ecological processes within the sanctuary. Specific concerns in this regard include the diversity, abundance, and size range of fish, including sand lance and herring, which serve as important prey for marine mammals.

With respect to size, the NOAA Condition Report concludes, based on an analysis of fifteen species included in NMFS research trawl data (1963–2000) from within the sanctuary, that all fifteen species showed decreasing trends in maximum length.[19] For seven of the species (white hake, goosefish, winter flounder, silver hake, cod, yellowtail flounder, and haddock), the decreases in length ranged from 15 to 49 percent.[20] The exact effect of these reductions in the size of fish within the sanctuary is unknown, but recent scientific studies have demonstrated that excessive removal of the largest predators within an ecosystem can result in a cascading effect through the lower (trophic) levels of the food web, thereby reducing its ecological integrity. In one study of the eastern Scotian Shelf ecosystem off Nova Scotia directed by Kenneth Frank of the Bedford Institute of Oceanography, a trophic cascade involving four trophic levels and nutrients was directly attributed to overfishing, primarily of cod.[21] The scientific literature on the phenomenon concludes that ecosystems that have experienced a trophic cascade generally are found to have low species diversity and simplified food webs.

Continued research will be required to monitor the effects of overfishing and to determine if steps can be taken to reverse current trends.

Whether or not this happens, if one of the results of overfishing throughout the Gulf of Maine has been a significant deterioration of biological communities and ecological processes within the sanctuary, the fisheries side of NOAA theoretically could be held accountable for violating the sanctuary side of NOAA's mandate to protect sanctuary resources.

Chapter 7

Whales Ho!

To the casual observer aboard a whale-watch vessel or ferry gazing over the blue-green water under a clear sky with the towers of Boston or the Provincetown Monument barely visible on the horizon, Stellwagen Bank may seem like paradise. That is, if you are not a whale.

For these giants of the sea, which aggregate in high numbers within the sanctuary, making it the whale-watching capital of the world, the risks of collision with vessels and entanglement in fishing gear are extreme. For starters, over twenty-five hundred large vessels, including gigantic container ships, barges, liquefied natural gas tankers, naval ships, ferries, and ocean liners transit the sanctuary every year going to and from the Port of Boston. Then there is the commercial fishing fleet of about three hundred vessels. In the spring and summer, traffic picks up with the addition of thousands of recreational boaters and fifteen whale-watch companies carrying more than one million visitors. On some summer weekends when whale-watching is reported to be especially good, a swarm of high-powered recreational boats descends on the large whale-watch boats to form an annoying "mosquito fleet" operated by some of the most irresponsible and inebriated boaters on the water.

For whales just passing through as they migrate along the coast and for those that come to feed, socialize, and nurse for months, the Stellwagen Bank area (including Boston Harbor and Cape Cod Bay) is a dangerous, even fatal place to be.

Ship Strikes and Entanglements

Even the most stoic researchers examining the problems of ship strikes and entanglements were taken aback when NOAA released a report in 2007 on serious injuries and mortalities among baleen whales along the eastern seaboard and Canadian Maritimes. Between 2001 and 2005, the agency verified that 42 ship strikes and 133 entanglements had occurred, resulting in 27 whale deaths caused by ship strikes and 26 deaths by entanglement.[1] The ship-strike mortalities included eight right whales, seven humpbacks, eight fins, two sei, and two minkes.

These numbers might not seem startling to some, but they are only a hint of what might be the actual killing rate, for out of a total of 292 confirmed deaths, the cause of death could not be determined for 223 animals, because the carcasses either were too badly decomposed or could not be retrieved for necropsy. Further obscuring the true dimensions of the problem is the fact that many serious injuries and mortalities are never reported. This has been borne out by the sight of large tankers entering ports with the carcasses of large whales draped over their bow bulbs.[2] In such instances, the captains and crews invariably claim that they were unaware that they had collided with anything.

As for entanglements, they rarely are witnessed. Studies of humpback whale scars conducted by the Provincetown Center for Coastal Studies, however, indicate that as many as 75 percent of all whales are entangled in fishing gear at some point in their lives (some more than once) and that only between 3 and 10 percent of entanglements are witnessed or reported.[3] The numbers in NOAA's report therefore "represent the minimum values for human-caused serious injury and mortality to large whale stocks." Twenty-seven fatal ship strikes, *minimum*. Twenty-six fatal entanglements, *minimum*.

While statistically humpback and fin whales seem just as likely to be struck as right whales, the death of a single right whale, especially a female, is catastrophic for the species, which currently totters on the brink of extinction.[4] Within the arcane lexicon of the Marine Mammal Protection Act, there is a somber term called the potential biological removal level (PBR), which is defined as "the maximum number of animals, not including natural mortalities that may be removed from a marine mammal stock while allowing that stock to reach or maintain its optimum sustainable population."[5] For the North Atlantic right whale, PBR is *zero*.[6] At an average rate of one or two fatal collisions per year and perhaps half as many deaths due to entanglement, the right whale crisis could not be more palpable.[7]

At the center of what can only be called a crusade to break the iron grip of right whale extinction is Scott Kraus, director of the New England Aquarium's Edgerton Research Laboratory. Kraus and a team of dedicated researchers have been surveying right whales from Florida to the Bay of Fundy for the past twenty-five years and maintain the official sightings catalogue, which is made available to scores of government and academic researchers in the United States, Canada, and abroad who are examining virtually every possible cause (and solution) of the species' failure to recover from centuries of exploitation.

Kraus sees hope in the dismal statistics relating to human-induced mortality, noting "that saving just two females per year could reverse the trend and that most of the actions that would need to be taken are already known."[8] Conservation efforts along the eastern seaboard to date have focused on locating right whales by means of air and vessel surveys, notices to mariners, public education, and rerouting shipping. Still to come, but meeting considerable industry resistance, are proposals to set speed limits and to designate certain hot spots as areas to be avoided.

Notice to Mariners

In the Northeast, the conservation effort began in earnest in 1997 in response to a federal lawsuit brought by Boston's idiosyncratic and self-proclaimed Prince of Whales, Richard Max Strahan.[9] While the suit made a number of novel and absurd allegations, U.S. District Court Judge Douglas Woodlock nevertheless inferred from various depositions that little was being done at either the state or the federal level to protect right whales and ordered that a working group be formed to develop a conservation plan for right whales in Massachusetts waters. The centerpiece of the plan was an aerial survey program using government and private aircraft to search for right whales in the near-shore waters of Massachusetts, including Cape Cod Bay and the Great South Channel to the south and east of Cape Cod in the winter and spring. The sightings from these surveys were then disseminated by NMFS to mariners, the Coast Guard, and port authorities, using the international NAVTEX system that automatically distributes offshore weather forecasts and advisories and navigational warnings via self-contained printing radio receivers, NOAA weather radio broadcasts, emails, and fax machines. A typical notice to mariners distributed by the Boston Pilots Association reads:

SPECIAL NAVIGATION NOTICE

Notice To Mariners

You are advised that the **endangered Right Whale** inhabits areas along the U.S. Eastern Seaboard. In the U.S. Northeast, right whales inhabit areas within the

Ambrose and Boston Harbor traffic lanes in the spring and summer. NOAA has designated Cape Cod Bay and the region east of Cape Cod as Critical Habitat for this species and has identified Stellwagen Bank National Marine Sanctuary as an additional area of importance. The whales also aggregate in the Precautionary Area within the Great South Channel in the spring. Mariners are requested to post a lookout for Right Whales as they approach these areas and to minimize their exit and entrance speeds to the extent possible to maintain safe handling of the vessel in the channels and precautionary areas to avoid ship–whale collisions. Intentional approach to Right Whales is prohibited and may result in a violation of federal or state laws.

However, because of poor weather conditions and the size of the search area, what was first envisioned as an early warning system soon became what is now called the Sighting Advisory System. Even within the comparatively small area of Cape Cod Bay (approximately 600 square miles) where flights are scheduled twice a week, flight crews are sometimes grounded for two weeks at a time in January and February. That means that a barge or tanker coming out of the Cape Cod Canal or along the outside of Cape Cod heading for Boston or other northern destinations may have no reliable information on where the whales actually are located. The goal is what is called near-real-time sightings data. The reality is more like navigating through a fog bank without radar. Moira Brown and Amy Knowlton, two scientists with the New England Aquarium who have flown hundreds of right whale surveys in small fixed-wing aircraft at elevations of 750 feet, frequently are asked, "Why do these strikes happen? Can't the whales hear an approaching ship and move out of the way? Can't the vessel captain see the whale(s) and avoid the collision?" Despite years of research, "the simple answer apparently is 'no.'"[10]

Mariners are expected to post lookouts at all times and the good ones do, but it is a rule that is often ignored or assigned to a crewmember with other tasks. Many fishermen who have spent years on the water will say that they rarely if ever see whales. The human mind has a way of concentrating on what it is trained to see. But even for the trained eye, whales in the sanctuary can be very difficult to spot. If a captain or lookout sees a spout in the distance, there is a very good chance that there are other whales in the vicinity. Motorists in New England are familiar with the cautionary rule of thumb regarding deer: If you see one, start looking for another. At sea, a similar expression circulates among marine mammal researchers that it is the "unseen whale" that you are most likely to collide with. That unseen whale could be about to breach; dramatic if you are aboard a stationary whale-watching boat but catastrophic if you are bearing down upon it . . . or it could be rising to the surface slowly for a short breath, barely breaking the surface before diving again without a splash . . . or it could be feeding just below the surface. Whatever the actual behavior, chances are very high that it will go unobserved. If the wind is blowing more than 11 to 16 knots (13 to 18 miles per hour), producing numerous whitecaps (Force 4 on the Beaufort scale), spotting a whale becomes extremely difficult unless it spouts. At night, they are invisible and do not show up on radar, except occasionally as a blur. Simply knowing where a whale *might* be hardly insures against a collision.

In a further effort to alert mariners to the presence, if not the precise location, of right whales, in 1999 the International Maritime Organization (IMO) adopted two mandatory ship reporting systems; one for the Northeast and one for the Southeast.[11] Under these systems, ships approaching the southern calving grounds along the Florida and Georgia coasts and northern feeding grounds in the Great South Channel and Cape Cod Bay are required to report in to the U.S. Coast Guard, which provides them with the latest information on right whale locations.

The consensus among scientists, resource managers, and mariners is that these various warning programs have heightened awareness and very likely have reduced ship strikes simply by placing vessels on alert, but the programs do not directly alter the course or speed of vessels. Ultimately, the best strategies are those that employ both caution, including limitations on speed, and avoidance.

Avoidance

The first instance of a regulatory avoidance strategy for right whales came in 1997, when NOAA prohibited all vessels from approaching within 500 yards. The rule has been publicized widely and by most accounts has been observed. Whale-watch captains on Stellwagen Bank in the early spring, desperate for whale sightings, often jokingly curse when they see a right whale's unique V-spout on the horizon and have to explain to their anxious, shivering passengers why they are moving out of the area. Still, the problem on Stellwagen Bank, where right whales could be feeding on a rich zooplankton resource almost anywhere within or around the sanctuary, is the "unseen whale."

Avoidance may not be as impossible a goal as it may first appear, since the whales come to Stellwagen Bank for one simple reason: food. Stormy Mayo, who has spent more than a quarter of a century studying right whale feeding, frequently emphasizes the point with colleagues by saying, "It's the habitat, dummy." Find the food resource and you very likely will find the whales. Protect the habitat and you very likely will protect the whales.

An outstanding example of this approach took effect in the Bay of Fundy in 2003. After twenty years of study, researchers from the New England Aquarium determined that one of the highest concentrations of right whales in the summer and fall of each year could be found feeding in the middle of the outbound shipping lanes from the Port of Saint John, New Brunswick. How many whales had already been injured or killed by tankers and freighters nobody knew, but the logic of avoidance, if navigationally feasible, was compelling. What followed was a series of skillful negotiations with private shipping interests, notably Irving Oil, the regional port authority Fundy Traffic, Transport Canada, the Canadian Coast Guard, and the Department of Fisheries and Oceans, that led to a plan to shift the lanes only a few miles, reducing the relative probability of collision by 80 percent. The IMO approved the plan in 2002, making it the first instance in the world of international shipping being rerouted for wildlife conservation purposes.

In July 2007, NOAA and the U.S. Coast Guard, also with IMO approval, implemented a similar shift for the traffic separation scheme servicing Boston Harbor designed to protect right, humpback, fin, and minke whales. Currently, commercial shipping in and out of Boston varies between about 175 and 225 ships a month. Based on over twenty-four years of sightings data, scientists were able to determine that by rotating the traffic lanes by 12 degrees beginning at a point just east of Provincetown, it might be possible for ships to transit Stellwagen Bank and reduce the risk of collisions. The realignment is expected to result in a 58 percent reduction in risk for right whales and an 81 percent risk reduction for other large whales, but the traffic lanes are not mandatory, as they are in the Bay of Fundy, and there are no speed limits. Greg Silber, with NOAA's Office of Protected Resources, and Richard Pace, with the Northeast Fisheries Science Center, have calculated that the probability of a serious injury or mortality increases from 45 percent to 75 percent as vessel speeds increase from 10 to 14 knots and exceed 90 percent at 17 knots.[12]

Speed Kills

The plain fact of the matter is that speed kills whales. Faced with the likely prospect of a lawsuit, NMFS published a proposed a rule in 2006 announcing its intention to establish mandatory and recommended traffic lanes and speed restrictions of 10 knots for vessels greater than 65 feet in overall length in specific locations during specific times.[13] For the southeastern calving grounds off the coasts of Florida and Georgia, the rule called for establishing mandatory east-west lanes between November 15 and April 15. For the Mid-Atlantic, NMFS would designate a migratory corridor from November 1 through April 30. Ships within 35 miles of port entrances would be required to reduce speed. In Cape Cod Bay, traffic coming in and out of the Cape Cod Canal would be advised, though not required, to transit the west side of the bay and reduce speed from January 1 through May 15. A speed restriction would be set for the Great South Channel as well from March 1 through April 30. NMFS also recommended designating the area immediately to the east of the Boston shipping lanes as an area to be avoided for vessels traveling further north, another action that would require international approval. In the event that right whales are reported outside these areas, NMFS would have the authority to designate temporary dynamic management areas within which mandatory routes and vessel speeds might be issued.

In February 2007, the proposed rule went to the White House's Office of Management and Budget for a mandatory ninety-day review. In June 2008, the Union of Concerned Scientists released internal NOAA documents that, according to Representative Henry Waxman (D-Ca.), "indicate that the delay in protecting the right whale appears to be due to objections raised by White House officials, including officials in the office of the vice president." Other published reports indicated that the White House was responding to pressure from the World Shipping Council, which has opposed the rule. The OMB's responsibility in such matters is supposed to be limited to ferreting out regulatory redundancies and weighing the cost effectiveness of regulations. The Bush administration is not the first to use the OMB review process as a means of stonewalling Congress and the courts, but it has done so with a vengeance with a wide range of environmental initiatives, including those coming from the administration itself. With the likelihood of litigation, the administration eventually relented and the new speed limits went into effect on December 9, 2008.

While the primary responsibility for marine mammal protection rests with NMFS and has to be approached from a regional, even international, perspective, the National Marine Sanctuary Program (NMSP) has broad authority under the National Marine Sanctuaries Act to take initiative in consultation with other federal agencies, including those within NOAA. The realignment of the Boston shipping lanes demonstrated this well. NMFS and the U.S. Coast Guard functioned as the lead agencies in developing the IMO proposal, but it was the Stellwagen Bank National Marine Sanctuary staff that assembled the data and analysis that justified the realignment.

Can and should the sanctuary do more to avoid collisions? The consensus among the sanctuary's advisors and the general public is that it should. Comments made in 1998 and 2002 during a series of scoping sessions revealed that the general public believes that a sanctuary should be managed by higher environmental, even ethical and aesthetic standards than other areas of open ocean.

Currently, no speed limits are posted in the sanctuary, despite overwhelming evidence that speed is a major contributing factor to serious injury and mortality among large whales.[14] Even with the traffic separation scheme now in place, a fully loaded supertanker traveling at 15 knots has very little maneuverability. A "crash stop" (a maneuver that calls for going from full ahead to full reverse) can take up to fifteen minutes and cover a distance of more than a mile and a half. At least within the shipping lanes, good seamanship and the sheer size of some of the vessels are limiting factors.

Outside the shipping lanes within the sanctuary, on the other hand, virtually anything is permitted. From mid-May to early October, a 90-minute, high-speed ferry service operates between Boston and Provincetown. The largest and fastest is the 600-passenger *Salacia* operated by Boston Harbor Cruises, a catamaran capable of speeds up to 40 knots (46 mph). As BHC's brochure notes, "That's faster than most speedboats." The *Salacia* also doubles from time to time as a whale watcher. Another fast catamaran, originally built for the New England Aquarium and now owned and operated by Water Transportation Alternatives, is the *Voyager III*, capable of carrying 350 passengers at speeds up to 30 knots (34.5 mph). The aquarium still uses it for its whale-watching program, and invites visitors in its promotional brochure to "enjoy the view as this high-speed catamaran whisks you safely to the whale feeding grounds." Another big boat is the mono-hull *Whale Watcher* that operates out of Barnstable Harbor on Cape Cod. It carries 392 passengers. Since the harbor is tidally restricted and the whales are usually 30 miles away, it requires lots of speed to make it out and back in three or four hours. The *Whale Watcher*'s powerful engines are capable of zipping along at 38 knots (44 mph). The slower whale-watch boats still cruise through the sanctuary in search of whales at about 18 knots (20 mph).

Unenforceable Guidelines

Voluntary guidelines first issued in 1988 and revised in 1999 by NMFS and the National Ocean Service (NOS) for the Northeast, including Stellwagen Bank, recommend that whale-watching vessels reduce speed when whales are sighted; to 13 knots (15 mph) when within 2 miles, to 10 knots (11.5 mph) within 1 mile, and to 7 knots (8mph) within ½ mile. The 1999 guidelines were developed by a committee made up largely of commercial operators after whale watchers collided with three whales in 1998, killing at least one.

In 2003 and 2004, Dave Wiley, who is now the research coordinator for the sanctuary, conducted a study funded by the International Fund for Animal Welfare on the whale-watching companies' compliance with the speed limits established by the guidelines. The study did not examine compliance with guidelines on close approaches to whales (see chapter 9). The results, published in the journal *Conservation Biology* in April 2008, revealed what has been observed widely but seldom discussed openly among conservationists for years; namely, everyone speeds. Wiley and his colleagues boarded a total of forty-six trips departing from each whale-watching port and discovered that every trip exceeded the voluntary speed limits. Several operators tried to dismiss the findings by explaining that there were not many whales around in 2003 and 2004 and captains were under pressure to rush their passengers, sometimes great distances, to see a whale.

The standard whale watch within the sanctuary is scheduled to last between three and four hours. Most companies guarantee a sighting and offer a free ticket for a future trip "in the unlikely event of no whale sightings," but no company relishes paying out $10,000 or more worth of tickets. Woe to the captain who gets "skunked" or does not return in time for the next trip.

Whale-watch captains from Boston and Hyannis have the added pressure of having to travel further to get to whales. The Boston boats are 30 miles from the feeding grounds and are required to move slowly through Boston Harbor.

The one company based in Hyannis has a tidally restricted harbor to contend with and must travel a similar distance to reach the feeding grounds.

For many passengers, it is their first trip ever on a large vessel. They have little sense of how fast they are traveling or reason to believe that it is a problem. For those who have been out before, they too may have no reason to be concerned and are just eager to get to the whales. The captains do not have to worry about Wiley's rangers and their hidden GPS devices or a flashing blue light from the nonexistent sanctuary marine patrol. Standard practice is to approach and enter the sanctuary as fast as weather and sea state allow. Only when in sight of whales or in the vicinity of a recent sighting do they slow down. What happens as the vessels approach the whales is a subject for later discussion.

Most of the whale-watch captains working the sanctuary are veterans and highly capable. All are licensed by the Coast Guard. Their license is their "ticket," which they value even more than company rules and policies. It explains why more accidents have not occurred. Still, neither the whale-watch operators nor the captains have any legal obligations to the sanctuary, making it the least-regulated commercial enterprise within the sanctuary.

Next comes a wide variety of smaller vessels that includes commercial fishing boats, including draggers and lobster boats mostly running between 10 and 15 knots, tuna and party boats with slightly higher speeds, weekend warriors in cigarette boats capable of speeds of more than 75 knots, and other overpowered craft that frequently move in on groups of whales like blue fish in a feeding frenzy.

For virtually all other vessels that engage in whale watching or pass through aggregations of whales, speed limits are ignored. Recreational boaters who have been urged to slow down generally claim that the whale-watching guidelines do not apply to them. Verbal confrontations and obscene hand gestures are frequently exchanged between whale-watch captains and recreational boaters.

As a rule, the smaller the boat, the less likely a collision will kill a whale, but every year reports and gruesome photos are circulated of whales with spiral propeller cuts over their backs and severed tailstocks that sometimes lead to fatal infections.

While the Endangered Species and Marine Mammal Protection Acts authorize stiff fines, imprisonment, and seizure of property for egregious violations, little enforcement is possible within the sanctuary and cases that are reported are almost never prosecuted. As for the whale-watching guidelines, NOAA enforcement officers and the Coast Guard openly complain that they more or less have their hands tied, since guidelines are unenforceable.

Ocean Noise

Even at reduced speeds, large vessels operating in areas of high whale concentrations pose a serious risk for whales; even more so in areas of large ship concentration such as the shipping lanes. Christopher Clark, director of Cornell University's Bioacoustics Research Program, is a world authority on the sounds of right whales and the increasingly noisy coastal environment in which right whales and other marine life struggle to survive. What he has discovered based on decades of research is that the noises of the ocean, including the natural "background" sound of waves, the sounds of cavitating ships' propellers, generators, mobile fishing gear, dredging, pile driving, oil exploration, and naval sonar, may be drowning out the sounds that right whales make to communicate with one another. The right whale's contact call is described as "a distinctive low-frequency glissando that rises from about 50 Hz (approximately an octave above the lowest note on a piano) to about 440 Hz (orchestral A on a piano) and lasts about one to two seconds."[15] This sound is overlapped entirely by the sound of ships. Susan Parks, also with the Cornell bioacoustics lab, estimates that the ambient noise levels of the western North Atlantic coastal environment have risen to such high levels that "the chance of two whales hearing each other today has been reduced to 10 percent of what it was a hundred years ago."[16] This startling discovery has led Parks and Clark to wonder if the species' drastically limited range of communication explains, at least in part, why the species has not recovered.

As yet, the problem of ocean noise remains unregulated, but Clark and his colleagues have applied their knowledge of right whale acoustics to protecting them from shipping. Recently, they placed ten acoustic buoys in the Boston shipping lanes 5 miles apart beginning at a point east of Truro on Cape Cod and across Stellwagen Bank to a point 5 miles west of the sanctuary boundary. Each buoy is equipped with an underwater hydrophone that can detect a right whale within 5 miles. The recorded sound is relayed to the surface, where a transmitter sends the signal to the lab via satellite. Ships in the area are then notified within twenty minutes of the last known location of the whale or group of whales.

The system is being paid for by Excelerate Energy owners and operators of Northeast Gateway, New England's first offshore liquefied natural gas port, located 13 miles southeast of Gloucester on the edge of the SBNMS boundary.[17] Construction of Northeast Gateway, which received swift approval by the Federal Energy Regulatory Commission and NMFS, was completed on December 21, 2007. Construction of a second facility by Neptune LNG in the same area is expected to begin in 2009. Together, the facilities will increase large tanker traffic by nearly two hundred ships per year, although as a condition of their license LNG tankers will be required to maintain speeds of 12 knots or less while in the traffic lanes except when transiting the Off Race Point Seasonal Management Area between March 1 and April 30, the Great South Channel Seasonal Management Area between April 1 and July 31, or when active right whale sightings, active acoustic detections, or both, have occurred in the vicinity of the tanker or at the port. As the tankers make their final approach, they will gradually reduce speed to 3 knots at a distance of about 2 miles and to 1 knot at a distance of 1,640 feet.[18]

Sanctuaries Bat Last

How ironic is it that in fifteen years the sanctuary, which was created in large part because it is an important habitat for marine mammals, has done so little to protect them? Despite a long tradition of freedom on the open water and pressure from vested interests, one might think that adopting a precautionary management strategy and regulating vessel traffic through the sanctuary and in close proximity to whales would have been the first order of business. But then, there is the "anarchy of agencies" within the Department of Commerce to contend with. There is much talk these days to the effect that there is "only one NOAA." But in reality, everyone knows that the National Marine Sanctuary Program bats last.

Inside the Beltway, there is an oft-told tale about the Secretary of Commerce's first week on the job. After endless briefings about international trade agreements, economic analysis and development, industrial safety, job training, and the census, a senior staffer attempts to inject a note of levity by adding, "Mr. Secretary, you are also in charge of the weather and the whales."

Chapter 8

The Accidental Hunt

The primary objective of this management must be to maintain the health and stability of the marine ecosystem; this in theory indicates that animals must be managed for their benefit and not for the benefit of commercial exploitation. The effect of this set of requirements is to insist that the management of animal populations be carried out with the interest of the animals as the prime consideration.

— House of Representatives, No. 707, 92nd Congress, 1st Session, December 4, 1971, in reference to the federal government's management responsibilities under the Marine Mammal Protection Act of 1972.

While Congress in 1972 may have been unsure about the purposes and goals of national marine sanctuaries, it had a clear sense of what the American people wanted when it came to the protection of whales. To this day, the Marine Mammal Protection Act (MMPA) stands as one of the most visionary pieces of environmental legislation, despite repeated efforts to weaken some of its strongest provisions. Among these is the "immediate goal that the incidental kill or incidental serious injury of marine mammals permitted in the course of commercial fishing operations be reduced to insignificant levels approaching zero mortality and serious injury rate."[1]

Entanglements

Notwithstanding the mandates of the MMPA, baleen whales throughout the Northeast continue to become entangled in fishing gear at an alarming rate. The 2007 NOAA report cited in chapter 7 with respect to collisions also verified 26 deaths between 2001 and 2005 resulting from 133 confirmed entanglements.[2] As in the case of vessel collisions, out of a total of 292 confirmed mortalities, the cause of death could be determined for only 69 animals

(24 percent). Even if half of the remaining animals died of natural causes, that would still leave more than 110 animals killed by humans; possibly half of this number by entanglement. It is impossible even to estimate how many deaths were never reported at all.

When it comes to estimating nonlethal entanglement injuries, on the other hand, researchers at the New England Aquarium and Provincetown Center for Coastal Studies have reported that about 75 percent of right whales and 65 percent of humpbacks bear scars from at least one entanglement.[3] Among humpbacks in the Gulf of Maine, it is estimated that between 10 and 25 percent of the population is entangled every year.

Ironically, very few eyewitness accounts of entanglements have been published, so the mechanics remain somewhat of a mystery. The effects, on the other hand, are vividly clear and heart wrenching; none more so than the 2001 case of right whale #1102, a large male severely wrapped in heavy lines bearing a deep infected wound on the top of its head. First spotted off Cape Cod on June 8, the whale the press called Churchill (after British Prime Minister Winston Churchill) evaded rescuers from the Provincetown Center for Coastal Studies and a dozen other institutions for one hundred days while traveling a distance of more than 4,000 miles along the eastern seaboard. Video footage on the national morning and evening television news broadcasts had viewers, including seasoned reporters, shaking their heads and weeping as day by day he turned a ghostly white and rotted away. The last signal from a telemetry tag that had been attached to the trailing fishing gear was received on September 16 and positioned Churchill 250 miles south of Nantucket.

The gruesome ordeal of Churchill's death is probably more common than most people care to think about. Occasionally, juvenile whales will get caught up in fishing gear and become anchored in place where they run the risk of drowning. This has occurred frequently in Canada, where many humpbacks have become entangled in fishing weirs set in shallow water and set free by fishermen and researchers. It is there that Jon Lien, a highly respected and legendary marine biologist at Memorial University of Newfoundland, first perfected the technique of large whale disentanglement. In New England waters, entanglement deaths are more likely to be the result of infection from wounds or starvation resulting from the whale's inability to feed properly. Whales, of course, grow; numerous cases are reported where ropes wrapped around a flipper or the tailstock have cut severely into the animal as it grew, resulting in an even slower and more torturous death. Occasionally, if the ropes do not cinch, a whale may free itself. A few instances have even been reported when the drag of a telemetry buoy attached to trailing gear by rescue teams preparing to stage a disentanglement or simply wanting to monitor a whale's condition actually has pulled the gear off. The primary East Coast rescue team at the Provincetown Center for Coastal Studies has sometimes jokingly referred to these narrow escapes as remote disentanglement.

Among right whales, entanglement ranks equally with ship strikes as a cause of death, which means, as Scott Kraus has said with respect to ship strikes, that "just saving two females a year could reverse the trend [toward extinction]."[4] But entanglement has become a growing problem for a number of baleen whales and sea turtles. In the 2007 NOAA report on mortalities and serious injury, the highest numbers of confirmed mortalities attributed to entanglement were among humpbacks (eight) and minkes (eleven).[5] Solving the entanglement problem, though most critical for the right whale at this time, will be beneficial to a variety of animals.

Synthetic Ropes

The problem essentially comes down to the types of ropes used in different fisheries and the manner in which fishing gear is deployed. Just about the time that the character played by Dustin Hoffman in the 1967 film *The Graduate* was being advised that his future might be in plastics, rope making for offshore fisheries went almost entirely synthetic. Among synthetic ropes, the most widely used is polypropylene. It is cheap, strong, light, long-lasting (nonbiodegradable), and for marine mammals, most deadly.

Although large whales have become entangled in a wide variety of active, abandoned, and lost fishing gear (also known as ghost gear), entanglements most often are associated with fixed gear used in trap or pot and gillnet fisheries. In the Northeast, traps are used to catch mostly lobster and some crabs in wooden or wire cages. In the case of an individual trap, a line runs from the gear to a buoy at the surface that usually bears the fisherman's permit number. The markings and colors are particular to that permit. However, these days, the common practice is to fish in trawls or strings of traps connected to one another by a common "ground" line. In the Stellwagen Bank National Marine Sanctuary (SBNMS), a typical trawl might consist of a string of two dozen traps spaced 100 to 180 feet apart. Because the traps are connected to one another on the seafloor, a trawl set only requires two buoy lines; one at each end of the set.

Almost no eyewitness accounts have been published of how whales become entangled in this gear, but the inferences drawn from literally scores of reports and successful disentanglements seems incontrovertible. Vertical buoy lines are a common cause of entanglements. In some areas, the traps are so numerous and densely set that the surface buoys pose a navigation hazard for any boat or large mammal moving in a straight line. A typical entanglement in a buoy minefield begins with a flipper or tail running along the vertical line, a sensation a whale probably initially does not feel or react to. But as the whale moves forward, the tension on the line increases until one of several things happens.

First, the line may break and slide off the whale's body like a wet noodle. If it does not, and the whale maintains its speed and direction, it eventually encounters the buoy, which is attached to a stick, causing the line to tug against the mass of the animal. At this point, the whale reacts by flipping its tail, turning sharply, rolling its entire body, or diving. In most instances, the evasive action works, but it is easy to imagine that any of these sharp moves could cause the line to wrap around a flipper, the tailstock, or even the entire body. Once this happens, the action becomes more violent and the whale in most instances tears the buoy line from the trap below and continues on its way, wrapped in line that it either will continue to try to shed by various maneuvers or ignore until it begins to cinch and lacerate. On occasion, the initial force of the whale against the line is not strong enough to snap the line and the whale swims on dragging one or more traps with it. Many reports also have been made of whales becoming anchored by the weight of a long trawl.

More recently, scientists and fisheries managers have come to realize that the ground lines may constitute an even greater threat to endangered whales than vertical buoy lines. Statistically, the ground lines in large trawl sets represent more linear feet of rope than the buoy lines. The problem is that the ground lines, which these days are often made of polypropylene, do not lie on the seafloor. They float; creating 15- to 20-foot-high arches that drift with the tides and currents. For a right whale foraging on zooplankton along the sea floor or a humpback pursuing sand lance buried in the sandy bottom, the ground lines are often just high enough to jam in their open mouths.

As the intensity of lobster fishing has increased in the Gulf of Maine in recent years, so have the number of entanglements involving head wraps and ropes jammed in the baleen plates. Although not initially lethal, baleen wraps often cause damage to the baleen plates as the whale tugs against the resistance of the traps. In these cases, if the trailing lines do not wrap around other body parts causing any number of bodily injuries, the whale's ability to feed normally may be restricted severely, eventually leading to malnutrition, stress, disease, and death.

Gillnets are anchored, wall-like nets made of monofilament webbing stretched between a buoyant float line running along the top of the net and a heavy sink line running along the bottom. The mesh size is designed for specific sizes of targeted species. Fish are caught by their gills once their heads pass through the mesh and their forward motion is stopped by their bodies. Gillnets can be set close to the bottom, in mid-water, or close to the surface. The height of the nets varies from 3 feet to as much as 12 feet depending on the target species. A single net can be 300 feet long and strings of nets can extend for more than a mile. The ends of the strings, as in the case of lobster trawls, are marked with a surface buoy that is attached to the gear with a line that must be strong enough to haul in the net. While gillnetting can be relatively selective in terms of the size and species of fish that are targeted, they can be as problematic as traps and pots for almost all marine mammals, sea turtles, and many species of seabirds. High-frequency acoustic alarms called pingers have proven effective in deterring harbor porpoises (*Phocoena phocoena*) from getting caught in bottom-set or sink nets, but some studies are underway to determine if this form of deterrence, which uses the echolocation abilities of the animals, does not also exclude them from their habitat. As for the larger baleen whales, the entanglement risks associated with gillnets are a function of how the gear is set and the ropes used to hold it in place.

Relative Interaction Potential

In an effort to determine where the risks of entanglement may be highest within the SBNMS, Dave Wiley, who coordinates research activities within the sanctuary, conducted a geographic information system (GIS) analysis several years ago. It consisted of mapping fishing activity and overlaying that data with sightings data of baleen whales, an idea first suggested by Stormy Mayo, who has been disentangling whales since 1984. The concurrence of the two data sets enabled Wiley to develop an index of what he calls the relative interaction potential (RIP).[6]

In general, the study found that the density of fixed gear was greatest in the western portions of the sanctuary and diminished to the east except for an area northeast of Stellwagen Bank and along a line delineating the Western

Gulf of Maine Closure Area. The trap fishery was in the sanctuary's north-western section off the coast of Cape Ann and in the southwestern portion of the sanctuary, especially in the area known as the Southwest Corner, where crab fishing intensified during the summer months. Lobster fishing during this time of the year was concentrated in shallow, near-shore waters outside the sanctuary. In the fall, as lobsters move offshore, traps are set in deeper waters just west of Stellwagen Bank. In the winter, lobstermen work these waters and the area just west of the sanctuary. Gillnetting was concentrated in the northern and eastern portions of the sanctuary, with the greatest activity occurring south of Jeffreys Ledge within a broad area along the northeast flank of Stellwagen Bank and in the northwest section of the sanctuary off Cape Ann.

Wiley's RIP index "suggested that the most likely sites of whale entanglement would be the [sanctuary's] southwest and northwest corners, followed by Jeffreys Ledge" and that "the highest RIPs occurred in the summer around the southwest corner of Stellwagen Bank." The intended application of this analysis was to identify "interaction hot spots" where NMFS or the SBNMS might impose seasonal closures, require the use of "whale-safe" gear, or conduct "intensive surveillance to facilitate rescue attempts." Under such a management regime, fishermen presumably would be free to fish elsewhere as they always have.

Nothing Incidental about It

While no fishermen setting fixed gear deliberately sets out to entangle a large whale (the cost of damaged and lost gear alone being a major disincentive), the fact remains that the interaction of fixed gear and whales in and around the SBNMS far exceeds what the Marine Mammal Protection Act refers to as "incidental takes." Were it not for the fact that fishermen are not entangling whales intentionally, what is now occurring in the sanctuary and elsewhere and being called incidental to "traditional fishing" would be called a hunt. If the hunt were being conducted by Japan or Iceland, a flotilla of protesters would be mobbing the fishermen.

Although the Wiley study has determined where and when whales are most at risk of becoming entangled within the SBNMS, in its first fifteen years, the sanctuary has done nothing to reduce the risk. Why? Because fisheries management and marine mammal protection are the primary responsibilities of

NMFS, which historically has subordinated the protection of whales to the economics of the fishing industry. Then too, there is the "traditional fishing" wild card dealt by NOAA in the 1993 SBNMS designation document. The combination of these two political realities has placed marine mammal protection effectively off limits to the sanctuary's management team.

Ignoring for now the question of whether SBNMS should be a true sanctuary (in the sense of refuge) for living creatures, where the "relative interaction potential" is reduced to some number approaching zero or where fixed gear might be prohibited altogether, the overall problem of marine mammal entanglement is not unique to the SBNMS and calls for broad-based solutions. This was the goal set by Congress in 1994 when it reauthorized and amended the Marine Mammal Protection Act, requiring NMFS, which it faulted for inaction, to develop "take" reduction plan(s)

> to reduce within 5 years of its implementation, the incidental mortality or serious injury of marine mammals incidentally taken in the course of commercial fishing operations to insignificant levels approaching a zero mortality and serious injury rate, taking into account the economics of the fishery, the availability of existing technology, and existing state and regional fishery management plans.[7]

The arcane term "take" means "to harass, hunt, capture or kill or attempt to harass, hunt, capture or kill any marine mammal."[8]

Atlantic Large Whale Take Reduction Team

A specific and pressing intent of the 1994 amendments was to reduce "takes" of North Atlantic right, humpback, minke, and fin whales in four fisheries: the New England sink gillnet fishery, the lobster trap/pot fishery in the Gulf of Maine and mid-Atlantic, the coastal gillnet fisheries in the mid-Atlantic, and the shark net fishery in the southeastern Atlantic. As further required by law, in 1996 NMFS assembled an unwieldy team of more than sixty fishermen, scientists, conservationists, and state and federal officials to help work on a take-reduction plan called the Atlantic Large Whale Take Reduction Team (ALWTRT). Given the size of the region, the diversity of affected fisheries, and the fact that the team was dominated by fishing interests, achieving meaningful consensus even about the severity of the problem proved difficult.

Some critics later would complain that the primary mission of the

ALWTRT was to give the appearance of trying to solve the problem while maintaining the status quo. The industry, emboldened by the Gingrich "revolution" in Congress, simultaneously began an all-out effort to undermine provisions of the Marine Mammal Protection and Endangered Species Acts.

The Massachusetts Gold Standard

The solution has never been as difficult as it has been made out to be. Entanglement is essentially about ropes in the water column. You can change the rope, alter the way in which it is deployed, or remove it altogether. It took Dan McKiernan, a fisheries biologist with the Massachusetts Division of Marine Fisheries (DMF), and a small team of scientists and fishermen less then three months in 1996 to figure it out after the U.S. District Court for the District of Massachusetts ordered the Commonwealth to "develop and prepare a proposal.... to restrict, modify or eliminate the use of fixed-fishing gear in coastal waters of Massachusetts listed as critical habitat for Northern Right whales in order to minimize the likelihood additional whales will actually be harmed by such gear."[9]

The DMF plan, which was submitted to the court on December 16, 1996, and immediately adopted, focused first on reducing the overall fishing effort in Cape Cod Bay from January 1 through May 15, when right whales move into the area to feed. The development of what has been billed loosely as "whale-safe" fishing gear has focused on replacing floating polypropylene surface lines with sinking lines, the use of weak links on buoy lines and between bridles on gillnets, and nonbuoyant ground lines. Other modifications have included the use of weak "tag lines" in place of the standard buoy lines. The function of the tag line is only to mark the end of the trawl and location of a stronger line lying on the bottom that is used to haul the pots. Sometimes stronger is better, as in the case of gillnets that traditionally have been held in place by weights. The DMF plan calls for anchoring the nets to increase the likelihood of breaking if a whale swims through the nets.

DMF's proactive, collaborative management style has earned it well-deserved national attention and high marks among fishermen and environmentalists alike. Although quick to act on the elimination of floating ground lines, DMF turned to the Atlantic Offshore Lobstermen's Association for assistance in the development of a durable, nonbuoyant "whale-safe alternative." When some fishermen complained about the cost of switching, DMF partnered with the Massachusetts Lobstermen's Association and International Fund for Animal Welfare in a buyout of all inshore lobstermen's ground lines. On January 1, 2007, it became unlawful to fish, store, or abandon any fixed gear in state waters with positively buoyant ground line.

While McKiernan and his team are not inclined to boast, one attorney for the Commonwealth appearing before a federal district court judge referred to the plan as the "gold standard" among Atlantic fisheries. The fact that no recent entanglements have been linked positively to fixed gear set in state waters is a very good sign. A collateral benefit has been the introduction of modified gear to the SBNMS, since most of the fishermen working the inshore state waters also fish within the sanctuary.[10]

On a broader scale, the goal of reducing entanglements, especially of right whales, "to insignificant levels approaching zero mortality" has proven to be more elusive. The initial recommendations of the ALWTRT in 1997, which closely resembled the Massachusetts regulations, called for an "aggressive gear research and development program" with priority given to the development of lightweight vertical tag lines, weak links for use at the top and bottom of buoy lines, biodegradable gear, sinking line, and smooth and nonsnagging lines. The fisheries targeted for gear modification included the New England multi-species gillnet fishery, the mid-Atlantic gillnet fishery, the Gulf of Maine lobster fishery, mid-Atlantic trap/pot fishery, and the shark and gillnet fisheries in the Southeast.

NMFS published an interim rule the same year incorporating most of the recommendations of the ALWTRT, including a general prohibition on the use of floating lines at the surface and water storage of inactive gear, and including time and area closures for the lobster, anchored gillnet, and shark fisheries. At the same time, the agency announced increased levels of funding for R&D and disentanglement training and operations.

The interim rule prompted instant controversy among some fisheries and the customary delays that characterize NMFS's rulemaking. The thirty-day comment period became sixty days, then ninety days, then six months, then a year. The final rule did not take effect until April 1999, five years after the passage of the 1994 MMPA amendments. By the end of the year, the Provincetown Center for Coastal Studies had confirmed entanglements of six right, nine humpback, three fin, and four minke whales; hardly "insignificant levels approaching zero mortality."

Over the course of the next five years, the plan would be amended several more times, still with little demonstrable effect. The problem lay in large part in NMFS's over-reliance on the ALWTRT as a consensus decisionmaking body and reluctance to impose broad-scale gear restrictions. For several years, in an apparent effort to minimize disruption to fisheries, NMFS experimented with a system of temporary closures called DAMs (for dynamic area management) triggered by the occurrence of a small group of right whales. The plan was for NMFS to take emergency action by publishing notice of a closure in the Federal Register, whereupon fishermen were to pull their gear. Scientists and fishermen alike argued that trying to manage a fishery around a moving group of whales was impractical if not ludicrous. To achieve a near-zero rate of mortality, broad-scale changes were needed.

The death of right whale #3107 in 2003 finally convinced NMFS that the take-reduction plan was not working and announced its intention to amend the plan by 2004. The agency held scoping meetings and published a proposed rule in 2005 calling for a more broad-based approach that especially raised the hackles of Maine lobstermen and their congressional allies, most notably Maine's senior senator Olympia Snowe. The proposed regulations languished for months, as the NOAA bureaucracy sought to avoid retaliatory budget cuts.

Meanwhile, between 2002 and 2007, confirmed entanglements of seven right, fourteen humpback, and four fin whales were reported, leading the Humane Society of the United States (HSUS) and Ocean Conservancy to sue NMFS in February 2007 for failure to protect the three species. The case was settled in July 2007, with NMFS agreeing to release the amended regulations by the end of the year.

Federal Gear Requirements

The 2007 amendments that went into effect in January 2008 rely on what NMFS calls broad-based gear modifications that include weak links, sinking and/or "neutrally buoyant" ground line, anchoring, and gear marking during specific times and in certain areas, doing away with the ill-fated SAM and DAM programs. The final rule, however, exempted 71 percent of Maine waters (a transparent concession to the state's powerful lobster industry) and significant portions of Long Island Sound on the grounds that "large whales are sighted infrequently and do not spend significant periods of time in these waters."[11]

With respect to Stellwagen Bank and adjacent Jeffreys Ledge, the new regulations prohibit the use of floating buoy lines, wet storage, and single traps (to minimize the number of vertical lines in the water column), and require weak links with a breaking strength of no more than 600 pounds.

Will any of this work? Because of the interannual variability of stock assessments, NMFS most likely will hold off making any final judgment for another five years. It seems reasonable to assume that the modified gear will result in some improvement, but the amount of potentially harmful gear that remains has led a number of knowledgeable observers to believe that no significant decrease will be measured in the rates of entanglement, serious injury, and mortality until regulations become universal and a greater effort is made to remove lines in the water column. Whales already have been found entangled in gear equipped with 600-pound weak links. In deeper offshore locations such as the Great South Channel, weak links with breaking strengths of up to 2,000 pounds are allowed.

As with the auto industry in the 1960s, when it argued that installing catalytic converters would be prohibitively costly and now when it argues that it cannot build hybrid cars that people can afford, the fishing industry bitterly complains that most of the truly innovative ideas that scientists have proposed for preventing entanglement are too costly. It is a strategy that has worked well in its dealings with NMFS, which treats the ALWTRT as a decisionmaking body rather than an advisory body. As one close observer of the process has noted, given this broad license, "fishermen have no incentive via consensus negotiation to agree to anything that restricts them, because they have a better alternative, which is to run to Congress."

In fairness to NMFS, immediately following passage of the landmark 1994 amendments to the MMPA, radical Republicans led by newly elected House Speaker Newt Gingrich set out to undo a long list of environmental laws and regulations dating back to the Nixon presidency. For a while, only the threat of a Clinton veto prevented laws such as the MMPA from being eviscerated. The threats of budget cuts to agencies such as the EPA and NOAA were more palpable. It is possible that NMFS found this predatory political environment a good time not to make waves.

The entanglement of endangered species raises challenging and frequently unanswered questions about government responsibility. In the case of *Strahan v. Coxe*, Judge Woodlock found that because right whales were becoming entangled in fishing gear, the Commonwealth of Massachusetts was liable for a take under the Endangered Species Act for permitting fishing.[12] Although the state's Division of Marine Fisheries responded quickly with a responsible and reasonably effective plan, the state appealed the ruling on the grounds that licensing fishermen "was not the proximate cause of the taking."[13] The state argued that issuing fishing licenses was equivalent to issuing driving licenses and that just as one would not hold the state responsible for a driver's accidents, the state should not be held accountable for a fisherman's incidental take. The First Circuit Court of Appeals did not buy the argument, affirmed the lower court's ruling, and concluded that "[A] governmental third party pursuant to whose authority an actor directly exacts a taking of an endangered species may be deemed to have violated the provisions of the ESA." While this may not have supported Strahan's belief in a covert conspiracy between the regulators and the regulated, it did make clear that resource managers must be equally proactive in implementing and enforcing the full range of authorities enacted by Congress.[14]

The company line of late has been that there is only "one NOAA," a line possibly created to offset the widespread belief that there may be no NOAA. It is intended to convey the notion that the agency is committed to a holistic approach to its many missions, best described as ecosystem-based management. But in reality, NOAA remains a house divided. With respect to national marine sanctuaries, which are administered by NOAA's National Ocean Service (NOS), there is little doubt that the technical orientation and commercial bias of NMFS dominates many of the critical discussions about living marine resources within the sanctuaries. It is even unclear, given its numerous and conflicting mandates and the political pressures under which it labors, whether NOAA is capable of viewing the public trust through anything but a commercial lens.

Chapter 9

Ecotourism Unlimited

Megaptera novaeangliae, Balaenoptera physalus, Eubalaena glacialis, Balaenoptera borealis. Their scientific names alone evoke mystery. To see any of these great and endangered whales in their natural environment is a thrilling, awe-inspiring experience.

Each year, approximately one million people from throughout the United States and around the world visit the Stellwagen Bank National Marine Sanctuary for the sole purpose of seeing these majestic creatures. The vast majority are transported by commercial whale-watch boats from a dozen or more companies operating about twenty vessels sailing out of Boston, Gloucester, Newburyport, Hyannis, Plymouth, and Provincetown, where whale watching in the Northeast began in 1975.[1]

If it were not for whale watching, the sanctuary would be known to no more than a few thousand commercial and recreational fishermen, scientists, divers, and conservationists. Indeed, if it had not been for whale watching and the public interest that it generated throughout the 1980s, it is possible that the legislation designating Stellwagen Bank as a national marine sanctuary might never have passed.

Big Business Uncritically Acclaimed

Chambers of commerce, especially in the smaller ports, tend to wax lyrical about whale watching and view it perhaps uncritically as a low-impact, environmentally friendly enterprise. Research institutions see it as an "opportunistic" platform for data collection (mostly in the relatively narrow field of population studies). Environmental advocacy groups, particularly those operating at the international level, cite the economic success and popularity of whale watching on Stellwagen Bank as proof that most people would rather pay to see a whale than to have it served to them in a restaurant.[2]

Most whale-watch companies hire naturalists to identify whales, dolphins, and seabirds and to talk about the behavior, conservation status, and migratory patterns of the wildlife they encounter.[3] Some collect sightings data that is shared with a consortium of research organizations. In terms of training and experience, they vary widely from active researchers with advanced degrees and certified teachers to undergraduates and self-trained wildlife observers. Captains and first mates occasionally chime in. Some are veterans with ten, twenty, and thirty years of experience who can identify individual humpbacks in a flash, much like old friends. An old favorite is a female named Salt who has been seen every year but one since 1976. Her site fidelity has earned her the title of Grand Dame of Stellwagen Bank. In 2007, she was spotted again with her tenth known calf, Soya.

The names of calves and adults spotted for the first time are selected by a group of naturalists and researchers at the end of each season and based on their interpretation of the unique pigmentation found on the underside of their tails; a technique that is now standard protocol among humpback whale researchers around the world. Salt was the first to be named and is an exception. She was named by the late Capt. Aaron Avellar of the Dolphin Fleet of Provincetown, not for her tail pigmentation, but for what looks like a sprinkling of white on her dorsal fin.

From a business perspective, whale watching has been a great success, reported to be a $35-million-a-year enterprise with a significant ripple effect. Actual financial information is hard to come by, as the companies are not licensed by the sanctuary or required to report to the sanctuary on how many trips they run or passengers they carry.[4] Rising fuel costs and a gradual but steady decline in passengers over the past five years has cast a pall over what was once touted as a fun-for-all business. Two noticeable consequences have been a growing reliance on larger and faster vessels and tighter schedules.

Larger and Faster

The commercial whale-watching vessels range in size from about 50 feet in length carrying thirty-five to forty passengers to over 140 feet capable of carrying four hundred passengers. Since the advent of whale watching, which predates the creation of the sanctuary, the cruising speed of vessels has increased from an average of 11 knots (12.7 mph) to 28 knots (32 mph) with maximum speeds doubling from 20 knots (23 mph) to 40 knots (46 mph).[5]

Its dependence on weather and the abundance and distribution of whales makes whale watching a bit like commercial fishing. Weather and, more importantly, sea state are critical factors. Cold and rain discourage most whale watchers, even if the seas are calm. But a warm sunny day on shore is no guarantee of a pleasant day at sea. Try as the companies may on their websites and with dockside chatter, no amount of spin fools all of the people all of the time. Once the word begins to spread that it is not a good time to go whale watching, it is difficult to convince people otherwise, even if conditions have improved. The lag time can be as much as three weeks. In any event, the good weather increases the pressure to pack the boats and move quickly.

The abundance of whales is the variable of most concern to whale watchers themselves, but a smart operator who depends heavily on charter groups and tours scheduled months in advance can sometimes slog through a dry year. There are ups and downs mostly having to do with the abundance of prey. For humpback whales, the critical factor is the abundance of sand lance.

For commercial operators, however, distribution is what matters most. If the whales are evenly distributed throughout the sanctuary, the captain generally heads out to the nearest location where whales have been seen previously. Spotting another whale watcher on station is a dead giveaway. Some chatter occurs over the VHF radio between captains, even from competing companies, but captains seldom want to share a hot spot. Some demonstrate great craftiness and intuitive abilities to determine where the whales might be. A flock of birds on the horizon possibly circling feeding whales or a slick on the surface indicating a possible upwelling might be all he needs to locate his catch of the day.

The distance traveled can vary from a short run of about 15 miles from Gloucester to Jeffreys Ledge in the northwest corner of the sanctuary to as much as 40 miles or more to the southwest corner. Boats traveling from Boston must move slowly through the inner and outer harbor and travel 25 miles just to reach the western boundary. The greater the distance, the more fuel and time it takes to get there.

Showtime

But for occasional seasickness, the roar of engines, and universally annoying loudspeakers used by naturalists, whale watching can be wildly entertaining. When the humpbacks are breaching or diving under the boats, gannets are plunging headlong into the water to feed on leftovers, and Atlantic white-sided dolphins are leaping in unison alongside; that's entertainment!

The industry prefers to call it ecotourism, but the marketing and presentation is heavily weighted toward entertainment. It is not staged, as the naturalists are quick to explain, but there is an element of prearrangement to the scene. The companies cannot control the weather or the exact number and location of the whales, but they alone control the type of vessel used, how fast it travels, where it goes, and how close to the animals it gets. The Coast Guard regulates the seaworthiness and carrying capacity of the vessels, but the sanctuary, which is charged with protecting the "resources" of the sanctuary, places no limits on how whale watching is conducted. The commercial operators are issued no permits, conform to no enforceable viewing standards, and as many vessels come and go as the market can bear and as often as they please. The recreational whale watchers are simply allowed to roam wildly.

Laissez-faire Policy

Were the sanctuary otherwise occupied with a crowded regulatory agenda, one might conclude that whale watching, widely considered to be a benign activity, was simply a low action priority. Instead, the industry is the beneficiary of a laissez-faire policy that derives from a mindset within the Congress and various agencies within NOAA captured by the term "living resources."

Congress first declared that national marine sanctuaries should be created among other purposes to "maintain for future generations the habitat, and ecological services, of the natural assemblage of *living resources* that inhabit these areas" [emphasis added].[6] It may seem a quibble to note that both living and nonliving "resources" generally are associated with money or the means of producing wealth and "use." The notion that "resources" are somehow to be possessed, used, and dominated is a human invention that in the case of living resources subordinates any intrinsic right to exist that those living resources might have. For some, the mandate to "maintain for future generations" may reflect a conservation ethic that is altruistic, but it is still distinctly anthropogenic when juxtaposed with the Endangered Species Act's mandate "to facilitate to the extent compatible with the primary objective of resource protection, all public and private uses of the resources of these marine areas not prohibited pursuant to other authorities."[7]

Relevance of Aesthetics

Whether the capacity to experience awe is unique to humans or not, wanting to encounter other species in the wild is, as the poet Alison Hawthorne

Deming puts it, "one of our better desires."[8] Awe can inspire a respect for nature with distinct spiritual and religious overtones. Many who have watched whales within the sanctuary claim to have experienced such feelings even in the din of the typical trip. But is the fulfillment of this desire, even in the interest of environmental education, in the best interest of the species? And if so, what are the standards for presenting this experience to the public?

It is not currently a matter of much concern, but the sanctuary's mandate to protect living resources extends to the aesthetic value they contribute to the sanctuary. By what aesthetic standard should wildlife observation be permitted? The National Park Service and U.S. Fish and Wildlife Service have wrestled with these kinds of issues for many years with some measure of success. Robert Underwood Johnson, one of the early champions of national parks, once wrote that "What is needed is the inculcation, by every agency, of *beauty as a principle*, that life may be made happier and more elevating for all the generations who shall follow us."[9]

Perhaps it is time for the National Marine Fisheries Service (NMFS) and National Marine Sanctuary Program (NMSP) to begin inculcating aesthetics into the management of whales and acknowledging that humans have a moral responsibility toward these animals. Even if there is doubt in the minds of some about this last issue, uncertainty requires a more deliberate and respectful approach than now exists.

Education or Edu-tainment?

Whether whale watching has significant educational value has not been a subject of much study. Considering that the standard whale watch is only three or four hours long (at least half of which is spent getting to and from the whales), it is highly unlikely that the experience results in any measurable advancement of knowledge or improvement of powers of observation. It is probably better described as a form of "edu-tainment," a term popularized by Ted Turner, the creator of Captain Planet. Many classroom teachers who incorporate whale watches into classroom curricula, on the other hand, believe the trips serve a great purpose, reinforcing other forms of instruction.

Practitioners of experiential education such as the Sea Education Association, Outward Bound, Mariner Scouts, and the Ocean Classroom Foundation have demonstrated convincingly the educational value, even the life-altering effect, of trips extending from a few days to an entire semester.

In 2006, the Provincetown Center for Coastal Studies and Ocean Classroom Foundation launched a program called MassSail to conduct teacher workshops and programs for middle school and high school students lasting up to two weeks aboard the schooner *Spirit of Massachusetts*. The programs focused on the coastal waters of Massachusetts with an emphasis on marine mammals and the Stellwagen Bank National Marine Sanctuary. Still, in Massachusetts and most of the country, there is no generally accepted working definition of environmental education. With the federal government's emphasis on leaving no child behind, in the narrowest sense, it should come as no surprise that the National Marine Sanctuary Program has left environmental education to others to define.

However one chooses to define the experience of whale watching, what is clear is that the educational, aesthetic, entertainment, conservation, and research values of the experience are determined entirely by the commercial operators, who are not licensed or regulated by the sanctuary in any way, and who make no financial contribution to the management of the sanctuary. If concessionaires have a tendency to undermine the purposes and policies of national parks, the commercial whale-watching industry operating within the sanctuary carry on as if they own the place.

Policy versus Practice

The immediate, long-term, and cumulative impacts on marine mammals from whale-watching activities has been a matter of concern in New England for longer than there has been a sanctuary, although in fairness to the sanctuary program, which has yet to place any restrictions on whale watching, the primary responsibility for protecting marine mammals rests with NMFS. The service has slowly begun to take action on preventing marine mammal entanglements (see chapter 8) and ship strikes (see chapter 7), despite efforts by the Bush White House to quash, delay, or otherwise water down wildlife regulations in general.

The issue that both NMFS and NMSP are uncomfortable dealing with is behavioral disturbance; in part because research is in its infancy; in part because interpretation of existing findings would require delving into matters of aesthetics and ethics. Federal policy, on the other hand, is clear:

Interacting with wild marine mammals should not be attempted, and viewing marine mammals must be conducted in a manner that does not harass the animals.

NMFS cannot support, condone, approve or authorize activities that involve closely approaching, interacting or attempting to interact with whales, dolphins, porpoises, seals or sea lions in the wild. This includes attempting to swim with, pet, touch or elicit a reaction from the animals. NMFS believes that such interactions constitute "harassment" as defined in the MMPA [Marine Mammal Protection Act].[10]

The Marine Mammal Protection Act defines the term harassment as "any act of pursuit, torment or annoyance which (A) has the potential to injure a marine mammal or marine stock in the wild; or (B) has the potential to disturb a marine mammal or marine stock in the wild by causing a disruption of behavioral patterns; including but not limited to migration, breathing, nursing, breeding, feeding, and sheltering."[11] The Marine Mammal Protection and Endangered Species Acts, notes one environmental historian, embody "the legal idea that a listed nonhuman resident of the United States is guaranteed, in a special sense, life and liberty."[12]

NMFS has implemented regulations under the Endangered Species Act limiting approaches to humpbacks to 100 yards in Hawaii and Alaska and to 500 yards for right whales in the North Atlantic. But in the Gulf of Maine and especially Stellwagen Bank, which is arguably the most intensively exploited whale-watching area in the world, the service has turned a blind eye toward commercial and recreational whale watchers, relying instead on unenforceable recommended viewing guidelines and educational brochures. Fortunately for right whales, the prime whale-watching season occurs when most right whales are in the Canadian Provinces and feeding grounds are as far east as Greenland.

The current guidelines, which have been in effect since 1999 following two potentially fatal collisions in 1998, address the issues of speed and direction, the number of vessels that can be close to animals at any one time, and close approaches, while astutely avoiding the issue of harassment. They are intended to apply to any vessel that might be considered to be whale watching, including commercial whale-watch boats, recreational boaters who specifically go out to the sanctuary to see the whales, commercial fishermen fishing around whales, and charter boats. They do not address the issue of vessel speed of whale watchers en route to the sanctuary and do not apply to boats in transit.

From a distance of between 2 and 1 mile from a whale, vessels are advised to reduce speed to 13 knots, to post a dedicated lookout, and to avoid sudden changes in speed and direction. Between 1 mile and ½ mile, speed is supposed to be reduced further to 10 knots and then down to 7 knots between ½ mile and 600 yards. Vessels are advised to avoid head-on approaches at all times.

Within 600 feet, the distance generally referred to as a close approach, vessels are supposed to parallel the course and speed of the whale up to the designated speed within that distance, which at that distance generally would be 7 knots. Captains are to approach and leave stationary whales at no more than idle or "no wake" speed, not to exceed 7 knots, not to intentionally drift down on whales, and not to approach within 100 feet of whales. If whales approach within 100 feet on their own, the captain is supposed to put the engines in neutral and not to reengage until the whales have been observed clear of the vessel.

When more than one vessel is in the area, only one vessel at a time is supposed to be within the so-called "close approach zone" and must limit its viewing time to fifteen minutes. A maximum of two vessels may stand by at a distance of ½ mile to 600 feet. The captains of the various vessels are supposed to coordinate viewing using their VHF radios.

Noncompliance

Noncompliance with the guidelines falls into several categories. The most obvious violation that has been observed widely is speeding. It occurs within every approach zone. The Wiley study reported an overall level of industry noncompliance of the recommended speeds of 78 percent.

Pursuit is common as well, as the whales are frequently on the move. Humpbacks pose less of a challenge, as they generally cruise at speeds under 10 miles per hour, although they are capable of bursts of 15 miles per hour or more. It is the fin whale that poses a challenge for many captains. Known as the greyhounds of the sea, these sleek and elegant creatures are capable of swimming 20 miles per hour. The best looks most people ever have of a finback are when they are feeding at the surface or cruising just below the surface. Captains who find themselves with a finback alongside often cannot resist the sport of chasing the animal. One can only imagine the startled reaction of a finback when it sees a giant hulk twice its length roaring along by its side.

By condoning close approaches of 100 feet by vessels while underway and by allowing whales to come closer when stationary, NMFS has encouraged a variety of questionable and potentially harmful practices. Drifting down has become so commonplace that whale watchers have come to expect it and register disappointment if they cannot get up close and personal. Drifting down occurs when wind and currents move the boat toward the whale, even when the engines are in neutral. A skillful captain can maneuver his boat to make it look as though the whale came to the boat, and sometimes, to the ultimate delight of the crowd, they do. It is the highlight of many passengers' trip. Is this normal behavior? Are the whales displaying some degree of "natural" curiosity? Does anyone care?

A sample of the enthusiasm generated by a close approach is contained in the following daily log:

> For over 30 minutes, Cajun circled the vessel. With our engines shut down, we drifted in the waves, as she circled us. From one side of the boat to the other, we all moved back and forth, looking and waiting to see where she'd appear next. Under the bow, off the port and starboard sides. She continued to circle the vessel. As she did, we could see the outline of her body and flukes below the bow and her white flippers glowing green through the water as it reflected through the plankton and algae. This close boat approach lasted so long, we were 20 minutes late returning to port for our second trip of the day, but it was well worth it![13]

Cutting in front of the path of a whale is another regular occurrence, although often difficult for nonmariners to observe from a distance. Nevertheless, if the course of the vessel and whale intersect at any point, even a half mile away, it is a potential collision course. At some point, the whale may feel threatened, and increase its swimming speed or veer off.

A variation of the chase is the "leapfrog." This occurs when a traveling whale dives and a vessel speeds ahead in anticipation of its resurfacing. This almost always involves exceeding the recommended speed limit for a short distance.

Habituation

Veteran operators recall that there was a time when the whales, especially humpbacks, did not approach the boats. The first scientist to report on habituation among whales in the region was the late William Watkins, a senior scientist at the Woods Hole Oceanographic Institution and a pioneer in the field of marine mammal acoustics.

A review of our whale observations of more than 25 years indicated that each of the species commonly observed within 35 km of Cape Cod reacted differently to stimuli from human activities, and that these responses have gradually changed with time. Over the years of exposure to ships, for example, minke whales (*Balaenoptera acutorostrata*) have changed from frequent positive interest to generally uninterested reactions, finback whales (*B. physalus*) have changed from mostly negative to uninterested reactions, right whales (*Eubalaena glacialis*) have apparently continued the same variety of responses with little change, and humpbacks (*Megaptera novaeangliae*) have dramatically changed from mixed responses that were often negative to often strongly positive reactions. These reactions appeared to result mostly from three types of stimuli: primarily underwater sound, then light reflectivity, and tactile sensation. The whale reactions were related to their assessment of the stimuli as attractive, uninteresting or disturbing, their assessment of the movements of the sources of the stimuli relative to their own positions, and their assessment of the occurrence of stimuli as expected or unexpected. Whale reactions were modified by their previous experience and current activity: habituation often occurred rapidly, attention to other stimuli or preoccupation with other activities sometimes overcame their interest or wariness of stimuli, and inactivity seemed to allow whales to notice and react to stimuli that otherwise might have been ignored. The changes over time in the reactions of whales to stimuli from human activities were gradual and constantly varying with increased exposure to these activities.[14]

Habituation is obviously a good thing for the business of whale watching, but is it a good thing for the whales? Is Stellwagen a sanctuary or a zoo where the animals are on full display for the sole benefit of the viewing public? Is it a right or privilege to watch whales?

Noise

Even if every operational guideline were adhered to strictly, there remains the issue of noise. A significant body of scientific literature shows that whales avoid loud sounds in the range of 110 to 120 decibels by abruptly altering course and taking abnormally longer dives. Whether these startled responses have any lasting behavioral effect is a subject that is being researched actively. In the meantime, the only explanation for allowing vessels in the sanctuary to approach whales so closely is that the whale-watching industry wants it that way. Their counterparts in almost every other major whale-watching center, on the other hand, have opted for a far more precautionary approach. In the Pacific Northwest, the best practices guidelines of the Whale Watch Operators Association Northwest urge vessels not to approach within 100 meters/yards of any whale.

Total Lawlessness

If the industry is in routine violation of what even it considers best practices, recreational whale watching is conducted in a regime of total lawlessness. The commercial industry, NMFS, and SBNMS have been wringing their hands over the situation for two decades, but nothing has been done to bring the situation under control.

In recent years, the Provincetown Center for Coastal Studies routinely documented and reported egregious examples of whale harassment on the part of recreational boaters and fishermen (mostly of tuna) to NOAA enforcement officers. A few choice examples include:

- A 50-foot charter fishing boat from Quincy with over thirty passengers aboard backing up over a group of humpbacks bubble feeding. Bubble clouds are created when a single whale or group of whales blows bubbles to confuse and trap schools of fish. The whales then rise slowly through the cloud of bubbles with their mouths agape. The scene of effervescent white and green water, mouths the size of pickup beds, and swarming birds looking for a free meal is breathtaking. In Hawaii and occasionally in the North Atlantic, a group of whales will arrange themselves in a circle and create a bubble ring. Aside from interfering with the whales' feeding, the propellers of the boat could have injured the whales' jaws or baleen plates.
- A pleasure boat from Boston with five adults and one child aboard traveling in excess of 15 knots weaves around commercial whale-watch boats and surfacing whales like a water skier on a slalom course. Most recreational boaters are unaware of any of the laws regarding whale protection and those that do often claim they only apply to the commercial whale-watch boats.
- Five adults in a sport-fishing boat from Marshfield trolling slowly head-on to a group of four or five whales that are forced to make an abrupt 90-degree turn to avoid collision. The no-approach zone is

roughly described as the area 30 degrees either side of the head of a whale.

- Three young men in a speed boat roar up to a bubble cloud in an apparent state of intoxication. With nobody at the controls, one of the men dives head first into the bubble cloud.
- A 25- to 30-foot tuna fishing boat from Scituate with five men aboard drags lures through a group of feeding humpbacks and narrowly misses a finback by about 15 feet.
- A recreational boat also from Scituate with a woman and two men aboard comes up behind a whale, forcing it to dive, and then travels over its path in pursuit.
- A slow-moving recreational boat with an obscene name from Waterford, Connecticut, with four adults and two children aboard enters a bubble cloud, forcing the group of whales to abandon feeding and one whale to dive.

In July and August, the recreational boaters often show up in great numbers and are referred to disdainfully by the commercial operators as the "mosquito fleet." Occasional arguments break out over the water or over the radio, often punctuated with obscene hand gestures. When the mosquito fleet is around, the recommended guideline about not having more than one vessel at a time within the close approach zone (100 feet to 300 feet) may as well not exist. In any event, the guidelines are not enforceable legal requirements applicable to either commercial or recreational whale watchers.

What is more disturbing is that even gross violations of the MMPA or ESA, such as those noted above, are rarely if ever prosecuted.[15]

The Necessity of Precaution

Just as government prosecutors are wont to say when they are presented with alleged violations of either the MMPA or ESA, it may take blood in the water to provoke a discussion of the right of marine mammals to be left alone. NMFS complains that the definition of harassment is too vague and not scientific. Scientists are more comfortable collecting biopsy samples and conducting necropsies than they are speaking to the issue of harassment and torment. The few who have, run the risk of being ridiculed by their colleagues.

One scientist who has not been afraid to speak up is Peter Tyack, a senior scientist at the Woods Hole Oceanographic Institution. Tyack has spent his career conducting research on the social behavior of acoustic communication of whales and dolphins. His work on the effects on whales of the Navy's low frequency array (LFA) sonar system for detecting enemy submarines has shown that underwater blasts definitely trigger abnormal behavior. Whether this results in irreparable harm, such as a disruption of reproductive rates, is a matter of conjecture and would require years of research. In the meantime, Tyack favors adopting a precautionary approach. "A lot of the controversy [over anthropogenic sound] depends on whether you want to give the animals or the noise makers the benefit of the doubt."[16]

One explanation given by NMFS for not regulating whale watching is that scientists still are not certain what constitutes disturbed behavior. For starters, whales are difficult to study, as most of their behavior occurs underwater. Then there is the issue of chronic underfunding of such studies, which many of the usual marine mammal funders (including NMFS) regard as a low priority. And finally, there are issues of interpretation, as most observational studies are unable to control other variables. Long-term impacts also may be disproportional, as some individual animals and groups — such as the humpbacks on Stellwagen Bank, which exhibit a high level of site fidelity — are subjected to intense levels of whale watching.

More research clearly is needed, but as the highly respected Canadian marine biologist Jon Lien has concluded, "What appears clear at present is that large numbers of vessels which persistently approach whales too closely, or move too quickly, or operate too noisily, or pursue the animals may interrupt their short-term performance of life processes."[17] Lien has urged his country to adopt a regulatory program based on the principle of precaution. "The precautionary approach," he explains, "requires that the exploitation of any resource does not proceed faster than knowledge about the impact of exploitation, and that it is done in a cautious manner which proactively avoids environmental harm. Thus research is required to show that a resource is not threatened by an activity if it is to proceed."

The precautionary approach happens to be recognized by no less of an authority than the International Whaling Commission, which has issued general principles for whale watching that go well beyond the NOAA guidelines for the Northeast or Stellwagen Bank in either principle or practice.[18] Is it asking too much of our "oceans agency" or the sanctuary to be proactive?

PART III

STARTING OVER

In part at risk and in part still pristine, the national marine sanctuaries are their own proof that they must be guarded for future generations. —Jean-Michel Cousteau

Chapter 10

Purposes and Policies Revisited

No unkindness is intended by the observation that if the act creating the Gerry E. Studds Stellwagen Bank National Marine Sanctuary were repealed by Congress tomorrow, the area would be no more vulnerable to disturbance and ruin than it has been for the past fifteen years. NOAA's own 2007 Condition Report gave the sanctuary a barely passing grade, which speaks volumes about the quality of its stewardship. Meanwhile, pressures within and around the sanctuary continue to mount; the latest being the completion of an LNG deepwater port and the startup of another just to the north of the sanctuary. A once-abundant and ecologically diverse fishing ground continues for some species to be fished to the point of collapse. And the great endangered whales that have given the sanctuary world renown may be more threatened today than before there was a sanctuary. For most commercial users of the sanctuary, it has more or less been business as usual.

Déjà Vu

Lest we forget the historical context of the 1992 designation, Stellwagen Bank was spared the imminent threat of sand and gravel mining by a specific prohibition.[1] On the other hand, with gasoline prices approaching $4 per gallon at the pump, it is also worth recalling that Congress and NOAA both waffled on the issue of prohibiting oil and gas exploration and development.

The loophole can be found in Article IV, Section 1 (Activities Subject to Regulation) of the Designation Document (see appendix D). Here it states that "exploring for, developing or producing oil, gas" may be subject to regulation, including prohibition "to the extent necessary and reasonable to ensure the protection and management of the conservation, recreational, ecological, historical, research, educational or esthetic resources and qualities of the area."

During the public hearings and comment period that preceded designation of Stellwagen Bank, many people expressed the view that oil and gas development was an inappropriate activity inside *any* national marine sanctuary.[2] In its final environmental impact statement on the original master plan, NOAA straddled the issue.[3] First it stated, "NOAA agrees that oil and gas development is *usually* an incompatible use of a national marine sanctuary" [emphasis added].[4] But the agency stopped short of imposing a prohibition, stating:

> Among the factors considered by NOAA were the historically low industry interest in the Stellwagen Bank area, based upon low estimates of recoverable oil and gas resources; the current Presidential moratorium on such activities, effective until the year 2000; and the ability of NOAA to protect the Sanctuary's living and non-living resources by listing the activity as "subject to regulation" at the time of designation. Moreover the general regulatory prohibitions against alteration of, or construction on, the seabed and discharges into the Sanctuary would prohibit most of the activities involved in exploration, development and production of hydrocarbon resources. Based upon these considerations, there appears to be little or no reason to specifically prohibit oil and gas activities in the Sanctuary at this time.[5]

In her comments on NOAA's draft environmental impact statement, the Massachusetts secretary of environmental affairs, Susan Tierney, asked for clarification on the agency's process for determining which activities to prohibit and which to make subject to regulation (including prohibition), noting that the same legal authorities that had led NOAA to believe that "the current management regime is adequate and would be appropriate" under sanctuary oversight to evaluate the appropriateness of oil and gas development also applied to sand and gravel mining.[6]

It was a tricky question that NOAA dodged with the following "trust us" response:

> Should circumstances related to recoverable resources and/or industry interest in development change in the future, NOAA will be able to make necessary determinations regarding the necessity for a prohibition on offshore hydrocarbon activities within Sanctuary boundaries at that time.[7]

While there still may be "low interest" in the Stellwagen Bank area, NOAA may no longer have any say in the matter. The Omnibus Energy Act of 2005, signed into law in July 2005, calls for an inventory of potential oil and gas resources in all federal waters, including within waters of *all national marine sanctuaries*. With this new law in place, whatever authority NOAA presumed to have in 1992 has vanished.

The implications of the Energy Act were not lost on supporters of the Cordell Bank and Gulf of Farallones National Marine Sanctuaries off the coast of California, where the threat of oil exploration served as the primary impetus for their designation in the 1980s.[8] Knowing that NOAA did not have the muscle within the administration to press for a prohibition, they turned to Congress. In April 2008, the House of Representatives passed a bill (H.R. 1187) introduced by Representative Lynn Woolsey (D-Ca.) and Representative Wayne Gilchrest (R-Md.) that would not only prohibit oil and gas exploration within the boundaries of both sanctuaries but double their size. A companion bill (S.2635) introduced by Senator Barbara Boxer is awaiting action in the Senate.

In 1989, NOAA had an opportunity to exclude all of Cordell Bank NMS from oil and gas leasing when it published its first regulations, but instead only prohibited leasing within a small area that amounted to less than 4 percent of the sanctuary.[9] Only two years before, Interior Secretary Donald Hodel had proposed opening up as many as 6.5 million acres off the California coast to oil leases. Representative Leon Panetta (D-Ca), who had led the congressional fight against leasing in Monterey Bay and later went on to become President Clinton's chief of staff, called the action a "declaration of war against the California coastline."

Runt of the Litter

NOAA's evasive response to Secretary Tierney regarding oil and gas exploration on Stellwagen Bank had little or nothing to do with scientific objectivity and everything to do with the fact that the national sanctuary program has throughout its thirty-six-year history been kept in check by the White House's Office of Management and Budget, the Department of the Interior (especially the Minerals Management Service), Department of Energy, and by other agencies within NOAA, most notably the National Marine Fisheries Service (NMFS). As the authors of one highly critical government-funded report once observed, "The sanctuary program has been managed as the runt of the NOAA litter."[10] Lastly, and it only may be an accident of history,

NOAA's placement within the Department of Commerce, which previously had a pro-business orientation and no public lands management experience, has shaped and arguably distorted the sanctuary program from the outset.[11]

Whatever the causes, the sanctuary program's propensity for avoiding controversy, deferring to other agencies, and accommodating just about any new or continued use raises serious questions about its utility as an ocean management regime. In 2000, Congress seems to have sensed the program's derailment when it declared a moratorium on the designation of any new sanctuaries, a move ostensibly designed to give the national program the opportunity to regroup and improve its management of existing agencies. The moratorium, together with increased funding during the Clinton administration, enabled the program to move forward with the development of management plans. However, it may have had an unintended effect of sidelining the sanctuary program from the growing national concern about ocean protection and management.

Nothing constructive would be gained by abolishing the Stellwagen Bank National Marine Sanctuary. What is needed is a management plan that fulfills the purposes and policies for which it was created. The management plan of 1993 clearly has produced disappointing results (see chapters 5 through 9) and not a single activity that might have been subject to regulation over the past fifteen years (including oil and gas exploration) has been regulated.

The amendments of 1992 that designated Stellwagen Bank included a requirement that all sanctuaries revise their management plans every five years. The obvious intent was to maintain the relevance and contemporaneousness of the plan and to regularly and fully engage the general public (as opposed to users) in the issues facing the sanctuary. Theoretically, the Stellwagen management plan should have been reviewed publicly and revised in 1998, 2003, and 2008. What happened during that ten-year period is the subject of later discussion (see chapter 11).

During the course of a management plan review, stakeholders and the general public have the opportunity (again, theoretically) to make adjustments to the existing plan based on current conditions and new scientific information, which in the case of Stellwagen Bank has been considerable enough to render the 1993 management plan obsolete. Management plan reviews also serve to enhance public understanding and support for the underlying purposes and policies of the national marine sanctuaries program, which are:

(1) ... to identify and designate as national marine sanctuaries areas of the marine environment which are of special national significance and to manage these areas as the National Marine Sanctuary System.[12]

The National Marine Sanctuaries website includes a short video that begins: "Did you ever want to own something really precious? Something beautiful? Well, you do. We all do. See those fourteen gems? Whether a whale breeding ground, a Civil War shipwreck, a coral reef, or a kelp forest, each spot has such unique value that it has been set aside by Congress."[13]

Congress actually had a more mundane mission in mind. It was not to "set aside" the crown jewels or precious gems of the U.S. oceans and Great Lakes but to establish a policy for coordinating management of offshore lands. In the late 1960s, Representative Hastings Keith (R-Ma.), Gerry Studds' predecessor, had in fact envisioned setting aside a large system of marine wilderness preserves, but by the early 1970s, the tide had turned, largely due to opposition from petroleum and fishing interests (see chapter 4). Instead of pressing for protection of areas where no commercial human use would be allowed, the emphasis was on "balanced," "dual," "varied," and "multiple use" of a significantly larger area than has since been designated or even contemplated by the national marine sanctuary program.

To the possible astonishment of some commercial users who regard the designation of Stellwagen Bank as a sanctuary as more meddlesome than meaningful, the term "multiple use" never appears in the act and certainly cannot be interpreted as an *inalienable* right. Put another way, a sanctuary is not a commercial zone. Conversely, while sanctuaries may have unique qualities, as in the case of Stellwagen Bank, sanctuary designation is not reserved for unique areas; indeed, the word "unique" never appears in the act either.

Congress stopped short of *setting aside* these areas, but by defining sanctuaries as areas of "special national significance" it clearly intended that they somehow be managed differently in accordance with their national significance. It is an important distinction, because it evokes the principle of the common good and the responsibilities of government under the public trust doctrine. Gerry Studds frequently reminded his constituents and colleagues that "the sanctuaries belong to all of us."

*   *   *

(2) . . . to provide authority for comprehensive and coordinated conservation and management of these marine areas, and activities affecting them, in a manner which complements existing regulatory authorities.[14]

Throughout the early debates over marine sanctuaries, the Department of the Interior insisted that it had authority to protect areas with ecological, environmental, and biological values under the Outer Continental Shelf Lands Act (OCSLA) and National Environmental Policy Act (NEPA). At the time, the Nixon administration's promotion of offshore oil development convinced many members of Congress otherwise. Much the same could be said today about the Bush administration.

To this day, you can still hear grumbling among middle-level bureaucrats within other federal agencies, and especially within the National Marine Fisheries Service, to the effect that national marine sanctuaries are "redundant" and that ample legal authority exists to protect the marine environment from abuse.[15] A "short list" of authorities includes the Outer Continental Shelf Lands Act, Magnuson-Stevens Fishery Conservation and Management Act, Sustainable Fisheries Act, Clean Water Act, Endangered Species Act, Marine Mammal Protection Act, Antiquities Act of 1906, Ports and Waterways Safety Act, Act to Prevent Pollution from Ships, National Historic Preservation Act, Coastal Zone Management Act, and Massachusetts Ocean Sanctuaries Act.

Despite what may seem to be a proliferation of authorities, Congress envisioned the National Marine Sanctuaries Act as a means of focusing upon specific areas of the ocean. Before there was a Stellwagen Bank National Marine Sanctuary, the 842-square-mile area that makes up the sanctuary was just a small part of the Gulf of Maine in the eyes of most other agencies. Designation of Stellwagen Bank as a special area in theory focuses governmental responsibility and makes coordination a legal requirement as opposed to a sound administrative principle. This stated purpose reflects the congressional finding that "while the need to control the effects of particular activities has led to enactment of resource-specific legislation, these laws cannot in all cases provide a coordinated and comprehensive approach to the conservation and management of special areas of the marine environment."[16]

* * *

(3) . . . to maintain the natural biological communities in the national marine sanctuaries, and to protect, and, where appropriate, restore and enhance natural habitats, populations, and ecological processes.[17]

Herein lies what might be considered the underlying "ocean ethic" or grand purpose of the National Marine Sanctuaries Act. It echoes the land ethic of Aldo Leopold that "A thing is right when it tends to preserve the integrity, stability, and beauty of the biotic community. It is wrong when it tends otherwise."[18]

Has the Stellwagen Bank National Marine Sanctuary been protected and managed in accordance with this stated purpose? Not yet.

*   *   *

(4) . . . to enhance public awareness, understanding, appreciation, and wise and sustainable use of the marine environment, and the natural, historical, cultural, and archeological resources of the National Marine Sanctuary System.[19]

Dan Basta, the director of the National Marine Sanctuary Program since 2000, has done more in eight years than all his predecessors over the previous twenty-eight years to increase public awareness and interest in marine sanctuaries. An unabashed media enthusiast, he presses his sanctuary superintendents to tap into the electronic age with hip websites, films, podcasts, and simulations to promote their sanctuaries and has teamed up with celebrities such as Sylvia Earle, Jean-Michel Cousteau, and others to spread the word.

Shortly after taking office, Basta told a group of Stellwagen Bank supporters that it was his goal to model the national marine sanctuary system after the national park system. Cousteau's PBS documentary series *America's Underwater Treasures* could not have been more "on message."[20] "In part at risk and in part still pristine, the national marine sanctuaries," said Cousteau, "are their own proof that they must be guarded for future generations."[21]

The program's effort to popularize the sanctuaries generally is regarded as a means of building support for their maintenance and operations, while broadening the public's understanding of the marine environment. The sanctuaries have been encouraged to build partnerships with educational institutions and to treat the sanctuaries as ocean classrooms.

*   *   *

(5) . . . to support, promote, and coordinate scientific research on, and long-term monitoring of, the resources of these marine areas.[22]

Stellwagen Bank and the other sanctuaries in the system often are referred to as laboratories for ocean research. Although a congressional moratorium has prevented the creation of new sanctuaries since 2000, previously the NMSP searched for areas that were "representative" of large area-wide marine ecosystems. By definition, being "representative" may discredit an area's "uniqueness," but the distinction is largely academic. Although it has had very little funding to initiate or support research, the Stellwagen Bank sanctuary has collaborated with numerous institutions and agencies to gain a better understanding of how the system works. The list includes the USGS on ocean floor mapping, National Undersea Research Center on habitat structure and disturbance, Cornell University on passive acoustic detection of whales, Massachusetts Water Resource Authority on water quality monitoring, and Provincetown Center for Coastal Studies on marine mammal abundance. Research funding, however, has been limited and inconsistent. In 2008, Stellwagen Bank's total research budget was less than $250,000 and included no plan for long-term monitoring, which most scientists agree is an essential management tool.

*　*　*

(6) . . . to facilitate to the extent compatible with the primary objective of resource protection, all public and private uses of the resources of these marine areas not prohibited pursuant to other authorities.[23]

If the National Marine Sanctuaries Act contains a litmus test, this is it. All uses not specifically prohibited, such as sand and gravel mining on Stellwagen Bank, must be compatible with *the primary objective of resource protection*. The statement reflects a purity of purpose that is undeniable. On the other hand, by not defining compatibility or the means by which it can be determined, Congress delegated broad authority to the secretary of commerce to shape each sanctuary. With the addition of the words "to facilitate," it also could be argued that Congress was promoting public and private uses.

In either case, the future of Stellwagen Bank and of all sanctuaries in the system ultimately rests on how and by whom compatibility is determined. After fifteen years, Stellwagen Bank has still not framed its future management in these terms.

*　*　*

(7) . . . to develop and implement coordinated plans for the protection and management of these areas with appropriate Federal agencies, State and local govern-

ments, Native American tribes and organizations, international organizations, and other public and private interests concerned with the continuing health and resilience of these marine areas.[24]

Congress initially perceived and the courts have upheld that regulatory gaps exist among the many agencies of government that have some authority over U.S. oceans and the Great Lakes. The solution was to develop and implement coordinated plans. For Stellwagen Bank, this has proven to be a formidable and time-consuming process.

*   *   *

(8) ... to create models of, and incentives for, ways to conserve and manage these areas, including the application of innovative management techniques.[25]

To date, only a small fraction of U.S. waters has been placed into the national marine sanctuary system, raising serious doubts among many marine experts that the program in its present form has broad application. The system's heavy reliance upon the consensus of commercial users and dependence on the cooperation of agencies with primary regulatory authority is cumbersome and possibly incapable of fulfilling its primary objectives. In the case of Stellwagen Bank, the sanctuary's management objectives relative to benthic habitat and marine mammal protection are subordinated to those of the National Marine Fisheries Service and New England Fisheries Management Council, and these two issues account for more than half of the sanctuary's responsibility.

*   *   *

(9) ... to cooperate with global programs encouraging conservation of marine resources.[26]

Today Stellwagen, tomorrow the world? Fulfilling this purpose seems fanciful at this time, since so little has been done to conserve marine resources even within the designated sanctuary. But to be generous, Stellwagen NMS has drawn some attention from beyond its boundaries. The realignment of the Boston shipping lanes required the approval of the International Maritime Organization (see chapter 8). For the IMO to involve itself in what otherwise might be considered a local conservation issue was a significant action that could lead to similar actions around the globe.[27] Stellwagen Bank has also recently created a diplomatic link with the Dominican Republic. Its national marine sanctuary on Silver Bank is the breeding ground for the humpback whales that travel north to the Gulf of Maine in the spring and summer. And there is potential for innovation in the areas of marine zoning that could have broader application, although in this area the United States has fallen behind a number of other countries.

Lastly, the specific enabling legislation for Stellwagen Bank (the Oceans Act of 1992) echoes the third basic purpose of the National Marine Sanctuaries Act (above), stating (emphasis added):

> The purpose of the regulations in this Part is to implement the designation of the Stellwagen Bank National Marine Sanctuary by regulating activities affecting the Sanctuary consistent with the terms of that designation in order *to protect and manage the conservation, ecological, recreational, research, educational, historical, cultural, and aesthetic resources and qualities of the area.*[28]

While the NMSP and its parent NOAA continue to consider what they might manage (while researching and monitoring the steady decline of most resources within the sanctuary), among the purposes for which all sanctuaries were created and the primary purpose for which Stellwagen Bank was created is *to protect and manage.* These are not tasks that require ten, fifteen, or twenty years of study, even if research and monitoring are ongoing activities. At some point, there must be the will to act.

Chapter 11

The Plan

In the opening scene of Samuel Beckett's famous play *Waiting for Godot,* a tramp by the name of Estragon is sitting in a wasteland beneath a dying tree trying to remove his boot. He continues to struggle throughout much of the first act while chattering gibberish with his companion Vladimir. At one point he mutters, "Nothing to be done." Eventually, he succeeds, looks into the boot, and finds nothing. The two men spend two days waiting for someone named Godot who never arrives and may not even exist. The only action in the play is waiting. The metaphysical implication, as one critic put it, is that "the act of waiting is never over . . . nothing is completed because nothing can be completed."[1]

It has been sixteen years since Congress created the Stellwagen Bank National Marine Sanctuary and laid out the basic purposes for which it should be protected and managed (see chapter 3). The enabling legislation — which identified the area as being of national significance for its biological productivity, uniqueness, and diversity — specifically prohibited sand and gravel mining, an imminent threat at the time, and identified a number of other activities that might be subject to future regulation. The assumption was that the National Marine Sanctuary Program (NMSP) would take further action to protect the sanctuary once it became organized and was able to set its priorities. That was 1992. The waiting public, like Estragon, has been staring into an empty boot ever since.

Management Plan Review (aka, "the Process")

By law, the NMSP is required to review its management plans for each of its thirteen sanctuaries every five years. The first management plan for the SBNMS was issued in July 1993.

The first sanctuary manager and one of the authors of the 1993 management plan was Brad Barr, a marine ecologist who had served as the critical areas coordinator for the Massachusetts Office of Coastal Zone Management. Barr's attempt to start the management plan review process in 1998 was nothing short of a disaster. Advance publicity was meager, notice was short, and the venues were less than ideal; even the weather was foul. One hearing had the misfortune of being held at the Cape Cod Community College in Barnstable during a winter rain storm. Either campus security was not notified in advance or the storm knocked out some of the outdoor lighting leading from the parking lots, but for a half hour some of those who showed up wandered through the darkness looking for the hearing room like mariners lost in the fog. The symbolism was unnerving.

The second round of scoping hearings more or less covered the same ground as the hearings that preceded passage of the SBNMS five years earlier. Supporters of the sanctuary generally complained that nothing had been accomplished in the first five years. Opponents, notably a handful of commercial fishermen, used the occasion to debunk the sanctuary idea altogether and to publicly accuse recently retired congressman Studds of reneging on his "promise" not to further burden fishermen with regulation, a relic position of many of the region's mobile-ear fishermen who view the sanctuary as just another layer of meddlesome bureaucracy.[2] Many who attended simply asked, What marine sanctuary?

Much like the owners of a failing ball club, the NMSP decided to replace the manager. Barr was reassigned to a position in headquarters and a lengthy search began within the NOAA bureaucracy for a successor. Unlike other established service agencies like the National Park Service, the sanctuary program did not have a large pool of experienced sanctuary staff to draw from. After three tries and some pressure from Representative Bill Delahunt, Gerry Studds' successor to the 10th Massachusetts congressional district, NOAA hired Craig MacDonald. A native New Englander, MacDonald had been working in Hawaii for the state as manager of ocean resources development. In that capacity, he worked closely with the Hawaiian Islands Humpback Whale National Marine Sanctuary, which was created at the same time as the Stellwagen Bank sanctuary, and was an author of the state's ocean resources management plan, at the time one of only two such state ocean policy plans in the nation.

By the time MacDonald took over as superintendent in 2000 (the position was upgraded from manager to superintendent to conform to the National

Park Service internal bureaucracy), the sanctuary was nearly eight years old and not a day closer to knowing how it would manage and protect its resources.

Rather than drafting a revised management plan based on the public comments collected in 1998, the national program office required Stellwagen to wait while it developed a standardized management plan review process based on lessons learned at other sanctuaries. Finally, MacDonald was instructed to start over with a new round of public scoping sessions in July 2002. By the end of the year, the SBNMS had heard from more than three hundred participants and received approximately twenty thousand written comments. The process identified more than two dozen issues having to do with alteration of seafloor habitat, ecosystem protection, water quality, marine mammal protection, maritime archaeology, enforcement, research needs, and public education.

By the time the SBNMS and the NMSP had collated the public comments from 1998 and 2002, it was 2003. By the legislative clock, another five years had passed and it was time to revise the phantom management plan of 1998. The sanctuary was then ten years old and still adrift.

The Role of the Advisory Council

Section 315 of the National Marine Sanctuaries Act authorizes the establishment of sanctuary advisory councils (SACs) comprised of voting public members and nonvoting representatives of federal and state agencies. The advisory council system is intentionally modeled after that employed by the National Park Service and, as with the national parks, their actual role and effectiveness varies somewhat from sanctuary to sanctuary depending on the composition of the council and management style of the superintendent.

The SBNMS appointed its first SAC in the mid-1990s. It met infrequently and meetings often devolved into tedious debates over the meaning of words such as "protect" and "restore" or subtle distinctions between the wordings of the sanctuary's enabling legislation and its designation document. Representatives from the New England Fisheries Management Council invariably used the occasions to bully the tiny SBNMS staff, reminding them and the SAC that anything having to do with fisheries management was off limits, whereupon one or more representatives of the fishing industry would say that Gerry Studds had "promised" fishermen the right to fish as they always had.[3] The meetings tended to reinforce the thinking of professional staff throughout the sanctuary system at the time that controversy was to be avoided at all cost.

The SAC was reconstituted in October 2001 and is made up of twenty-one members, fifteen voting public members and six nonvoting ex officio members representing state and other federal agencies. Twelve public members represent specific constituent interests; namely, marine transportation, recreational fishing, fixed-gear commercial fishing, mobile-gear commercial fishing, marine-related business and industry, research, conservation, and education. three at-large members represent the general public. Each public member has a designated alternate.[4]

Following the second round of scoping meetings, the sanctuary staff and SAC condensed hundreds of public comments into four general categories: capacity building, ecosystem protection, marine mammal protection, and maritime heritage management. To address these broad topics, working groups were created to develop action plans in eleven areas: administrative capacity and infrastructure, interagency cooperation, public outreach and education, compatibility determination, ecosystem-based management, ecosystem alteration, water quality, marine mammal behavioral disturbance, marine mammal vessel strikes, marine mammal entanglement, and maritime heritage management.

Each working group was chaired by a public member of the SAC and was comprised of a dozen or more users, citizens, academicians, and agency representatives with relevant knowledge of the respective issues. Altogether more than two hundred people served voluntarily on the working groups that met on average about five times over a period of nine months from October 2003 to July 2004. By the end of this period, the working groups had developed 244 specific actions that they believed should be taken over the course of the next five years.

In October and November 2004, the SAC reviewed, amended, and ranked each action as a high, medium, or low priority. However, the SAC was not asked to participate in the writing of the actual management plan, an activity that superintendents of some other sanctuaries believe leads to a sense of "ownership" that proves valuable when ushering the plan through the political process. For MacDonald, the role of the SAC was meant to be purely advisory.

With the help of paid consultants, MacDonald and his staff then reviewed the SAC's recommendations internally (setting their own priorities and taking into account anticipated funding) and began writing a draft management plan. It was not seen again by the SAC for four years.

By all accounts, the level of discussion within the working groups was constructive and cooperative, despite obvious areas of disagreement, especially when matters of regulation and agency jurisdiction arose. Some participants were known to have held back criticisms of the process or the final recommendations of the working group, knowing that the recommendations were not likely to go far or that the working group was not the right venue for conflict resolution. Conflicts directly or indirectly concerning fisheries management, for example, ultimately would be resolved by the National Marine Fisheries Service and the New England Fisheries Management Council or the courts.

What ultimately diminished the value of the working-group process was the lack of any budgetary guidance. Instead of being asked to develop action plans based on realistic levels of funding (e.g., What would you do first if you had only $1 million in funding available over the next five years?), they were let loose like teenagers in a shopping mall with their parents' charge cards. Only after the process was completed did the sanctuary staff develop budgets for each action plan, and what they came up with was staggering. Programmatic costs (excluding federal labor costs) for implementing all of the action plans were estimated to cost $22 million. To put this figure in perspective, the annual operating, research, and facilities budget of the sanctuary has never exceeded $2.5 million. The operations, research, and facilities budget for the *entire* national marine sanctuary program was only about $45 million in FY08.

By 2006, some of the SAC members and alternates involved in the 2004 planning process had moved on to other things and other places, and others' terms were about to expire. The majority kept waiting, assuming with some justification that the Bush administration's action plan for Stellwagen Bank was simply to let the next administration deal with it.

NMSP director Dan Basta denies that the Bush/Cheney White House had anything to do with the delays. But when National Marine Fisheries Service regulations on fishing gear modification and vessel speed reductions aimed at protecting right whales first surfaced, the White House definitely expressed its displeasure, leading some SAC members to assume that the sanctuary program was also under close scrutiny and leaving them disinclined to propose any new regulations. Whether the 2008 presidential election or the fact that Bush's rival in 2004 is the junior senator from the "blue state" of

Massachusetts had anything to do with the plan's delay, were frequent topics of speculation.

With public interest in the sanctuary waning, the patience of some SAC members at a near breaking point, and MacDonald at a loss for words to explain what was happening, the SAC complained directly to NOAA administrator, retired Navy admiral Conrad Lautenbacher, Jr., noting:

> The lack of approval of the draft plan stands in stark contrast to NOAA's own findings in its recently released Stellwagen Bank Condition Report (2007). The Report raises serious warnings about the ecological health of the Sanctuary and surrounding waters. The management of Stellwagen Bank must be strengthened with science-based solutions that balance the ecology with the needs of a diverse set of stakeholders.

The letter, dated December 4, 2007, was drafted by SAC chair Susan Farady, a project manager at the time with the New England regional office of the Ocean Conservancy, and co-chair Sally Yozell, director of marine conservation for the eastern U.S. region of The Nature Conservancy. Yozell was former deputy assistant secretary of commerce for oceans and atmosphere during the Clinton administration and a one-time aide to Senator John Kerry. More than anyone on the SAC, Yozell was savvy to the machinations of the Washington bureaucracy and the extremes to which it can go in pursuit of inaction. The admiral never replied to the letter.

The Roll-Out

On May 6, 2008, the sanctuary finally "rolled out" a 366-page document entitled *Stellwagen Bank National Marine Sanctuary Draft Management Plan and Environmental Assessment* for public comment at a series of eight public hearings in June held in Maine, New Hampshire, and Massachusetts, and ninety-day review ending August 4 (later extended to October 3). Maintaining this schedule, NOAA would make whatever changes it considered appropriate and issue a final management plan and environmental assessment sometime in early 2009 during the startup of a new administration, meaning that the clock was still running on a management plan review that had dragged out over the last two years of the Clinton administration and two full terms of the Bush administration, making Stellwagen Bank the slowest-moving sanctuary in the nation. By way of contrast, the Hawaiian Islands Humpback National Marine Sanctuary, created the same year as Stellwagen Bank, completed its first management plan review in 2002 and had begun its second in early 2008. Earlier in the year, a program audit conducted by NOAA's Office of Inspector General criticized the NMSP for the glacial pace of some sanctuaries and recommended that the NMSP director hold "superintendents [who] have ongoing management plan reviews accountable for completing them within established timeframes."[5]

The weighty document, lavishly printed and containing a wealth of information gathered from hundreds of scientific papers, consultations with other agencies, and meetings of the SAC and working groups, received a chilly reception by the SAC at its official unveiling in Boston on May 6, 2008. NOAA had kept a tight embargo on the plan throughout its four-year preparation, even shielding it from the SAC's executive committee, but its title had been hinted at for several years. According to MacDonald, it was to be a draft management plan and *environmental assessment*, not an environmental impact statement. Stripping away the legalese, what this meant was that after more than ten years of deliberation, the possibility existed that the plan for the next five years might be nothing more than a plan for more planning and deliberation; that NOAA never intended to propose any new rules for the sanctuary.

Yozell, who could not refrain from speed reading the opening pages of the plan while MacDonald labored through a lengthy Power Point presentation of its contents during the official roll-out, stopped dead at page 6 upon reading:

> At this time, NOAA is not proposing any regulations or changes to the designation document and an environmental assessment accompanies this management plan, rather than an environmental impact statement pursuant to requirements of the National Environmental Policy Act and Council on Environmental Quality regulations. However, a suite of regulatory initiatives that derives from the strategies presented in the draft management plan ultimately could be considered.[6]

One explanation given earlier by MacDonald for separating what might be called "the plan" from any regulatory elements was that it would trigger a regulatory review that could further delay the adoption of a new management plan. He cited the example of the Channel Islands NMS, which incorporated a proposal for the creation of a number of ecological reserves in its

1999 draft plan. The reserve proposals triggered some initial resistance in both California and Washington, D.C., and extensive regulatory review lasting several years. What MacDonald did not say was that by 2006 both the plan and reserves for the Channel Islands NMS were in place. The Channel Islands experience would seem to corroborate the observation of other sanctuary superintendents that there is not enough energy in the world to do both separately — that it is better to keep the stakeholders engaged, even in controversy, than to put off tough decisions.

The underlying assumption of MacDonald's approach could only have been that in the case of Stellwagen Bank, the public will, political leadership, and process for resolving conflicts does not exist. On the issue of conflict resolution, the sanctuary has been hoist on its own petard as it has been a consummate proponent of consensus decisionmaking, a practice that it has taken to extraordinary, even absurd, extremes. But when the moment of decision came, MacDonald must have realized that he did not have significant enough support to ride out the storm that would follow.

Disappointment, Confusion, and Anger

One of the first to express confusion and disbelief over the draft management plan — or non-plan — was Gib Chase, a retired official with the U.S. Fish and Wildlife Service and an early proponent of the sanctuary. Chase served from 1996 to 2000 as an SAC member and from 2001 to 2004 as an alternate. Throughout his tenure, he prodded the sanctuary staff and fellow SAC members to get on with the business of managing the sanctuary.

"A national designation of any kind," says Chase,

> carries with it an expectation of management protection befitting the purposes for which the site was designated, be it a park, wildlife refuge, forest, seashore, natural scenic monument, or marine sanctuary. Until and unless NOAA acts to ensure the compatibility of commercial and recreational uses of Stellwagen Bank National Marine Sanctuary, the mission of the sanctuary and its primary purpose to conserve, protect, and enhance the biodiversity and ecological integrity of the site will be compromised. Continuing to ignore the mandated compatibility requirement is a breech of public trust and responsibility.[7]

The "compatibility requirement" that Chase repeatedly refers to appears first in the National Marine Sanctuary Act, which states that one of the purposes of national marine sanctuaries is "to maintain the natural biological communities in the national marine sanctuaries, and to protect, and, where appropriate, restore and enhance natural habitats, populations, and ecological processes," and again in the sanctuary's designation document, which authorizes the sanctuary to regulate and if necessary prohibit human activities "to ensure the protection and management of the conservation, recreational, ecological, historical, research, educational or aesthetic resources and qualities of the area."[8]

Frustrated and angered by the sanctuary's unwillingness to carry out its primary mission, Chase recently suggested that "in the fifteen years since its designation the biological value of the bank or sanctuary may have been denigrated to the point that it is no longer worthy of such recognition."

Chase recalls participating in a series of underwater research submersible dives in June 1976 conducted by NOAA as part of the Man Undersea Science and Technology (MUST) Program. The team made dives at Stellwagen, Jeffreys Ledge, Tillies Bank, and Cashes Ledge. On one occasion, Chase dove on a boulder field at 180 feet. "The attached epibenthic communities and fish life were spectacular. Commercial fishing and recreational boating were a non-factor at that time. However, by 1992 and the designation of the site as a national marine sanctuary, that had changed drastically." NOAA's own Condition Report confirms that the seafloor continues to undergo annual disturbance, possibly resulting in a condition that is no longer recoverable to its original state, whatever that might have been.

By the end of June 2008, the many sanctuary proponents who had time to examine the draft plan were echoing Gib Chase's criticism that the draft management plan so long in the making was not a management plan but an interagency "consultation report." SAC chairman Susan Farady, who most observers believe had maintained a spirit of cooperation and civility at SAC meetings while still advocating for marine protected areas for the Ocean Conservancy, quickly distanced herself from the draft plan. In an alert to thousands of Conservancy members and friends, she declared the sanctuary to be "in crisis" and accused its managers of not protecting it. "Tell the managers," she wrote, "that you expect them to make this place a sanctuary in fact as well as in name."[9] The Conservancy's priorities for the next five years included enacting regulations to reduce whale disturbance by all commercial and recreational vessels, development of a zoning plan for the sanctuary designating areas suitable for commercial and recreational use as well as "no-take" and "limited-use" areas, and banning fishing on forage species such as sand lance and herring. Priscilla Brooks, director of the Conservation Law Foundation's marine conservation program and another long-time SAC member, denounced the plan as "woefully inadequate" and urged the sanctuary to regulate all commercial and recreational activities within its boundaries.

Commercial and recreational fishermen, on the other hand, regarded the sheer heft and policy focus of much of the document as advance notice of the sanctuary program's intent to cross over into the presumed exclusive jurisdictions of the fisheries service and regional fisheries management council. As one fisherman attending the Plymouth hearing muttered, "Anything this thick cannot be good." Others were more direct. Tom DePersia, who owns and operates three charter boats out of Marshfield and represents an association of one hundred charter boats, complained, "we were promised that the sanctuary would not interfere with fishing," and threatened that any "direct or indirect effort" to do so would trigger a "move to rescind the designation."[10] Ed Barrett, a member of the SAC representing mobile-gear fishermen, quietly but angrily stated that a growing number of his constituents now favor "eliminating the sanctuary altogether."[11] Numerous other fishermen took the occasion to remind sanctuary officials at the public hearings that Gerry Studds had "promised" that their future access to the sanctuary would never be threatened and that he "would roll over in his grave" if he knew what was intended.

What seemed to have triggered a general outpouring of frustration and anger on the part of fishermen was the authors' lengthy review of the scientific literature on biodiversity and ecosystem-based management and several key findings that pointed to fishing—especially commercial fishing—as the source of many environmental problems. "On an annual basis," the plan states, "virtually every square kilometer of the sanctuary is physically disturbed by fishing."[12] MacDonald, who used this line during his introduction of the plan at each of the eight public hearings on the draft plan, might just as well have shouted "Fire!" Use of the word "disturb" set off verbal rockets from Maine to Rhode Island.

The management plan offered no detailed examination of current efforts of National Marine Fisheries Service or the NEFMC to convert to an ecosystem-based management approach to fisheries management or to implement the provisions of the Sustainable Fisheries Act.

Susan Playfair, author of the sympathetic examination of the New England groundfishing fleet *Vanishing Species: Saving the Fish, Sacrificing the Fisherman*, called some of the language in the report "highly inflammatory" and urged the sanctuary program to develop a plan that treats commercial fishing as the "primary compatible use" within the sanctuary.[13] Ed Barrett simply called for "a plan that embraces" fishermen. Gerry Studds might have agreed.

Chapter 12

Potential Actions

Public reaction to the NOAA Stellwagen Bank National Marine Sanctuary draft management plan continued to run negative from all quarters throughout the summer of 2008. Those hoping for a decisive plan of action that, at the very least, would halt the deterioration of the sanctuary documented in the 2007 NOAA Condition Report were disappointed and expressed a sense of betrayal over the management plan review process. Those opposed to any effort by the sanctuary to limit commercial uses found cause for concern, especially in the document's lengthy treatments of ecosystem alteration and the principles of conservation biology. Had NOAA put forth even a simple plan of action, public comment might have focused on the pros and cons of specific actions. Instead, the hearings were a replay of the 1998 and 2002 public scoping sessions.

Even NOAA's preferred no-action alternative stirred some legal wrangling. By postponing any new management actions, was NOAA contributing to further environmental degradation of the sanctuary? If so, a full environmental impact statement might be required. Others argued that while no actions were being proposed, the tone and intent of the document was to amend the designation document, for which congressional approval would be required.

"NOAA's Plan"

The authorship of the document also stirred confusion. Throughout the public hearings, sanctuary superintendent Craig MacDonald told audiences, "This is NOAA's plan, not the sanctuary's plan." He offered no explanation of what this meant. Was he referring to differences between the sanctuary and the national program office or differences between the sanctuary program and other offices? Not likely, since nowhere in the document was there a single indication that the National Marine Fisheries Service (NMFS) and National Marine Sanctuary Program (NMSP) had a shared vision for the sanctuary. Instead, the document states only that "This draft management plan serves as a *non-regulatory framework* for addressing the issues facing the Stellwagen Bank sanctuary over the next five years" [emphasis added]. For those knowledgeable about the process, the obvious message was that the NMFS, buttressed by the New England fisheries lobby, had over the course of the two-year internal review once again deployed its smothering defense against the NMSP's weak offense.

Despite the ongoing debate within NOAA and the decision not to propose new regulations in the draft plan "at this time," the plan goes on to state that "a suite of regulatory initiatives that derives from the strategies presented in the draft management plan ultimately could be considered" over the coming five years.[1] The strategies presumably under consideration, 102 of them, were described in some detail in chapter 7 of the document.[2]

NOAA stopped short of describing exactly what the sanctuary proposed to work on from 2009 to 2013, but it offered four "examples" of "potential management actions" in a provocative timeline labeled "Proposed Management Continuum." The authors' use of the words "examples," "potential," and "proposed" reinforced the argument advanced by Gib Chase and others that the document was not a management plan but a discourse on the principles of biodiversity and ecosystem-based management, and an introduction to the issues and strategies that *might* be included in a *future* plan. Whatever the intent, NOAA listed whale watching, maritime heritage, forage base management, habitat zoning, and compatibility analysis as examples of activities that might be subject to management actions in the near future. Assuming management actions are proposed, each would be subject to full NEPA review at that time.

Marine Mammal Behavioral Disturbance

The potential management actions regarding marine mammal behavioral disturbance might best be described as low-hanging fruit—actions long overdue. The working group on marine mammal behavioral disturbance identified three broad objectives aimed at reducing disturbance and harassment by vessels, aircraft, and noise.[3] Strategies included the development of research programs to determine the effects of vessels and aircraft on marine mammals and the development of a "noise budget" for the sanctuary. The strategy directly affecting whale watching and the tuna fleet most likely would involve regulating vessel speed and close approaches and probably could be accomplished in six months at little cost. The draft management plan, however, outlines a slower and more costly pace requiring five years and an expenditure of more than $200,000 (excluding federal labor costs). The research components of the plan, according to the plan, would require more than $1.5 million (excluding federal labor costs) over the same period. Over the course of five years, implementation of the full marine mammal behavior disturbance action plan is estimated to cost more than $2 million. Given the sanctuary's total annual operating budget of about $1.5 million, it seems unrealistic that the sanctuary will make much headway. In this area, the sanctuary needs to ask itself what can be done now based on the best available information. The situation seems to be calling for a regulatory regime predicated on the precautionary approach advanced by Jon Lien and others.[4]

Maritime Heritage

Also qualifying as low-hanging fruit is a proposed maritime heritage program, the goals of which are to inventory, assess, protect, manage, and interpret prehistoric (possible paleontological remains from the last ice age) and historic archaeological resources (primarily shipwrecks) in the sanctuary. An important first step is identifying and nominating sites eligible for listing on the National Register of Historic Places and developing strategies for protecting them from disturbance by fishing gear, anchors, and scuba divers. Education, public outreach, and, most importantly, on-the-water patrols will be the principal tools for carrying this out.

Several scuba-diving clubs and diving charter operators were quick to protest any limits on access or implementation of a permit system for diving on the wrecks, arguing that there had been no known cases of scavenging. Commercial fishermen also protested the characterization that modern mobile gear was disturbing the wrecks. Attention to date has focused on the wrecks of the steamship *Portland* and schooners *Frank A. Palmer, Louise B. Crary*, and *Paul Palmer*, which are now listed on the National Register. The estimated five-year cost of carrying out this action plan is a staggering $800,000. As in the case of minimizing marine mammal behavioral disturbance, a great deal could be accomplished for little money with some swift action aimed at the key sites that have been identified over the past fifteen years. Public interest most likely will determine what priority this receives in upcoming budgets.

Protection of Forage Base

The third potential management activity identified in the draft plan concerns protection of the sanctuary's forage base, primarily American sand lance (*Ammodytes dubius*) and Atlantic herring (*Clupea harengus*). These days, the forage base is one of Craig MacDonald's primary interests and he talks about it with the fervor of an ocean explorer fresh off an expedition.

Several months before the release of the draft management plan, Mac-Donald found time to reflect on his eight years at the sanctuary and how the planning process (distinct from the management plan, which he was still forbidden to discuss), had begun to define the significance of the sanctuary at a level of sufficient detail to enable managers and the general public to chart its course for the future.

"When you look at the volume that is taken out of this place in terms of pounds of biomass [fish landings] and factor in the amount of by-catch that is discarded," says MacDonald, "and then you look at the biogenic habitat disturbance and possible destruction caused by some of the fishing practices, you realize that for all of that to be sustained you have to have phenomenal primary production. And where is this happening? Primarily in the water column and in some of the shallower sites." MacDonald describes it as "the epiphany of the management planning process. We weren't initially thinking of that component of the ecosystem. In retrospect all I can say is, duh."[5]

The sanctuary's high nutrient concentrations, upwellings, turbulence, and connectivity with other portions of the Gulf of Maine all favor high productivity. Generally, where there is an abundance of phytoplankton — signifying high primary productivity — there will be an abundance of animals. Where there is a scarcity of phytoplankton — signifying low primary productivity — there will be a scarcity of animals.

"What nurtures this productivity," says MacDonald, "is water quality. If you protect water quality, you sustain primary productivity. And if you protect the forage base, the critical driver of this place, you attract whales, cod, and seabirds. This to me is the lifeblood of the place." But MacDonald stopped short of saying how he proposes to protect the forage base, either because that might be construed as a proposed rule that might trigger NEPA review, setting the planning process back another year or more, or because the inter-connectivity of species that make up the ecosystem is not understood suffi-ciently. Or it could be that MacDonald and the sanctuary program are waiting for the public (and next administration) to choose what kind of sanctuary they want to have.

The sand lance (also called sand eel) is a slender little schooling fish that plays a large role in the life of the sanctuary. Sand lance prefer sand and fine gravel substrates, where they deposit and bury their eggs during the winter months and remain during the rest of the year.[6] They mature during their first or second year, growing to between 6 and 9 inches, and live most of their lives throughout the water column, feeding and schooling during the day over these same substrates where they burrow at night. Schools of sand lance can number in the tens of thousands.

Trawl surveys conducted by the Northeast Fisheries Science Center have found that sand lance occur in greater abundance within the sanctuary than in any other area in the southern Gulf of Maine. In marked contrast with the eastern North Atlantic, where a very similar species of sand lance (*Ammodytes marinus*) is the largest single species fishery in the North Sea, there is no fish-ery for sand lance in the Gulf of Maine; something that bodes well for the entire food web of the sanctuary. In economic terms, this also means that any actions taken now to protect the role that sand lance play in the forage base could be taken at virtually no cost to the fishing industry.

One of the most palpable associations within the complex Stellwagen Bank ecosystem is that of baleen whales (primarily humpbacks and finbacks) and sand lance. Overlays of trawl survey data and whale sighting data show that the abundance and distribution of whales corresponds with the abundance and distribution of sand lance. When the abundance of sand lance is down, for whatever reason, the whales go elsewhere to feed on herring and other small fish, and in the northern reaches of the Gulf of Maine, on krill.

The abundance or scarcity of sand lance has not been an issue of much concern for fisheries managers, since the species is not targeted commercially at this time. But if the sanctuary's managers want to manage the area as a sanc-tuary for marine mammals, protecting sand lance habitat needs to be a high priority. This would require working with NMFS and the NEFMC on a plan to protect spawning areas from disturbance.

Equally, if not more important, is the status of Atlantic herring (*Clupea harengus*; not to be confused with river herring), a small, pelagic, migratory schooling fish that plays a critical role in the Gulf of Maine ecosystem. The Atlantic States Marine Fisheries Commission (ASMFC), which manages the species in state waters, claims that it "may be the most important fish in the northeastern United States because of its vast role in the ecosystem and its importance to the fishing industry."[7]

In the Gulf of Maine, Atlantic herring are preyed upon by many species, including cod, haddock, silver hake, bluefish, spiny dogfish, summer flounder, sharks, bluefin tuna, and marine mammals. The commercial fishery provides bait for the lobster, blue crab, and tuna fisheries of New England. Juvenile herring are canned and sold as sardines in the United States, while a strong overseas market exists for salted herring.

Herring are distributed widely from Labrador to Cape Hatteras. They migrate from summer feeding grounds along the Maine coast and Georges Bank to southern New England and the mid-Atlantic in winter. Spawning occurs in the late summer and early fall, beginning in northern regions and progressing southward. Herring eggs typically are deposited on gravel substrates and are preyed upon heavily by flounder, cod, and skates. Herring prey on a wide variety of zooplankton and larvae, including that of sand lance. They mature in four years, by which time they have grown to approximately 12 inches in length and weigh about a pound.[8] Studies have shown that humpback whales and fin whales may switch in the winter from feeding on sand lance on Stellwagen Bank, where they are less abundant prior to spawning, to herring in deeper waters over Tillies Bank and Jeffreys Ledge.

The Gulf of Maine and Georges Bank offshore herring fishery collapsed in 1977 due primarily to intense foreign fishing, which was halted by passage of the Magnuson Act in 1976. At the height of the assault, landings were estimated to be 470,000 metric tons. The species did not begin to recover until the late 1980s and government fisheries managers now believe it has recovered to stock levels of the 1960s, a claim that is disputed widely by New England fishermen and conservation groups.[9]

The dispute revolves around the impact of an industrial-scale domestic fleet of about twenty mid-water trawlers that has replaced the foreign vessels. The trawlers run up to 175 feet in length and deploy massive 1½-inch mesh nets the width of football fields that sweep up just about everything in their path, including many other regulated species that are discarded. By way of contrast, the highly regulated groundfish fleet uses 6½-inch mesh nets to minimize the impact on juveniles and other undersized fish. The impact of the mid-water trawlers has been greatest in the inshore waters of the Gulf of Maine, including the area in and around Stellwagen Bank. While only 18 percent of the herring population is found in inshore waters, approximately 60 percent of the landings have been taken from this area.

The Herring Alliance, a coalition of marine conservation organizations working to curb overfishing, has been leading an effective campaign aimed at educating the general public about the impact of the huge mid-water trawlers and convincing government managers that action must be taken. One issue that is particularly galling to groundfishermen, who are highly observed and regulated these days, is that only a tiny number of the mid-water herring trawlers carry government observers aboard.

Beginning in the summer of 2007, the inshore waters of the Gulf of Maine were closed to mid-water trawlers from June through September. Within months, more herring, striped bass, tuna, and whales were reported. The Alliance is now lobbying managers in the interest of smaller New England groundfishermen and biodiversity to take additional regulatory measures, including a ban on all mid-water trawling in areas already closed to groundfishing and within 50 miles of shore. These two measures alone would close off not only all of the sanctuary but also the Western Gulf of Maine Closure Area, which overlaps 22 percent of the sanctuary.

The controversy over herring illustrates a continuing difference between the missions of NMFS and the sanctuary, despite significant progress on the part of the service to embrace the principles of ecosystem-based management. Andy Read, a marine biologist at Duke University, notes that "the fishery management plan may not adequately consider the importance of herring as prey for marine mammals, seabirds, and piscivorous [fish-eating] fish."[10] Stock assessments conducted by fishery managers, he explains, do not specifically account for the consumption by these predators. "Instead, as in most fisheries stock assessments, predation is subsumed with the natural mortality rate, and no empirical estimates of herring consumption are used in the models."

In a study published in 2003 in *Conservation Ecology*, Read and Carrie Brownstein, using the most recent estimates of abundance and the best available data on diet, estimated the total annual consumption of herring by eight marine mammal species in the Gulf of Maine to be between 93,802 and 189,898 metric tons.[11] The study did not estimate predation by piscivorous fish and seabirds, but their broad conclusion was that "the consumption of herring by these upper trophic level predators may have exceeded the estimate of natural mortality used in stock assessment models by more than fourfold." The intention of this and similar studies has been to move fisheries managers "beyond a single-species approach to management of our public fishery resources" and "toward formal consideration of trophic relationships."

Development of a forage base management plan for the sanctuary would require that the sanctuary's managers and scientific advisors become involved more directly in the fisheries management process carried out by the NEFMC and NMFS than they have to date. In the long run, that would be a test of whether there is one NOAA or two.

Habitat Zoning

The draft management plan also discusses the possibility of introducing within the next five years some form of habitat zoning, designed to reduce alteration of benthic habitat by the laying of submarine cables, pipelines, and mobile fishing gear. The laying of cables and pipelines is already a prohibited activity, but existing regulations do allow for the issuance of special use permits on a case-by-case basis. The sanctuary has defended its issuance in 2001 of such a permit for the Hibernia Transatlantic optic cable on the grounds that the spatial extent of impact of laying the cable was "equivalent to 88 minutes spent fishing with a standard scallop dredge. . . . This represents 0.0027 percent of the sanctuary by area" (see chapter 6).[12] By comparison, nearly every square mile of the sanctuary outside the Western Gulf of Maine Closure Area "is dragged by mobile fishing gear at least once per year on average."[13]

Notwithstanding significant and economically painful efforts on the part of the NEFMC and NMFS to reduce the overall groundfishing effort and area available to bottom trawlers, disturbance (and in some instances permanent destruction) of benthic habitat continues to occur within the sanctuary.

The concept of zoning the sanctuary based on classification and mapping of benthic habitats is receiving a great deal of interest and much of the preliminary field work has been completed. The USGS has surveyed the entire sanctuary using high-resolution multi-beam imagery and documented the makeup of substratum types. The survey will require further ground-truthing by means of underwater video and sediment sampling, but the USGS already has classified more than a dozen substrata that fall within the three major types that make up the sanctuary: gravel, sand, and mud.

In general terms, the seafloor of the sanctuary is comprised of 38 percent gravel (including piled boulder reefs), 34 percent sand, and 28 percent mud. Among specific benthic habitats, hard bottom and mud substrata appear to be the most sensitive to the impact of mobile gear, requiring a decade or more to "recover." Sand habitats, on the other hand, may recover in a matter of months. These generalizations have been confirmed by the National Undersea Research Center at the University of Connecticut at Avery Point, which has monitoring stations located within and outside the WGoMCA.

In theory, habitat zoning combined with appropriate regulations might enable NOAA to achieve the twin objectives of sustainable fisheries management and resource protection, much as community zoning boards and planners attempt to control land use development in the best interest of the community.

For such a plan to work, the sanctuary and fisheries managers still would need to come a long way both intellectually and politically. In principle, especially under the One-NOAA banner, this already is underway and generally is referred to as ecosystem-based management (EBM). But in the trenches, NMFS's primary focus is on the recovery of depleted commercial stocks and its primary constituency is the fishing community. The NOAA Sanctuary Program, on the other hand, is directed to "protect, and, where appropriate, restore and enhance natural habitats, populations and ecological processes." The two missions overlap, but for NMFS, the goal is the attainment of a sustainable commercial fishery. For the NOAA Sanctuary Program, the goal is ecological integrity irrespective of its commercial benefit.

At the present time, the two missions partly merge in Amendment 13 to the Northeast Multi-species Fishery Management Plan, which in time should increase protection of the ecological integrity of the sanctuary by reducing the overall fishing effort and establishing permanent essential fish habitat (EFH) closed areas among other things.[14] Amendment 13 went into effect on May 1, 2004, and is just the latest attempt to meet the goals of the 1996 Sustainable Fisheries Act. It has been a slow process and of necessity focused on the entire Gulf of Maine, of which the sanctuary is only a small part.

Still, it is important to ask when and if the NEFMC and NMFS will accept responsibility for the special significance and needs of the sanctuary. Not soon, seems to be the answer, as evidenced by the council's rejection of a June 2007 proposal to designate the sanctuary as a Habitat Area of Particular Concern. NOAA defines HAPCs as

discrete subsets of essential fish habitat that provide extremely important ecological functions or are especially vulnerable to degradation. Councils may designate a specific habitat area as an HAPC based on one or more of the following
reasons: (1) the importance of the ecological function provided by the habitat,
(2) the extent to which the habitat is sensitive to human-induced environmental
degradation, (3) whether, and to what extent, development activities are, or will
be, stressing the habitat type, and (4) rarity of the habitat type.[15]

HAPC designation is intended as a means of setting conservation priorities and does not confer additional protection or restrictions upon an area.
Nevertheless, when the resolution was introduced by NMFS's regional director Patricia Kurkul, fishermen jumped all over it. Ron Smolowitz, a fisherman
from East Falmouth, Massachusetts, charged that the proposal was political and not based on science and called for a stepped approach that put off
discussions of fishing threats to habitats to a latter date. Vito Giacolone, representing the Gloucester based Northeast Seafood Coalition, argued that
"documentation [of fishing impacts] does not exist. . . . We agree completely
that Stellwagen is an exceptional area," he said, but then added, "This is purely
a maneuver to control fishing activity in the sanctuary."[16]

Supporting Kurkul's proposal was David Pierce, deputy director of the
Massachusetts Division of Marine Fisheries. Pierce, who is both an ex officio
voting member of the NEFMC and ex officio nonvoting member of the SAC,
is a soft-spoken marine scientist and ordained deacon in the Catholic Church
who seems genuinely convinced of the legitimacy of both the fisheries management and sanctuary management processes; a true renaissance man in an
age of ecosystem-based management.

Pierce told the council that the sanctuary merits being designated an
HAPC and that if the council did not approve the resolution, "it might send
a signal to the sanctuary and the program nationwide that the council does
not take the sanctuary seriously."[17] That may have been the statement of the
decade.

Pierce went on to explain that the sanctuary was an EFH for fifteen or
more species, including white hake, pollock, witch flounder, winter flounder,
American plaice, cod, yellowtail flounder, haddock, and red hake. "Every part
of it may be an EFH for some species." Still, the measure failed to pass.

While the future of the sanctuary will not turn on the council's position
on this issue, it demonstrates that any effort on the part of the sanctuary in

the near future to introduce habitat zoning through the SAC will be resisted. On the other hand, if in the course of the next few years the goals of Amendment 13 are not met to the satisfaction of the courts and Congress, the need for radical reform of both management regimes may be required. If there is one reoccurring and unifying thought threading its way through "NOAA's draft management plan," as MacDonald calls it, it is that that time has already come.

Chapter 13

Vision and Goals

A thing is right when it tends to preserve the integrity, stability, and beauty of the biotic community. It is wrong when it tends otherwise.

— Aldo Leopold, *A Sand County Almanac*, 1949

Compatible with what? This is a question the sanctuary has been asking itself since its creation. Congress did not provide much guidance when it comes to determining what activities are compatible with Stellwagen Bank's sanctuary status, a criticism that applies to one extent or another to the entire sanctuary system. Instead of adopting a methodology for determining compatibility as the Department of the Interior has for the National Wildlife Refuge System, the National Marine Sanctuary Program has dealt with unanticipated uses or threats to sanctuaries on a case-by-case basis. Some might prefer to call it crisis management, with the outcome invariably compromising the purposes for which the sanctuary was first created.

The Prime Directive

The Sanctuaries Act, written twenty years ago, states only that the Secretary of Commerce is "to facilitate to the extent compatible with the primary objective of resource protection, all public and private uses of the resources of these marine areas not prohibited pursuant to other authorities."[1] And while the mission of the Stellwagen Bank sanctuary found in the Oceans Act of 1992 ("to ensure the protection and management of the conservation, recreational, ecological, historical, research, educational or esthetic resources and qualities of the area") reemphasizes resource protection, it offers little guidance on how this should be carried out.[2] Judging from some of the actions and inactions of the sanctuary over its first fifteen years, resource protection has been carried out more as a balancing act than as a prime directive consonant with a clear vision of what the sanctuary ought to be.

The only use of the term "multiple use" in the Sanctuaries Act is in Section 1445A(b) in reference to advisory council members being persons "interested in the protection and multiple use management of sanctuary resources." But the mandate to "facilitate . . . all public and private uses . . . not prohibited pursuant to other authorities" sounds very much like the language in the Multiple Use Act of 1960 that gave official sanction to the principle of multiple use on national forests, stating: "The Secretary of Agriculture is authorized and directed to develop and administer the renewable surface resources of the national forests for multiple use and sustained yield of the several products and services obtained therefrom."[3]

Four years later, in the Multiple Use Reclassification Act, which applies to lands administered by the Bureau of Land Management (BLM), Congress defined multiple use to mean "the management of the various surface and subsurface resources so that they are utilized in the combination that will best meet the present and future needs of the American people."[4] Implied in this definition is the principle of sustained yield, but throughout the 1960s and 1970s, land managers either felt they had license to authorize uses far in excess of what the land could bear or succumbed to the pressures of leaseholders and their congressional allies. In response to public outcry over what often was often called "multiple abuse," millions of acres of public land eventually were reclassified as primitive and wilderness areas. Tension continues over public land management policies to this day, although a gradual adoption of a more holistic approach to management issues has begun to take effect, as a new generation of land managers educated in the principles of conservation biology has risen through the ranks. Still, it is hard not to draw comparisons between the Forest Service and BLM of a generation ago with the national marine sanctuary program of today.

Despite general dissatisfaction over the sanctuary's failure to fulfill its conservation mission and occasional threats by some commercial users to de-list it, the Gerry E. Studds Stellwagen Bank National Marine Sanctuary survives. It survived the political strife of the Gingrich era, during which Gerry Studds was stripped of the chairmanship of the Merchant Marine and Fisheries Committee, and a concerted effort was made to repeal or weaken key provisions of the Endangered Species and Marine Mammal Protection Acts. It survived the

anti-environmentalism and stupor of the Bush administration. And, despite
the numerous shortcomings of the 2008 draft management plan, a vision of
the sanctuary not unlike the one Gerry Studds first espoused is beginning
to emerge. It is the vision of a "people's sanctuary" in which all resources are
held in public trust and protected by the government for the benefit of all,
now and in the future.

The Vision Thing

As part of the management plan review process, the Sanctuary Advisory
Council (SAC) was asked to write a vision statement, capturing in words
its collective view of what the Stellwagen Bank National Marine Sanctuary
ought to be like in the near future. The SAC briefly discussed a timeframe
of five to ten years but preferred to dwell on broad goals rather than a schedule by which to achieve them. In July 2005, after fourteen motions, the SAC
unanimously adopted the following statement:

> The Stellwagen Bank National Marine Sanctuary is teeming with a great diversity
> and abundance of marine plants and animals supported by diverse, healthy habi-
> tats in clean ocean waters. The ecological integrity of the sanctuary is protected
> and fully restored for current and future generations. Human uses are diverse and
> compatible with maintaining natural and cultural resources.[5]

The statement is not likely to find its way into any anthologies of environmental wisdom, but it represents a portrait of the sanctuary that reasonably captures public comments made during the scoping sessions of 1998
and 2002 and the interests represented on the SAC. The council deliberately
avoided using technical terms like "biodiversity" and "ecosystem-based management" that had been the subjects of much discussion by various working
groups in the preceding months. Instead, the members talked about a place
"teeming" with life, a somewhat nostalgic reminder of earlier days when fishermen could go out to the bank without the aid of a compass or depth finder.
They just knew they were there by the profusion of life around them in the
plankton-rich waters: birds circling, whale lunging, and schools of fish breaking the surface.

By recalling such times, the SAC was calling for a return to an earlier condition. Nobody was so foolish as to envision (or at least not to express) a

pre-colonial pristine state. Most would have settled on a mid-twentieth-century state: before the invasion of the foreign fishing fleets, before the mismanagement and rapid decline of the domestic fisheries, before the urbanization of the New England coastline.

There was much discussion and some heated debate over the feasibility of achieving even a post–Second World War environmental state, but in the end, most agreed that it was essential to try and that the "ecological integrity of the sanctuary [must be] protected and fully restored for current and future generations."

Finally, the SAC's vision statement returns to the issue of the compatibility of human uses: "Human uses are diverse and compatible with maintaining natural and cultural resources." The statement makes clear that the SAC does not view the sanctuary as an area closed off to human activity. In this respect, it is consistent with the Sanctuaries Act ("to facilitate to the extent compatible with the primary objective of resource protection, all public and private uses of the resources of these marine areas not prohibited pursuant to other authorities"), but the emphasis on biodiversity, ecological integrity, and full restoration sets a very high standard for compatibility; higher than any currently in place in the Gulf of Maine.

Noah's Ark or Absolute Wilderness?

With this vision of a "fully restored" ecosystem, the SAC has taken a giant step toward answering a question that has hobbled it for years; namely, What is resource protection? To restore the sanctuary fully to the state observed and recorded in living memory will require an extraordinary effort and some tough choices. Perhaps the toughest and first is a societal choice of what the sanctuary ought to be. If the draft management plan containing the vision statement is adopted, the spectrum of choices automatically will narrow. But still, the goals of restoration will have to be set.

Peter Auster, who has been documenting the loss of biodiversity within the sanctuary for more than a decade, remarks, "We need to decide what our goal is? If we are happy with the Noah's ark scenario where there is two of everything, we can all go home."[6] Even during the heaviest fishing effort of recent history, Stellwagen Bank supported two of everything. Today, with Amendment 13 to the Northeast Multi-species Fishery Management Plan in effect, conditions will improve to some degree.[7]

At the opposite end of the broadest possible spectrum would be the wilderness scenario that Auster describes as a sanctuary "where human effects [would be] minimal and transient on wild populations of animals." A subcommittee of the sanctuary working group on ecosystem-based management picked up on this notion and defined what it called the "absolute wilderness scenario" as follows:

> in a true wilderness state, all disruptive activities must cease. The SBNMS would become a totally protected, non-extractive reserve. In addition, the borders of the sanctuary would have to be extended so as to encompass Jeffreys Ledge and adjacent areas of high topographic relief, such as the "Fingers." This would yield two important benefits. First, areas rich in both herring (to the north) and sand lance (mostly Stellwagen Bank) would be protected, thus providing insurance against low-abundance years for [either] of these primary forage species. Second, a crucial feeding area for the North Atlantic right whale would be protected. In addition, the core protected area encompassing the two banks should be surrounded by an easement of additional grounds in which activities that severely disrupt habitat and the distribution and abundance of wildlife are curtailed.[8]

The full sixteen-member working group, comprised of academics, fishing industry representatives, conservationists, and government representatives from the National Marine Fisheries Service, New England Fishery Management Council, Massachusetts Division of Marine Fisheries, and Massachusetts Coastal Zone Management, agreed that absolute wilderness was not an appropriate goal. For starters, it would eliminate all fishing, an action not envisioned in the original designation of the sanctuary and one most likely to create enormous political upheaval. Even if the idea had widespread support, Congress would have to amend the designation to establish an absolute wilderness. Second, an element of optimism remains among fisheries managers that the goals of the Sustainable Fisheries Act will in time be met. Finally, some scientific disagreement exists about whether the level of biodiversity associated with a wilderness state actually could be attained at the scale of Stellwagen Bank, since the sanctuary is not a closed system.

Middle Ground

Somewhere between the Noah's Ark and absolute wilderness scenarios lie the objectives of the Sanctuaries Act, on the one hand, and the Magnuson-Stevens and Sustainable Fisheries Acts on the other. The two acts were intended to be complementary but their goals are different. An example that illustrates the tension between the two has to do with the age and size of fish. One of the goals of the sanctuary is to restore "old-growth fish," especially among biologically important fish populations. It is well known that larger females produce a greater number of eggs, but researchers have now found that among some species, including cod, haddock, and rockfish, that experienced spawners, now referred to as "big old fat females" or BOFFs, produce bigger eggs containing a higher volume of oil, resulting in faster-growing, healthier larvae. One study by researchers at Boston University has shown that a doubling of the growth rate of larval Atlantic cod can increase survival rates by five to ten times.[9] Another study analyzed thirty-eight years of NMFS trawl survey data and concluded that the maximum length of fifteen species of ecologically and commercially important species had declined by an average of 20 percent. For Atlantic cod, the decrease in maximum length was 27 percent.

From the perspective of the sanctuary, it has "become abundantly clear that high numbers of larger, older fish are what ultimately sustain fish populations."[10] As Craig MacDonald explains, "our goal is to allow some fish to regain a larger size and begin looking at what happens to associated communities."[11] While the sanctuary makes no claim that the recovery of cod will be improved markedly depending upon how the sanctuary is managed, MacDonald adds that managing cod—which is considered a keystone species for the sanctuary and for the Gulf of Maine as a whole—is a perfectly valid goal at the scale of the sanctuary. "There is a lot that can be done that could result in greater diversity, more robust community structure, and recovery of spatial heterogeneity." Supporting this point of view is a finding that 35 percent of the cod population of the sanctuary is resident year-round, which means that for a subset of the total Gulf of Maine population, spawning fidelity is very site-related.[12]

"We are not proposing to manage stocks," says MacDonald, "and we are not particularly interested in population dynamics and the whole notion of population ecology that NMFS needs to manage on a regional scale. However, we are extremely interested in community ecology or the relationships between populations and habitat. We are not saying that there ought to be no fishing, but we are saying, Can we please think of how fishing affects certain aspects of the sanctuary?"

From a fisheries management point of view, on the other hand, the primary goal is *optimum sustainable yield*, "taking into account the protection of marine ecosystems."[13] But the pressure to produce "the amount of fish which will provide the greatest overall benefit to the nation particularly with respect to food production and recreational opportunity" remains the dominant consideration. In the short run, cropping out big fish that are slow growing may increase turnover and total biomass, but a growing body of scientific literature is finding that reported increases in yields may not be sustainable. Add to this the ecological impacts of current fishing practices and the prospects of major alteration of the food web, and the irreversible destruction of essential biological communities within the sanctuary becomes palpable. "Things have to be done differently," concludes MacDonald. "The status quo will not lead to a sanctuary teeming with wildlife."

Conversely, the status quo seems to be what another subcommittee of the ecosystem-based management working group aimed to preserve. This group's vision was called the sustainable use scenario and its action plan was

> designed to protect sanctuary resources through existing best management practices . . . [focusing] on sustainable use with emphasis on maintaining benefits that are produced in the waters of the Stellwagen Bank National Marine Sanctuary.[14]

The membership of the subcommitee was comprised of representatives of the Massachusetts Bay ground fishermen and lobster fishermen and the state's Division of Marine Fisheries. Not surprisingly, the subcommittee's report went on to insist upon the exclusive jurisdiction of the New England Fisheries Management Council and NMFS.

Management Myopia

Management of fisheries and the sanctuary are at a crossroads. The legislative intent of the Sanctuaries Act and the Magnuson-Stevens and Sustainable Fisheries Acts are theoretically compatible. But "cross-speak" issues continue to complicate communications; differences, for example, between the disciplines of conservation biology and population dynamics. Then, too, there is the unwieldy two-tiered system of fisheries management established by Congress that assigns the development of fisheries management plans to regional management councils dominated by fishermen. The congressional intent was to put informed "stakeholders" at the table, but in practice the system has in effect conferred ownership of a public trust resource to commercial uses. However, in the case of marine sanctuaries, Congress authorized the creation of advisory councils in which fishing interests are represented but not given management responsibility.

The difference between the two management structures has led to much acrimony and was the focus of a 2008 report by the Department of Commerce's Office of Inspector General. The report included the following finding:

> Despite many attempts to improve collaboration, persistent disagreements and lack of communication between NMSP and NMFS have played a role in causing long delays in several sanctuary management plan reviews, and a disproportionate amount of resources and time have been spent by NMFS and NOS deciding whether NMFS or the sanctuary program should regulate fishing in sanctuaries. This confuses and fatigues community members and can compromise NOAA's ability to gain public trust.[15]

A key recommendation of the report was that the under secretary of commerce for oceans and atmosphere take the necessary actions to ensure that the National Marine Sanctuary Program and National Marine Fisheries Service improve communications and issue "clear guidance" on how to collaborate more effectively. Specific recommendations included greater levels of staff participation on interagency advisory councils and working groups, especially in the early development of sanctuary management plans and condition reports.

Improving internal communications is a beginning, but at some point Congress or the courts need to step in and clarify not only how but when the sanctuary program's needs for greater resource protection are to be acted upon by fishery management councils and NMFS. As Pat Kurkul, NMFS regional administrator told the New England Fisheries Management Council during the 2007 debate over the proposed designation of the sanctuary as a Habitat Area of Particular Concern, "The sanctuary standard for resource protection is actually higher than that of HAPCs."[16] Still, the council disapproved the designation, preferring to stay the course of achieving sustainable use on a regional scale, one fish species at a time. The vote seemed to be an invitation for someone to litigate.

Urban Wilderness

On a more constructive note, and in keeping with the vision statement, the same subcommittee that defined (and dismissed) absolute wilderness as a viable management goal developed an alternate scenario to both absolute wilderness and sustainable use called the "urban wilderness scenario."

> It is virtually impossible to manage SBNMS as a true wilderness, because many of the organisms that move through the sanctuary are severely impacted outside of its borders. In addition, SBNMS waters are under burgeoning pressure as the regional human population increases in numbers and wealth, thus elevating the demand for use of coastal waters for commercial and recreational fishing, boating and wildlife watching. In other words, *humans are part of the ecosystem* [emphasis added].[17]

Whether humans should be included in the definition of "ecosystem" is often debated but essentially irrelevant in the context of management alternatives, since the objective of management is some degree of control of human activity *within* the ecosystem. So, while humans may not have been a part of the ecosystem, they are now. The choices then come down to: (1) doing things in ways that are less disturbing to the ecosystem (while still pursuing current societal objectives); or (2) turning back the clock.

Option 1 more or less characterizes most of the nation's pollution control laws and resource management plans, which are based on the firm belief in the existence of technological fixes to problems. Option 2 is less empirical and usually requires a fundamental change in behavior, most often necessitated by crisis.

So, is it man *and* nature or man *versus* nature? Context and perspective are the keys to resolving the debate. If your management objective is restoration to, say, a pre-colonial state, your working definition of ecosystem either would not include humans or would treat humans as an invasive, predatory species. To "fully restore" the ecosystem of today's sanctuary (as the SAC vision statement prescribes), on the other hand, probably cannot be accomplished without making adjustments for the presence of humans and the societal benefits of human activity, while at the same time attempting to moderate that activity.

The legislative intent of both the Sanctuaries Act and the Stellwagen Bank designation clearly was to accommodate some level of human activity, so for management purposes, this acknowledgment of humans being part of the ecosystem found in the urban wilderness scenario is appropriate. The subcommittee went on to define urban wilderness as an area where the management goal:

> is the defense and restoration of such wilderness values as can be achieved in the context of proximity to the heavily settled watersheds and heavily impacted waters of the Gulf of Maine. The urban wilderness scenario employs zoning and impact restrictions to preserve a substantial portion of the ecological services that wilderness would provide. . . . The primary mechanism for achieving and maintaining wilderness values is the close monitoring of the ecosystem to allow for more informed and confident decisions in response to changes in human impacts and system state. The core of the program is a well-designed network of research areas and monitoring activities. These provide the data-stream required to manage human activities within the sanctuary in an adaptive manner, and to thus maintain the viability of human activity in a self-supporting system. . . . The urban wilderness scenario differs from "sustainable use" in system attributes such as the size-frequency distribution of organisms, the ecological resiliency of the sanctuary, and the emphasis on maximizing standing biomass and species diversity rather than gross rates of biomass production. . . . The return of natural ecological processes to a sanctuary that is nonetheless subject to some level of extraction and modification can be effected by safeguarding certain attributes of the system.[18]

The urban wilderness scenario conforms most closely to the vision statement included in the draft management plan, yet the draft management plan in its description of various action plans for *future* consideration omits any mention of the three scenarios discussed by the working group or the actions that would be required to implement them.

The draft plan limits itself to the *process* of ecosystem-based management, such as research, monitoring, and modeling activities; nothing, however, is specified that would guarantee that the condition of the sanctuary would be improved in five or ten years. Could it be that NOAA found the SAC's vision statement too controversial or too far ahead of the balance it hopes to strike between competing interests and values? As the draft management plan reads, NOAA appears to be forcing collaboration between sanctuary and fisheries management under the banner of sustainable use without actually saying so.

Adoption of the urban wilderness scenario would not necessarily require ceding fisheries management in the sanctuary to the sanctuary, but it would cause NOAA to lay out a series of nonnegotiable requirements; including:

1. Protecting the forage base of the sanctuary by prohibiting fishing of Atlantic and river herring and two species of sand lance;

2. Expanding the sanctuary borders to the north to include extensive areas of bottom that support herring and to the south to include areas that support sand lance;

3. Zoning portions of the sanctuary as off limits to the extraction of large brood fish with the possible exception of catch-and-release recreational fishing;

4. Zoning some areas for full protection to enhance and restore biodiversity and to provide untouched reference areas for adaptive management;

5. Allowing fishing based on ecosystem parameters, not just demographic criteria such as maximum sustained yield;

6. Requiring the use of low-impact fishing gear within specific areas, the goal being sustainability within the sanctuary; and

7. Minimizing degradation of the trophic system that supports all marine mammals and other harmful interactions with them.[19]

Ecological Reserves

Shortly before leaving office, President Bill Clinton attempted to put the nation back on track with respect to ocean management and protection by reviving some of the ideas of the late 1960s that formed the intellectual backdrop to what became the National Marine Sanctuaries Act. On a blistering hot day in late May 2000, he visited the island of Martha's Vineyard in the Bay State and issued an executive order calling upon the Departments of Commerce and Interior "to protect the significant natural and cultural resources within the marine environment for the benefit of present and future generations by strengthening and expanding the Nation's system of marine protected areas (MPAs). An expanded and strengthened comprehensive system of marine protected areas," added Clinton, "would enhance the conservation of our nation's natural and cultural marine heritage and the ecologically and economically sustainable use of the marine environment for future generations."[20]

The executive order defined a "marine protected area" broadly as "any area

of the marine environment that has been reserved by federal, state, territorial, tribal, or local laws or regulations to provide lasting protection for part or
all of the natural and cultural resources." The definition includes all existing
marine sanctuaries, fishery closure areas, coastal wildlife refuges, and a variety
of other unique areas that provide some degree of protection. For all its shortcomings, Stellwagen Bank is a marine protected area under this definition.

But the clear intent of the executive order was both to expand the sanctuary system and to encourage the creation of even more protective measures
based on three related principles. First, the identification and prioritization of
natural and cultural resources should be science-based. Second, ocean planning must take a holistic view that examines the ecological linkages among
marine protected areas which should include "ecological reserves in which
consumptive uses of resources are prohibited." Third, the minimum area of
ecological (or marine) reserves should be based on biological assessments as
opposed to arbitrary or political boundaries.

A month after issuing his executive order on MPAs, Clinton temporarily resolved the long-standing debate within the Congress and six presidential administrations over oil and gas exploration. With the stroke of a pen,
he prohibited exploration in any national marine sanctuary through the
year 2012.[21]

Congress seems to have turned a deaf ear to the President during reauthorization of the act later that year by declaring a moratorium on the creation
of any new sanctuaries, but it did give him authority to establish the 139,000-
square-mile Northwestern Hawaiian Islands Coral Reef Ecosystem Reserve,
which he did via Executive Order 13178 on December 4, 2000.[22] While the
Clinton order contained no regulations, it nevertheless bought time for the
National Marine Sanctuary Program to begin a lengthy public planning process for its eventual designation as a sanctuary.

Then, in June 2006, in a surprise move not in keeping with his stance on
most environmental issues, President George H. Bush issued a proclamation re-designating the reserve as the Papahānaumokuākea Marine National
Monument.[23] The proclamation included a regulatory package that prohibits
all fishing, making it what National Marine Sanctuary Program director Dan
Basta calls "the largest marine protected area on the planet."[24] The newly created national monument will be administered by the National Marine Sanctuary Program.

Bush credited documentary filmmaker Jean-Michel Cousteau and marine biologist Sylvia Earle, currently explorer-in-residence at the National Geographic Society, with the idea of setting the area aside. He received widespread and unqualified praise for the proclamation. Elliott Norse, president of the Marine Conservation Biology Institute, told MSNBC that it was "the start of a new era of protecting places in the sea before they're degraded beyond recognition."[25]

The significance of the Clinton and Bush proclamations cannot be overstated, but if there is to be a "new era" of ocean protection, the President, Congress, and the American people must view the ocean not as a *resource* to be possessed and used, but as a *living environment* for which we have both practical and moral responsibilities to protect and use wisely and equitably — both for our own survival and for the life forms therein. The challenge lies not just in identifying and protecting the last pristine and far-away remnants of a dying sea, but in restoring those areas that we either have neglected in the past or managed poorly. In the case of Stellwagen Bank and many other places along the continental shelf, that challenge requires us to look beyond the short horizon of sustainability to a fully restored ecosystem, a goal that is attainable even in the context of the National Marine Sanctuaries Act.

It is not too late for the Gerry E. Studds Stellwagen Bank National Marine Sanctuary to start over.

Appendixes

APPENDIX A

Acronyms

COE	Army Corps of Engineers (also Army Corps)
CZMA	Coastal Zone Management Act (16 U.S.C. §§451 *et seq.*)
DOI	Department of the Interior (also Interior)
DEIS	Draft Environmental Impact Statement
EEZ	Exclusive Economic Zone
EIS	Environmental Impact Statement
EPA	Environmental Protection Agency
ESA	Endangered Species Act (16 U.S.C. §§1531–1543)
HMMFC	House Merchant Marine and Fisheries Committee
MMPA	Marine Mammal Protection Act (16 U.S.C. §§1361 *et seq.*)
MPRSA	Marine Protection, Research, and Sanctuaries Act (16 U.S.C. §§1431 *et seq.*)
MSFCMA	Magnuson-Stevens Fishery Conservation and Management Act (16 U.S.C. §§1801 *et seq.*)
NCCOS	National Centers for Coastal Ocean Science
NEFMC	New England Fisheries Management Council (also the Council)
NEPA	National Environmental Policy Act (42 U.S.C. §§4321 *et seq.*)
NMFS	National Marine Fisheries Service (now NOAA Fisheries Service)
NMSA	National Marine Sanctuaries Act (16 U.S.C. §§1431 *et seq.* as amended by Public Law 106-513)
NMSP	National Marine Sanctuaries Program
NOAA	National Oceanic and Atmospheric Administration
NOS	National Ocean Service
OCS	Outer Continental Shelf
OCSLA	Outer Continental Shelf Lands Act (43 U.S.C. §§1331 *et seq.*)
ONMS	Office of National Marine Sanctuaries
SBNMS	Gerry E. Studds Stellwagen Bank National Marine Sanctuary (also the Sanctuary)

National Marine Sanctuaries Act

Title 16, Chapter 32, §§1431 *et seq.* United States Code (U.S.C.), as amended by Public Law 106-513, November 2000

Sec. 1431. Findings, Purposes, and Policies; Establishment of System

(a) FINDINGS. — The Congress finds that —
   (1) this Nation historically has recognized the importance of protecting special areas of its public domain, but these efforts have been directed almost exclusively to land areas above the high-water mark;
   (2) certain areas of the marine environment possess conservation, recreational, ecological, historical, scientific, educational, cultural, archeological, or

esthetic qualities which give them special national, and in some cases international, significance;

(3) while the need to control the effects of particular activities has led to enactment of resource-specific legislation, these laws cannot in all cases provide a coordinated and comprehensive approach to the conservation and management of special areas of the marine environment; and

(4) a Federal program which establishes areas of the marine environment which have special conservation, recreational, ecological, historical, cultural, archeological, scientific, educational, or esthetic qualities as national marine sanctuaries managed as the National Marine Sanctuary System will—

(A) improve the conservation, understanding, management, and wise and sustainable use of marine resources;

(B) enhance public awareness, understanding, and appreciation of the marine environment; and

(C) maintain for future generations the habitat, and ecological services, of the natural assemblage of living resources that inhabit these areas.

(b) PURPOSES AND POLICIES. — The purposes and policies of this chapter are —

(1) to identify and designate as national marine sanctuaries areas of the marine environment which are of special national significance and to manage these areas as the National Marine Sanctuary System;

(2) to provide authority for comprehensive and coordinated conservation and management of these marine areas, and activities affecting them, in a manner which complements existing regulatory authorities;

(3) to maintain the natural biological communities in the national marine sanctuaries, and to protect, and, where appropriate, restore and enhance natural habitats, populations, and ecological processes;

(4) to enhance public awareness, understanding, appreciation, and wise and sustainable use of the marine environment, and the natural, historical, cultural, and archeological resources of the National Marine Sanctuary System;

(5) to support, promote, and coordinate scientific research on, and long-term monitoring of, the resources of these marine areas;

(6) to facilitate to the extent compatible with the primary objective of resource protection, all public and private uses of the resources of these marine areas not prohibited pursuant to other authorities;

(7) to develop and implement coordinated plans for the protection and management of these areas with appropriate Federal agencies, State and local governments, Native American tribes and organizations, international organizations, and other public and private interests concerned with the continuing health and resilience of these marine areas;

(8) to create models of, and incentives for, ways to conserve and manage these areas, including the application of innovative management techniques; and

(9) to cooperate with global programs encouraging conservation of marine resources.

(c) ESTABLISHMENT OF SYSTEM. — There is established the National Marine Sanctuary System, which shall consist of national marine sanctuaries designated by the Secretary in accordance with this chapter.

Sec. 1432. Definitions

As used in this chapter, the term —

(1) "draft management plan" means the plan described in section 1434(a)(1) (C)(v) of this title;

(2) "Magnuson-Stevens Act" means the Magnuson-Stevens Fishery Conservation and Management Act (16 U.S.C. §1801 *et seq.*);

(3) "marine environment" means those areas of coastal and ocean waters, the Great Lakes and their connecting waters, and submerged lands over which the United States exercises jurisdiction, including the exclusive economic zone, consistent with international law;

(4) "Secretary" means the Secretary of Commerce;

(5) "State" means each of the several States, the District of Columbia, the Commonwealth of Puerto Rico, the Commonwealth of the Northern Mariana Islands, American Samoa, the Virgin Islands, Guam, and any other commonwealth, territory, or possession of the United States;

(6) "damages" includes —

(A) compensation for —

(i) (I) the cost of replacing, restoring, or acquiring the equivalent of a sanctuary resource; and (II) the value of the lost use of a sanctuary resource pending its restoration or replacement or the acquisition of an equivalent sanctuary resource; or

(ii) the value of a sanctuary resource if the sanctuary resource cannot be restored or replaced or if the equivalent of such resource cannot be acquired;

(B) the cost of damage assessments under section 1443(b)(2) of this title;

(C) the reasonable cost of monitoring appropriate to the injured, restored, or replaced resources;

(D) the cost of curation and conservation of archeological, historical, and cultural sanctuary resources; and

(E) the cost of enforcement actions undertaken by the Secretary in response to the destruction or loss of, or injury to, a sanctuary resource;

(7) "response costs" means the costs of actions taken or authorized by the Secretary to minimize destruction or loss of, or injury to, sanctuary resources, or to minimize the imminent risks of such destruction, loss, or injury, including costs related to seizure, forfeiture, storage, or disposal arising from liability under section 1443 of this title;

(8) "sanctuary resource" means any living or nonliving resource of a national marine sanctuary that contributes to the conservation, recreational, ecological, historical, educational, cultural, archeological, scientific, or aesthetic value of the sanctuary; and

(9) "exclusive economic zone" means the exclusive economic zone as defined in the Magnuson-Stevens Act; and

(10) "System" means the National Marine Sanctuary System established by section 1431 of this title.

Sec. 1433. Sanctuary Designation Standards

(a) STANDARDS.—The Secretary may designate any discrete area of the marine environment as a national marine sanctuary and promulgate regulations implementing the designation if the Secretary determines that—

    (1) the designation will fulfill the purposes and policies of this chapter;

    (2) the area is of special national significance due to—

        (A) its conservation, recreational, ecological, historical, scientific, cultural, archaeological, educational, or esthetic qualities;

        (B) the communities of living marine resources it harbors; or

        (C) its resource or human-use values;

    (3) existing State and Federal authorities are inadequate or should be supplemented to ensure coordinated and comprehensive conservation and management of the area, including resource protection, scientific research, and public education;

    (4) designation of the area as a national marine sanctuary will facilitate the objectives stated in paragraph (3); and

    (5) the area is of a size and nature that will permit comprehensive and coordinated conservation and management.

(b) FACTORS AND CONSULTATIONS REQUIRED IN MAKING DETERMINATIONS AND FINDINGS—

    (1) Factors.—For purposes of determining if an area of the marine environment meets the standards set forth in subsection (a) of this section, the Secretary shall consider—

        (A) the area's natural resource and ecological qualities, including its contribution to biological productivity, maintenance of ecosystem structure, maintenance of ecologically or commercially important or threatened species or species assemblages, maintenance of critical habitat of endangered species, and the biogeographic representation of the site;

(B) the area's historical, cultural, archaeological, or paleontological significance;

(C) the present and potential uses of the area that depend on maintenance of the area's resources, including commercial and recreational fishing, subsistence uses, other commercial and recreational activities, and research and education;

(D) the present and potential activities that may adversely affect the factors identified in subparagraphs (A), (B), and (C);

(E) the existing State and Federal regulatory and management authorities applicable to the area and the adequacy of those authorities to fulfill the purposes and policies of this chapter;

(F) the manageability of the area, including such factors as its size, its ability to be identified as a discrete ecological unit with definable boundaries, its accessibility, and its suitability for monitoring and enforcement activities;

(G) the public benefits to be derived from sanctuary status, with emphasis on the benefits of long-term protection of nationally significant resources, vital habitats, and resources which generate tourism;

(H) the negative impacts produced by management restrictions on income-generating activities such as living and nonliving resources development;

(I) the socioeconomic effects of sanctuary designation;

(J) the area's scientific value and value for monitoring the resources and natural processes that occur there;

(K) the feasibility, where appropriate, of employing innovative management approaches to protect sanctuary resources or to manage compatible uses; and

(L) the value of the area as an addition to the System.

(2) Consultation. — In making determinations and findings, the Secretary shall consult with —

(A) the Committee on Resources of the House of Representatives and the Committee on Commerce, Science, and Transportation of the Senate;

(B) the Secretaries of State, Defense, Transportation, and the Interior, the Administrator, and the heads of other interested Federal agencies;

(C) the responsible officials or relevant agency heads of the appropriate State and local government entities, including coastal zone management agencies, that will or are likely to be affected by the establishment of the area as a national marine sanctuary;

(D) the appropriate officials of any Regional Fishery Management Council established by section 302 of the Magnuson-Stevens Act (16 U.S.C. §1852) that may be affected by the proposed designation; and

(E) other interested persons.

Sec. 1434. Procedures for Designation and Implementation

(a) SANCTUARY PROPOSAL—

(1) Notice. — In proposing to designate a national marine sanctuary, the Secretary shall —

(A) issue, in the Federal Register, a notice of the proposal, proposed regulations that may be necessary and reasonable to implement the proposal, and a summary of the draft management plan;

(B) provide notice of the proposal in newspapers of general circulation or electronic media in the communities that may be affected by the proposal; and

(C) no later than the day on which the notice required under subparagraph (A) is submitted to the Office of the Federal Register, submit a copy of that notice and the draft sanctuary designation documents prepared pursuant to paragraph (2), including an executive summary, to the Committee on Resources of the House of Representatives, the Committee on Commerce, Science, and Transportation of the Senate, and the Governor of each State in which any part of the proposed sanctuary would be located.

(2) Sanctuary Designation Documents. — The Secretary shall prepare and make available to the public sanctuary designation documents on the proposal that include the following:

(A) A draft environmental impact statement pursuant to the National Environmental Policy Act of 1969 (42 U.S.C. §4321 et seq.).

(B) A resource assessment that documents —

(i) present and potential uses of the area, including commercial and recreational fishing, research and education, minerals and energy development, subsistence uses, and other commercial, governmental, or recreational uses;

(ii) after consultation with the Secretary of the Interior, any commercial, governmental, or recreational resource uses in the areas that are subject to the primary jurisdiction ofthe Department of the Interior; and

(iii) information prepared in consultation with the Secretary of Defense, the Secretary of Energy, and the Administrator of the Environmental Protection Agency, on any past, present, or proposed future disposal or discharge of materials in the vicinity of the proposed sanctuary. Public disclosure by the Secretary of such information shall be consistent with national security regulations.

(C) A draft management plan for the proposed national marine sanctuary that includes the following:

(i) The terms of the proposed designation.

(ii) Proposed mechanisms to coordinate existing regulatory and management authorities within the area.

(iii) The proposed goals and objectives, management responsibilities, resource studies, and appropriate strategies for managing sanctuary resources of the proposed sanctuary, including interpretation and education, innovative management strategies, research, monitoring and assessment, resource protection, restoration, enforcement, and surveillance activities.

(iv) An evaluation of the advantages of cooperative State and Federal management if all or part of the proposed sanctuary is within the territorial limits of any State or is superjacent to the subsoil and seabed within the seaward boundary of a State, as that boundary is established under the Submerged Lands Act (43 U.S.C. §1301 *et seq.*).

(v) An estimate of the annual cost to the Federal Government of the proposed designation, including costs of personnel, equipment and facilities, enforcement, research, and public education.

(vi) The proposed regulations referred to in paragraph (1)(A).

(D) Maps depicting the boundaries of the proposed sanctuary.

(E) The basis for the determinations made under section 1433(a) of this title with respect to the area.

(F) An assessment of the considerations under section 1433(b)(1) of this title.

(3) Public Hearing. — No sooner than thirty days after issuing a notice under this subsection, the Secretary shall hold at least one public hearing in the coastal area or areas that will be most affected by the proposed designation of the area as a national marine sanctuary for the purpose of receiving the views of interested parties.

(4) Terms of Designation. — The terms of designation of a sanctuary shall include the geographic area proposed to be included within the sanctuary, the characteristics of the area that give it conservation, recreational, ecological, historical, research, educational, or esthetic value, and the types of activities that will be subject to regulation by the Secretary to protect those characteristics. The terms of designation may be modified only by the same procedures by which the original designation is made.

(5) Fishing Regulations. — The Secretary shall provide the appropriate Re-

gional Fishery Management Council with the opportunity to prepare draft regulations for fishing within the Exclusive Economic Zone as the Council may deem necessary to implement the proposed designation. Draft regulations prepared by the Council or a Council determination that regulations are not necessary pursuant to this paragraph, shall be accepted and issued as proposed regulations by the Secretary unless the Secretary finds that the Council's action fails to fulfill the purposes and policies of this chapter and the goals and objectives of the proposed designation. In preparing the draft regulations, a Regional Fishery Management Council shall use as guidance the national standards of section 301(a) of the Magnuson-Stevens Act (16 U.S.C. §1851) to the extent that the standards are consistent and compatible with the goals and objectives of the proposed designation. The Secretary shall prepare the fishing regulations, if the Council declines to make a determination with respect to the need for regulations, makes a determination which is rejected by the Secretary, or fails to prepare the draft regulations in a timely manner. Any amendments to the fishing regulations shall be drafted, approved, and issued in the same manner as the original regulations. The Secretary shall also cooperate with other appropriate fishery management authorities with rights or responsibilities within a proposed sanctuary at the earliest practicable stage in drafting any sanctuary fishing regulations.

(6) Committee Action. — After receiving the documents under subsection (a) (1)(C) of this section, the Committee on Resources of the House of Representatives and the Committee on Commerce, Science, and Transportation of the Senate may each hold hearings on the proposed designation and on the matters set forth in the documents. If within the forty-five day period of continuous session of Congress beginning on the date of submission of the documents, either Committee issues a report concerning matters addressed in the documents, the Secretary shall consider this report before publishing a notice to designate the national marine sanctuary.

(b) TAKING EFFECT OF DESIGNATIONS—

(1) Notice. — In designating a national marine sanctuary, the Secretary shall publish in the Federal Register notice of the designation together with final regulations to implement the designation and any other matters required by law, and submit such notice to the Congress. The Secretary shall advise the public of the availability of the final management plan and the final environmental impact statement with respect to such sanctuary. The Secretary shall issue a notice of designation with respect to a proposed national marine sanctuary site not later than 30 months after the date a notice declaring the site to be an active candidate for sanctuary designation is published in the Federal Register under regulations issued under this Act, or shall publish not later than

such date in the Federal Register findings regarding why such notice has not been published. No notice of designation may occur until the expiration of the period for Committee action under subsection (a)(6) of this section. The designation (and any of its terms not disapproved under this subsection) and regulations shall take effect and become final after the close of a review period of forty-five days of continuous session of Congress beginning on the day on which such notice is published unless, in the case of a national marine sanctuary that is located partially or entirely within the seaward boundary of any State, the Governor affected certifies to the Secretary that the designation or any of its terms is unacceptable, in which case the designation or the unacceptable term shall not take effect in the area of the sanctuary lying within the seaward boundary of the State.

(2) Withdrawal of Designation. — If the Secretary considers that actions taken under paragraph (1) will affect the designation of a national marine sanctuary in a manner that the goals and objectives of the sanctuary or System cannot be fulfilled, the Secretary may withdraw the entire designation. If the Secretary does not withdraw the designation, only those terms of the designation not certified under paragraph (1) shall take effect.

(3) Procedures. — In computing the forty-five-day periods of continuous session of Congress pursuant to subsection (a)(6) of this section and paragraph (1) of this subsection —

(A) continuity of session is broken only by an adjournment of Congress sine die; and

(B) the days on which either House of Congress is not in session because of an adjournment of more than three days to a day certain are excluded.

(c) Access and Valid Rights

(1) Nothing in this chapter shall be construed as terminating or granting to the Secretary the right to terminate any valid lease, permit, license, or right of subsistence use or of access that is in existence on the date of designation of any national marine sanctuary.

(2) The exercise of a lease, permit, license, or right is subject to regulation by the Secretary consistent with the purposes for which the sanctuary is designated.

(d) Interagency Cooperation

(1) Review of Agency Actions. —

(A) In General. — Federal agency actions internal or external to a national marine sanctuary, including private activities authorized by licenses, leases, or permits, that are likely to destroy, cause the loss of, or injure any sanctuary resource are subject to consultation with the Secretary.

(B) Agency Statements Required. — Subject to any regulations the Secretary may establish each Federal agency proposing an action described in subparagraph (A) shall provide the Secretary with a written statement describing the action and its potential effects on sanctuary resources at the earliest practicable time, but in no case later than 45 days before the final approval of the action unless such Federal agency and the Secretary agree to a different schedule.

(2) Secretary's Recommended Alternatives. — If the Secretary finds that a Federal agency action is likely to destroy, cause the loss of, or injure a sanctuary resource, the Secretary shall (within 45 days of receipt of complete information on the proposed agency action) recommend reasonable and prudent alternatives, which may include conduct of the action elsewhere, which can be taken by the Federal agency in implementing the agency action that will protect sanctuary resources.

(3) Response to Recommendations. — The agency head who receives the Secretary's recommended alternatives under paragraph (2) shall promptly consult with the Secretary on the alternatives. If the agency head decides not to follow the alternatives, the agency head shall provide the Secretary with a written statement explaining the reasons for that decision.

(4) Failure to Follow Alternative. — If the head of a Federal agency takes an action other than an alternative recommended by the Secretary and such action results in the destruction of, loss of, or injury to a sanctuary resource, the head of the agency shall promptly prevent and mitigate further damage and restore or replace the sanctuary resource in a manner approved by the Secretary.

(e) REVIEW OF MANAGEMENT PLANS. — Not more than five years after the date of designation of any national marine sanctuary, and thereafter at intervals not exceeding five years, the Secretary shall evaluate the substantive progress toward implementing the management plan and goals for the sanctuary, especially the effectiveness of site-specific management techniques and strategies, and shall revise the management plan and regulations as necessary to fulfill the purposes and policies of this chapter. This review shall include a prioritization of management objectives.

(f) LIMITATIONS ON DESIGNATION OF NEW SANCTUARIES—

(1) Finding Required. — The Secretary may not publish in the Federal Register any sanctuary designation notice or regulations proposing to designate a new sanctuary, unless the Secretary has published a finding that —

(A) the addition of a new sanctuary will not have a negative impact on the System; and

(B) sufficient resources were available in the fiscal year in which the finding is made to —

(i) effectively implement sanctuary management plans for each sanctuary in the System; and

(ii) complete site characterization studies and inventory known sanctuary resources, including cultural resources, for each sanctuary in the System within 10 years after the date that the finding is made if the resources available for those activities are maintained at the same level for each fiscal year in that 10-year period.

(2) Deadline. — If the Secretary does not submit the findings required by paragraph (1) before February 1, 2004, the Secretary shall submit to the Congress before October 1, 2004, a finding with respect to whether the requirements of subparagraphs (A) and (B) of paragraph (1) have been met by all existing sanctuaries.

(3) Limitation on Application. — Paragraph (1) does not apply to any sanctuary designation documents for —

(A) a Thunder Bay National Marine Sanctuary; or

(B) a Northwestern Hawaiian Islands National Marine Sanctuary.

Sec. 1435. Application of Regulations; International Negotiations, and Cooperation

(a) REGULATIONS. — This chapter and the regulations issued under section 1434 of this title shall be applied in accordance with generally recognized principles of international law, and in accordance with treaties, conventions, and other agreements to which the United States is a party. No regulation shall apply to or be enforced against a person who is not a citizen, national, or resident alien of the United States, unless in accordance with —

(1) generally recognized principles of international law;

(2) an agreement between the United States and the foreign state of which the person is a citizen; or

(3) an agreement between the United States and the flag state of a foreign vessel, if the person is a crewmember of the vessel.

(b) NEGOTIATIONS. — The Secretary of State, in consultation with the Secretary, shall take appropriate action to enter into negotiations with other governments to make necessary arrangements for the protection of any national marine sanctuary and to promote the purposes for which the sanctuary is established.

(c) INTERNATIONAL COOPERATION. — The Secretary, in consultation with the Secretary of State and other appropriate Federal agencies, shall cooperate with other governments and international organizations in furtherance of the purposes and policies of this chapter and consistent with applicable regional and mutilateral arrangements for the protection and management of special marine areas.

Sec. 1436. Prohibited Activities

It is unlawful for any person to —

(1) destroy, cause the loss of, or injure any sanctuary resource managed under law or regulations for that sanctuary;

(2) possess, sell, offer for sale, purchase, import, export, deliver, carry, transport, or ship by any means any sanctuary resource taken in violation of this section;

(3) interfere with the enforcement of this chapter by —

(A) refusing to permit any officer authorized to enforce this chapter to board a vessel, other than a vessel operated by the Department of Defense or United States Coast Guard, subject to such person's control for the purposes of conducting any search or inspection in connection with the enforcement of this chapter;

(B) resisting, opposing, impeding, intimidating, harassing, bribing, interfering with, or forcibly assaulting any person authorized by the Secretary to implement this chapter or any such authorized officer in the conduct of any search or inspection performed under this chapter; or

(C) knowingly and willfully submitting false information to the Secretary or any officer authorized to enforce this chapter in connection with any search or inspection conducted under this chapter; or

(4) violate any provision of this chapter or any regulation or permit issued pursuant to this chapter.

Sec. 1437. Enforcement

(a) IN GENERAL. — The Secretary shall conduct such enforcement activities as are necessary and reasonable to carry out this chapter.

(b) POWERS OF AUTHORIZED OFFICERS. — Any person who is authorized to this chapter may —

(1) board, search, inspect, and seize any vessel suspected of being used to violate this chapter or any regulation or permit issued under this chapter and any equipment, stores, and cargo of such vessel;

(2) seize wherever found any sanctuary resource taken or retained in violation of this chapter or any regulation or permit issued under this chapter;

(3) seize any evidence of a violation of this chapter or of any regulation or permit issued under this chapter;

(4) execute any warrant or other process issued by any court of competent jurisdiction;

(5) exercise any other lawful authority; and

(6) arrest any person, if there is reasonable cause to believe that such person has committed an act prohibited by section 1436(3) of this title.

(c) CRIMINAL OFFENSES—

(1) Offenses. —A person is guilty of an offense under this subsection if the person commits any act prohibited by section 1436(3) of this title.

(2) Punishment. —Any person that is guilty of an offense under this subsection —

(A) except as provided in subparagraph (B), shall be fined under title 18, imprisoned for not more than 6 months, or both; or

(B) in the case of a person who in the commission of such an offense uses a dangerous weapon, engages in conduct that causes bodily injury to any person authorized to enforce this chapter or any person authorized to implement the provisions of this chapter, or places any such person in fear of imminent bodily injury, shall be fined under title 18, imprisoned for not more than 10 years, or both.

(d) CIVIL PENALTIES—

(1) Civil Penalty. —Any person subject to the jurisdiction of the United States who violates this chapter or any regulation or permit issued under this chapter shall be liable to the United States for a civil penalty of not more than $100,000 for each such violation, to be assessed by the Secretary. Each day of a continuing violation shall constitute a separate violation.

(2) Notice. — No penalty shall be assessed under this subsection until after the person charged has been given notice and an opportunity for a hearing.

(3) In Rem Jurisdiction. —A vessel used in violating this chapter or any regulation or permit issued under this chapter shall be liable in rem for any civil penalty assessed for such violation. Such penalty shall constitute a maritime lien on the vessel and may be recovered in an action in rem in the district court of the United States having jurisdiction over the vessel.

(4) Review of Civil Penalty. —Any person against whom a civil penalty is assessed under this subsection may obtain review in the United States district court for the appropriate district by filing a complaint in such court not later than 30 days after the date of such order.

(5) Collection of Penalties. — If any person fails to pay an assessment of a civil penalty under this section after it has become a final and unappealable order, or after the appropriate court has entered final judgment in favor of the Secretary, the Secretary shall refer the matter to the Attorney General, who shall recover the amount assessed in any appropriate district court of the United States. In such action, the validity and appropriateness of the final order imposing the civil penalty shall not be subject to review.

(6) Compromise or Other Action by Secretary. — The Secretary may compromise, modify, or remit, with or without conditions, any civil penalty which is or may be imposed under this section.

(e) FORFEITURE—

(1) In General. — Any vessel (including the vessel's equipment, stores, and cargo) and other item used, and any sanctuary resource taken or retained, in any manner, in connection with or as a result of any violation of this chapter or of any regulation or permit issued under this chapter shall be subject to forfeiture to the United States pursuant to a civil proceeding under this subsection. The proceeds from forfeiture actions under this subsection shall constitute a separate recovery in addition to any amounts recovered as civil penalties under this section or as civil damages under section 1443 of this title. None of those proceeds shall be subject to set-off.

(2) Applications of the Customs Laws. — The Secretary may exercise the authority of any United States official granted by any relevant customs law relating to the seizure, forfeiture, condemnation, disposition, remission, and mitigation of property in enforcing this chapter.

(3) Disposal of Sanctuary Resources. — Any sanctuary resource seized pursuant to this chapter may be disposed of pursuant to an order of the appropriate court, or, if perishable, in a manner prescribed by regulations promulgated by the Secretary. Any proceeds from the sale of such sanctuary resource shall for all purposes represent the sanctuary resource so disposed of in any subsequent legal proceedings.

(4) Presumption. — For the purposes of this section there is a rebuttable presumption that all sanctuary resources found on board a vessel that is used or seized in connection with a violation of this chapter or of any regulation or permit issued under this chapter were taken or retained in violation of this chapter or of a regulation or permit issued under this chapter.

(f) PAYMENT OF STORAGE, CARE AND OTHER COSTS. —

(1) Expenditures. —

(A) Notwithstanding any other law, amounts received by the United States as civil penalties, forfeitures of property, and costs imposed under paragraph (2) shall be retained by the Secretary in the manner provided for in section 9607(f)(1) of title 42.

(B) Amounts received under this section for forfeitures and costs imposed under paragraph (2) shall be used to pay the reasonable and necessary costs incurred by the Secretary to provide temporary storage, care, maintenance, and disposal of any sanctuary resource or other property seized in connection with a violation of this chapter or any regulation or permit issued under this chapter.

(C) Amounts received under this section as civil penalties and any amounts remaining after the operation of subparagraph (B) shall be used, in order of priority, to —

(i) manage and improve the national marine sanctuary with respect to which the violation occurred that resulted in the penalty or forfeiture;

(ii) pay a reward to any person who furnishes information leading to an assessment of a civil penalty, or to a forfeiture of property, for a violation of this chapter or any regulation or permit issued under this chapter; and

(iii) manage and improve any other national marine sanctuary.

(2) Liability for Costs. — Any person assessed a civil penalty for a violation of this chapter or of any regulation or permit issued under this chapter, and any claimant in a forfeiture action brought for such a violation, shall be liable for the reasonable costs incurred by the Secretary in storage, care, and maintenance of any sanctuary resource or other property seized in connection with the violation.

(g) SUBPOENAS. — In the case of any hearing under this section which is determined on the record in accordance with the procedures provided for under section 554 of title 5, the Secretary may issue subpoenas for the attendance and testimony of witnesses and the production of relevant papers, books, electronic files, and documents, and may administer oaths.

(h) USE OF RESOURCES OF STATE AND OTHER FEDERAL AGENCIES. — The Secretary shall, whenever appropriate, use by agreement the personnel, services, and facilities of State and other Federal departments, agencies, and instrumentalities, on a reimbursable or nonreimbursable basis, to carry out the Secretary's responsibilities under this section.

(i) COAST GUARD AUTHORITY NOT LIMITED. — Nothing in this section shall be considered to limit the authority of the Coast Guard to enforce this or any other Federal law under section 89 of title 14.

(j) INJUNCTIVE RELIEF. — If the Secretary determines that there is an imminent risk of destruction or loss of or injury to a sanctuary resource, or that there has been actual destruction or loss of, or injury to, a sanctuary resource which may give rise to liability under section 1443 of this title, the Attorney General, upon request of the Secretary, shall seek to obtain such relief as may be necessary to abate such risk or actual destruction, loss, or injury, or to restore or replace the sanctuary resource, or both. The district courts of the United States shall have jurisdiction in such a case to order such relief as the public interest and the equities of the case may require.

(k) AREA OF APPLICATION AND ENFORCEABILITY. — The area of application and enforceability of this chapter includes the territorial sea of the United States, as described in Presidential Proclamation 5928 of December 27, 1988, which is subject to the sovereignty of the United States, and the United States exclusive economic zone, consistent with international law.

(l) NATIONWIDE SERVICE OF PROCESS. — In any action by the United States under this chapter, process may be served in any district where the defendant is found, resides, transacts business, or has appointed an agent for the service of process.

Sec. 1439. Regulations

The Secretary may issue such regulations as may be necessary to carry out this chapter.

Sec. 1440. Research, Monitoring, and Education.

(a) IN GENERAL. — The Secretary shall conduct, support, or coordinate research, monitoring, evaluation, and education programs consistent with subsections (b) and (c) of this section and the purposes and policies of this chapter.

(b) RESEARCH AND MONITORING. —

   (1) In General. — The Secretary may —

   (A) support, promote, and coordinate research on, and long- term monitoring of, sanctuary resources and natural processes that occur in national marine sanctuaries, including exploration, mapping, and environmental and socioeconomic assessment;

   (B) develop and test methods to enhance degraded habitats or restore damaged, injured, or lost sanctuary resources; and

   (C) support, promote, and coordinate research on, and the conservation, curation, and public display of, the cultural, archeological, and historical resources of national marine sanctuaries.

   (2) Availability of Results. — The results of research and monitoring conducted, supported, or permitted by the Secretary under this subsection shall be made available to the public.

(c) EDUCATION. —

   (1) In General. — The Secretary may support, promote, and coordinate efforts to enhance public awareness, understanding, and appreciation of national marine sanctuaries and the System. Efforts supported, promoted, or coordinated under this subsection must emphasize the conservation goals and sustainable public uses of national marine sanctuaries and the System.

   (2) Educational Activities. — Activities under this subsection may include education of the general public, teachers, students, national marine sanctuary users, and ocean and coastal resource managers.

(d) Interpretive Facilities.—

(1) In General.—The Secretary may develop interpretive facilities near any national marine sanctuary.

(2) Facility Requirement.—Any facility developed under this subsection must emphasize the conservation goals and sustainable public uses of national marine sanctuaries by providing the public with information about the conservation, recreational, ecological, historical, cultural, archeological, scientific, educational, or esthetic qualities of the national marine sanctuary.

(e) Consultation and Coordination.—In conducting, supporting, and coordinating research, monitoring, evaluation, and education programs under subsection (a) of this section and developing interpretive facilities under subsection (d) of this section, the Secretary may consult or coordinate with Federal, interstate, or regional agencies, States or local governments.

Sec. 1441. Special Use Permits

(a) Issuance of Permits.—The Secretary may issue special use permits which authorize the conduct of specific activities in a national marine sanctuary if the Secretary determines such authorization is necessary—

(1) to establish conditions of access to and use of any sanctuary resource; or

(2) to promote public use and understanding of a sanctuary resource.

(b) Public Notice Required.—The Secretary shall provide appropriate public notice before identifying any category of activity subject to a special use permit under subsection (a) of this section.

(c) Permit Terms.—A permit issued under this section—

(1) shall authorize the conduct of an activity only if that activity is compatible with the purposes for which the sanctuary is designated and with protection of sanctuary resources;

(2) shall not authorize the conduct of any activity for a period of more than 5 years unless renewed by the Secretary;

(3) shall require that activities carried out under the permit be conducted in a manner that does not destroy, cause the loss of, or injure sanctuary resources; and

(4) shall require the permittee to purchase and maintain comprehensive general liability insurance, or post an equivalent bond, against claims arising out of activities conducted under the permit and to agree to hold the United States harmless against such claims.

(d) Fees.—

(1) Assessment and Collection.—The Secretary may assess and collect fees for the conduct of any activity under a permit issued under this section.

(2) Amount. — The amount of a fee under this subsection shall be equal to the sum of —

(A) costs incurred, or expected to be incurred, by the Secretary in issuing the permit;

(B) costs incurred, or expected to be incurred, by the Secretary as a direct result of the conduct of the activity for which the permit is issued, including costs of monitoring the conduct of the activity; and

(C) an amount which represents the fair market value of the use of the sanctuary resource.

(3) Use of Fees. — Amounts collected by the Secretary in the form of fees under this section may be used by the Secretary —

(A) for issuing and administering permits under this section; and

(B) for expenses of managing national marine sanctuaries.

(4) Waiver or Reduction of Fees. — The Secretary may accept in-kind contributions in lieu of a fee under paragraph (2)(C), or waive or reduce any fee assessed under this subsection for any activity that does not derive profit from the access to or use of sanctuary resources.

(e) VIOLATIONS. — Upon violation of a term or condition of a permit issued under this section, the Secretary may —

(1) suspend or revoke the permit without compensation to the permittee and without liability to the United States;

(2) assess a civil penalty in accordance with section 1437 of this title; or

(3) both.

(f) REPORTS. — Each person issued a permit under this section shall submit an annual report to the Secretary not later than December 31 of each year which describes activities conducted under that permit and revenues derived from such activities during the year.

(g) FISHING. — Nothing in this section shall be considered to require a person to obtain a permit under this section for the conduct of any fishing activities in a national marine sanctuary.

Sec. 1442. Cooperative Agreements, Donations, and Acquisitions

(a) AGREEMENTS AND GRANTS. — The Secretary may enter into cooperative agreements, contracts, or other agreements with, or make grants to, States, local governments, regional agencies, interstate agencies, or other persons to carry out the purposes and policies of this chapter.

(b) AUTHORIZATION TO SOLICIT DONATIONS. — The Secretary may enter into such agreements with any nonprofit organization authorizing the organization to solicit private donations to carry out the purposes and policies of this chapter.

(c) DONATIONS. — The Secretary may accept donations of funds, property, and services for use in designating and administering national marine sanctuaries under this chapter. Donations accepted under this section shall be considered as a gift or bequest to or for the use of the United States.

(d) ACQUISITIONS. — The Secretary may acquire by purchase, lease, or exchange, any land, facilities, or other property necessary and appropriate to carry out the purposes and policies of this chapter.

(e) USE OF RESOURCES OF OTHER GOVERNMENT AGENCIES. — The Secretary may, whenever appropriate, enter into an agreement with a State or other Federal agency to use the personnel, services, or facilities of such agency on a reimbursable or nonreimbursable basis, to assist in carrying out the purposes and policies of this chapter.

(f) AUTHORITY TO OBTAIN GRANTS. — Notwithstanding any other provision of law that prohibits a Federal agency from receiving assistance, the Secretary may apply for, accept, and use grants from other Federal agencies, States, local governments, regional agencies, interstate agencies, foundations, or other persons, to carry out the purposes and policies of this chapter.

Sec. 1443. Destruction or Loss of, or Injury to, Sanctuary Resources

(a) LIABILITY. — Liability

(1) Liability to United States. — Any person who destroys, causes the loss of, or injures any sanctuary resource is liable to the United States for an amount equal to the sum of—

(A) the amount of response costs and damages resulting from the destruction, loss, or injury; and

(B) interest on that amount calculated in the manner described under section 2705 of title 33.

(2) Liability In Rem. — Any vessel used to destroy, cause the loss of, or injure any sanctuary resource shall be liable in rem to the United States for response costs and damages resulting from such destruction, loss, or injury. The amount of that liability shall constitute a maritime lien on the vessel and may be recovered in an action in rem in any district court of the United States that has jurisdiction over the vessel.

(3) Defenses. — A person is not liable under this subsection if that person establishes that—

(A) the destruction or loss of, or injury to, the sanctuary resource was caused solely by an act of God, an act of war, or an act or omission of a third party, and the person acted with due care;

(B) the destruction, loss, or injury was caused by an activity authorized by Federal or State law; or

(C) the destruction, loss, or injury was negligible.

(4) Limits to Liability. — Nothing in sections 181 to 188 of title 46, Appendix, or section 192 of title 46, Appendix, shall limit the liability of any person under this chapter.

(b) RESPONSE ACTIONS AND DAMAGE ASSESSMENT. —

(1) Response Actions. — The Secretary may undertake or authorize all necessary actions to prevent or minimize the destruction or loss of, or injury to, sanctuary resources, or to minimize the imminent risk of such destruction, loss, or injury.

(2) Damage Assessment. — The Secretary shall assess damages to sanctuary resources in accordance with section 1432(6) of this title.

(c) CIVIL ACTIONS FOR RESPONSE COSTS AND DAMAGES. —

(1) The Attorney General, upon request of the Secretary, may commence a civil action against any person or vessel who may be liable under subsection (a) of this section for response costs and damages. The Secretary, acting as trustee for sanctuary resources for the United States, shall submit a request for such an action to the Attorney General whenever a person may be liable for such costs or damages.

(2) An action under this subsection may be brought in the United States district court for any district in which —

(A) the defendant is located, resides, or is doing business, in the case of an action against a person;

(B) the vessel is located, in the case of an action against a vessel; or

(C) the destruction of, loss of, or injury to a sanctuary resource occurred.

(d) USE OF RECOVERED AMOUNTS. — Response costs and damages recovered by the Secretary under this section shall be retained by the Secretary in the manner provided for in section 9607(f)(1) of title 42, and used as follows:

(1) Response Costs. — Amounts recovered by the United States for costs of response actions and damage assessments under this section shall be used, as the Secretary considers appropriate —

(A) to reimburse the Secretary or any other Federal or State agency that conducted those activities; and

(B) after reimbursement of such costs, to restore, replace, or acquire the equivalent of any sanctuary resource.

(2) Other Amounts. — All other amounts recovered shall be used, in order of priority —

(A) to restore, replace, or acquire the equivalent of the sanctuary resources that were the subject of the action, including for costs of monitoring and the costs of curation and conservation of archeological, historical, and cultural sanctuary resources;

(B) to restore degraded sanctuary resources of the national marine sanctuary that was the subject of the action, giving priority to sanctuary resources and habitats that are comparable to the sanctuary resources that were the subject of the action; and

(C) to restore degraded sanctuary resources of other national marine sanctuaries.

(3) Federal-State Coordination. — Amounts recovered under this section with respect to sanctuary resources lying within the jurisdiction of a State shall be used under paragraphs (2)(A) and (B) in accordance with the court decree or settlement agreement and an agreement entered into by the Secretary and the Governor of that State.

(e) STATUTE OF LIMITATIONS. — An action for response costs or damages under subsection (c) of this section shall be barred unless the complaint is filed within 3 years after the date on which the Secretary completes a damage assessment and restoration plan for the sanctuary resources to which the action relates.

Sec. 1444. Authorization of Appropriations

There are authorized to be appropriated to the Secretary —

(1) to carry out this chapter —

(A) $32,000,000 for fiscal year 2001;

(B) $34,000,000 for fiscal year 2002;

(C) $36,000,000 for fiscal year 2003;

(D) $38,000,000 for fiscal year 2004;

(E) $40,000,000 for fiscal year 2005; and

(2) for construction projects at national marine sanctuaries, $6,000,000 for each of fiscal years 2001, 2002, 2003, 2004, and 2005.

Sec. 1445. USS *Monitor* Artifacts and Materials

(a) CONGRESSIONAL POLICY. — In recognition of the historical significance of the wreck of the United States ship *Monitor* to coastal North Carolina and to the area off the coast of North Carolina known as the Graveyard of the Atlantic, the Congress directs that a suitable display of artifacts and materials from the United States ship *Monitor* be maintained permanently at an appropriate site in coastal North Carolina.

(b) DISCLAIMER. — This section shall not affect the following:

(1) Responsibilities of Secretary. — The responsibilities of the Secretary to

provide for the protection, conservation, and display of artifacts and materials from the United States ship *Monitor*.

(2) Authority of Secretary.—The authority of the Secretary to designate the Mariner's Museum, located at Newport News, Virginia, as the principal museum for coordination of activities referred to in paragraph (1).

Sec. 1445a. Advisory Councils

(a) ESTABLISHMENT.—The Secretary may establish one or more advisory councils (in this section referred to as an "Advisory Council") to advise and make recommendations to the Secretary regarding the designation and management of national marine sanctuaries. The Advisory Councils shall be exempt from the Federal Advisory Committee Act.

(b) MEMBERSHIP.—Members of the Advisory Councils may be appointed from among—

(1) persons employed by Federal or State agencies with expertise in management of natural resources;

(2) members of relevant Regional Fishery Management Councils established under section 1852 of this title; and

(3) representatives of local user groups, conservation and other public interest organizations, scientific organizations, educational organizations, or others interested in the protection and multiple use management of sanctuary resources.

(c) LIMITS ON MEMBERSHIP.—For sanctuaries designated after November 4, 1992, the membership of Advisory Councils shall be limited to no more than 15 members.

(d) STAFFING AND ASSISTANCE.—The Secretary may make available to an Advisory Council any staff, information, administrative services, or assistance the Secretary determines are reasonably required to enable the Advisory Council to carry out its functions.

(e) PUBLIC PARTICIPATION AND PROCEDURAL MATTERS.—The following guidelines apply with respect to the conduct of business meetings of an Advisory Council:

(1) Each meeting shall be open to the public, and interested persons shall be permitted to present oral or written statements on items on the agenda.

(2) Emergency meetings may be held at the call of the chairman or presiding officer.

(3) Timely notice of each meeting, including the time, place, and agenda of the meeting, shall be published locally and in the Federal Register, except that in the case of a meeting of an Advisory Council established to provide assistance

regarding any individual national marine sanctuary the notice is not required to be published in the Federal Register.

(4) Minutes of each meeting shall be kept and contain a summary of the attendees and matters discussed.

Sec. 1445b. Enhancing Support for National Marine Sanctuaries

(a) AUTHORITY. — The Secretary may establish a program consisting of —

(1) the creation, adoption, and publication in the Federal Register by the Secretary of a symbol for the national marine sanctuary program, or for individual national marine sanctuaries or the System;

(2) the solicitation of persons to be designated as official sponsors of the national marine sanctuary program or of individual national marine sanctuaries;

(3) the designation of persons by the Secretary as official sponsors of the national marine sanctuary program or of individual sanctuaries;

(4) the authorization by the Secretary of the manufacture, reproduction, or other use of any symbol published under paragraph (1), including the sale of items bearing such a symbol, by official sponsors of the national marine sanctuary program or of individual national marine sanctuaries;

(5) the creation, marketing, and selling of products to promote the national marine sanctuary program, and entering into exclusive or nonexclusive agreements authorizing entities to create, market or sell on the Secretary's behalf;

(6) the solicitation and collection by the Secretary of monetary or in-kind contributions from official sponsors for the manufacture, reproduction or use of the symbols published under paragraph (1);

(7) the retention of any monetary or in-kind contributions collected under paragraphs (5) and (6) by the Secretary; and

(8) the expenditure and use of any monetary and in-kind contributions, without appropriation, by the Secretary to designate and manage national marine sanctuaries. Monetary and in-kind contributions raised through the sale, marketing, or use of symbols and products related to an individual national marine sanctuary shall be used to support that sanctuary.

(b) CONTRACT AUTHORITY. — The Secretary may contract with any person for the creation of symbols or the solicitation of official sponsors under subsection (a) of this section.

(c) RESTRICTIONS. — The Secretary may restrict the use of the symbols published under subsection (a) of this section, and the designation of official sponsors of the national marine sanctuary program or of individual national marine sanctuaries to ensure compatibility with the goals of the national marine sanctuary program.

(d) Property of United States. — Any symbol which is adopted by the Secretary and published in the Federal Register under subsection (a) of this section is deemed to be the property of the United States.

(e) Prohibited Activities. — It is unlawful for any person —

(1) designated as an official sponsor to influence or seek to influence any decision by the Secretary or any other Federal official related to the designation or management of a national marine sanctuary, except to the extent that a person who is not so designated may do so;

(2) to represent himself or herself to be an official sponsor absent a designation by the Secretary;

(3) to manufacture, reproduce, or otherwise use any symbol adopted by the Secretary under subsection (a)(1) of this section, including to sell any item bearing such a symbol, unless authorized by the Secretary under subsection (a)(4) of this section or subsection (f) of this section; or

(4) to violate any regulation promulgated by the Secretary under this section.

(f) Collaborations. — The Secretary may authorize the use of a symbol adopted by the Secretary under subsection (a)(1) of this section by any person engaged in a collaborative effort with the Secretary to carry out the purposes and policies of this chapter and to benefit a national marine sanctuary or the System.

(g) Authorization for Non-Profit Partner Organization to Solicit Sponsors

(1) In General. — The Secretary may enter into an agreement with a non-profit partner organization authorizing it to assist in the administration of the sponsorship program established under this section. Under an agreement entered into under this paragraph, the Secretary may authorize the non-profit partner organization to solicit persons to be official sponsors of the national marine sanctuary system or of individual national marine sanctuaries, upon such terms as the Secretary deems reasonable and will contribute to the successful administration of the sanctuary system. The Secretary may also authorize the non-profit partner organization to collect the statutory contribution from the sponsor, and, subject to paragraph (2), transfer the contribution to the Secretary.

(2) Reimbursement for Administrative Costs. — Under the agreement entered into under paragraph (1), the Secretary may authorize the non-profit partner organization to retain not more than 5 percent of the amount of monetary contributions it receives from official sponsors under the agreement to offset the administrative costs of the organization in soliciting sponsors.

(3) Partner Organization Defined. — In this subsection, the term partner organization" means an organization that —

(A) draws its membership from individuals, private organizations, corporations, academic institutions, or State and local governments; and

(B) is established to promote the understanding of, education relating to, and the conservation of the resources of a particular sanctuary or 2 or more related sanctuaries.

Sec. 1445nt. Short Title

This title may be cited as the "National Marine Sanctuaries Act."

Sec. 1445c. Dr. Nancy Foster Scholarship Program

(a) ESTABLISHMENT. — The Secretary shall establish and administer through the National Ocean Service the Dr. Nancy Foster Scholarship Program. Under the program, the Secretary shall award graduate education scholarships in oceanography, marine biology or maritime archeology, to be known as Dr. Nancy Foster Scholarships.

(b) PURPOSES. — The purposes of the Dr. Nancy Foster Scholarship Program are —

(1) to recognize outstanding scholarship in oceanography, marine biology, or maritime archeology, particularly by women and members of minority groups; and

(2) to encourage independent graduate level research in oceanography, marine biology, or maritime archeology.

(c) AWARD. — Each Dr. Nancy Foster Scholarship —

(1) shall be used to support graduate studies in oceanography, marine biology, or maritime archeology at a graduate level institution of higher education; and

(2) shall be awarded in accordance with guidelines issued by the Secretary.

(d) DISTRIBUTION OF FUNDS. — The amount of each Dr. Nancy Foster Scholarship shall be provided directly to a recipient selected by the Secretary upon receipt of certification that the recipient will adhere to a specific and detailed plan of study and research approved by a graduate level institution of higher education.

(e) FUNDING. — Of the amount available each fiscal year to carry out this chapter, the Secretary shall award 1 percent as Dr. Nancy Foster Scholarships.

(f) SCHOLARSHIP REPAYMENT REQUIREMENT. — The Secretary shall require an individual receiving a scholarship under this section to repay the full amount of the scholarship to the Secretary if the Secretary determines that the individual, in obtaining or using the scholarship, engaged in fraudulent conduct or failed to comply with any term or condition of the scholarship.

(g) MARITIME ARCHEOLOGY DEFINED. — In this section the term "maritime archeology" includes the curation, preservation, and display of maritime artifacts.

National Marine Sanctuaries

Designation References

Channel Islands National Marine Sanctuary. — 45 F.R. 65198, Oct. 2, 1980; 15 C.F.R. part 922, subpart G.

Cordell Bank National Marine Sanctuary. — 54 F.R. 22417, May 24, 1989; 15 C.F.R. part 922, subpart K; Pub. L. 100-627, title II, Sec. 205(a)(1), Nov. 7, 1988, 102 Stat. 3217.

Fagatele Bay National Marine Sanctuary. — 51 F.R. 15878, Apr. 29, 1986; 15 C.F.R. part 922, subpart J.

Florida Keys National Marine Sanctuary. — 15 C.F.R. part 922, subpart P; Pub. L. 101-605, Nov. 16, 1990, 104 Stat. 3089, as amended by Pub. L. 102-587, title II, Secs. 2206, 2209, Nov. 4, 1992, 106 Stat. 5053, 5054.

Flower Garden Banks National Marine Sanctuary. — 56 F.R. 63634, Dec. 5, 1991; 60 F.R. 10312, Feb. 24, 1995; 15 C.F.R. part 922, subpart L; Pub. L. 100-627, title II, Sec. 205(a)(2), Nov. 7, 1988, 102 Stat. 3217; Pub. L. 102-251, title I, Sec. 101, Mar. 9, 1992, 106 Stat. 60; Pub. L. 104-283, Sec. 8, Oct. 11, 1996, 110 Stat. 3366.

Gerry E. Studds Stellwagen Bank National Marine Sanctuary (former Stellwagen Bank National Marine Sanctuary). — 58 F.R. 53865, Oct. 19, 1993; 59 F.R. 53348, Oct. 24, 1994; 15 C.F.R. 922, subpart N; Pub. L. 102-587, title II, Sec. 2202, Nov. 4, 1992, 106 Stat. 5048; Pub. L. 104-283, Secs. 9(g), 11, Oct. 11, 1996, 110 Stat. 3368, 3369.

Gray's Reef National Marine Sanctuary. — 46 F.R. 7942, Jan. 26, 1981; 15 C.F.R. part 922, subpart I.

Gulf of the Farallones National Marine Sanctuary (former Point Reyes–Farallon Islands National Marine Sanctuary). — 46 F.R. 7936, Jan. 26, 1981; 15 C.F.R. part 922, subpart H; 62 F.R. 3788, Jan. 27, 1997.

Hawaiian Islands Humpback Whale National Marine Sanctuary. — 15 C.F.R. part 922, subpart Q; Pub. L. 102-587, title II, subtitle C, Secs. 2301–2308, Nov. 4, 1992, 106 Stat. 5055-5059; Pub. L. 104-283, Sec. 7, Oct. 11, 1996, 110 Stat. 3365.

Monitor National Marine Sanctuary. — 40 F.R. 5349, Feb. 5, 1975; 40 F.R. 21706, May 19, 1975; 15 C.F.R. part 922, subpart F.

Monterey Bay National Marine Sanctuary. — 57 F.R. 43310, Sept. 18, 1992; 15 C.F.R. part 922, subpart M; Pub. L. 100-627, title II, Sec. 205(a)(3), Nov. 7, 1988, 102 Stat.

3217; Pub. L. 102-368, title I, Sec. 102, Sept. 23, 1992, 106 Stat. 1119; Pub. L. 102-587, title II, Sec. 2203, Nov. 4, 1992, 106 Stat. 5048.

Olympic Coast National Marine Sanctuary. — 59 F.R. 24586, May 11, 1994; 15 C.F.R. 922, subpart O; Pub. L. 100-627, title II, Sec. 205(a)(4), Nov. 7, 1988, 102 Stat. 3217; Pub. L. 102-587, title II, Sec. 2207, Nov. 4, 1992, 106 Stat. 5053.

Thunder Bay National Marine Sanctuary and Underwater Preserve. — 65 F.R. 39042, June 19, 2000; 15 C.F.R. part 922, subpart R.

Designation Document for the Stellwagen Bank National Marine Sanctuary

On November 4, 1992, the Oceans Act of 1992 became law (Pub. L. 102-587). Section 2202 of Title II of that Act, known as the National Marine Sanctuaries Program Amendments Act of 1992 ("NMSPAA"), designated an area of waters and submerged lands, including the living and non-living resources within those waters, as described in Article II, as the Stellwagen Bank National Marine Sanctuary.

Article I. Effect of Designation

Title III of the Marine Protection, Research and Sanctuaries Act of 1972, as amended (the "Act" or "MPRSA"), 16 U.S.C. 1431 *et seq.* authorizes the issuance of such final regulations as are necessary and reasonable to implement the designation, including managing and protecting the conservation, recreational, ecological, historical, research, educational and esthetic resources and qualities of the Stellwagen Bank National Marine Sanctuary. Section 1 of Article IV of this Designation Document lists activities of the type that either are to be regulated, or may have to be regulated subsequently in order to protect Sanctuary resources and qualities. Listing does not necessarily mean that a type of activity will be regulated; however, if a type of activity is not listed it may not be regulated, except on an emergency basis, unless Section 1 of Article IV is amended to include the type of activity by the procedures outlined in section 304(a) of the MPRSA.

Article II: Description of the Area

The Stellwagen Bank National Marine Sanctuary (the "Sanctuary") boundary encompasses a total of approximately 638 square nautical miles (approximately 2,181 square kilometers) of ocean waters, and the submerged lands thereunder, over and surrounding the submerged Stellwagen Bank and additional submerged features, offshore the Commonwealth of Massachusetts. The boundary encompasses the entirety of Stellwagen Bank; Tillies Bank to the northeast of Stellwagen Bank; and southern portions of Jeffreys Ledge, to the north of Stellwagen Bank. Portions of the Sanctuary are adjacent to three coastal ocean areas designated by the Commonwealth of Massachusetts as Ocean Sanctuaries. The northwestern border coincides with the North Shore Ocean Sanctuary. The southern border coincides with the seaward limit of Commonwealth jurisdictional waters adjacent to the Cape Cod Bay Ocean Sanctuary; and is also tangential to the Cape Cod Ocean Sanctuary. The western border of the Stellwagen Bank Sanctuary occurs approximately 25 miles east of Boston, Massachusetts. Appendix I to this Designation Document sets the precise Sanctuary boundary.

Article III: Characteristics of the Area that Give It Particular Value

Stellwagen Bank is a glacially deposited, primarily sandy feature measuring nearly twenty miles in length, occurring in a roughly southeast-to-northwest direction between Cape Cod and Cape Ann, Massachusetts. It is located at the extreme southwestern corner of the Gulf of Maine, and forms a partial "gateway" to Cape Cod Bay, situated shoreward and southwest of the Bank.

The presence of the Bank feature contributes to a particular combination of physical and oceanographic characteristics which results in two distinct peak productivity periods annually, when overturning and mixing of coastal waters with nutrient-rich waters from deeper strata produce a complex system of overlapping mid-water and benthic habitats. From the time of Colonial settlement, this area has supported an abundant and varied array of fisheries, which continue to provide livelihoods for an active commercial fleet. Important fisheries include bluefin tuna, herring, cod, haddock, winter and summer flounder, silver hake, pollack, ocean pout, lobster, shrimp, surf clam and sea scallop. The commercial value of fish caught (exclusive of bluefin tuna) within Sanctuary waters exceeded $15 million in 1990.

The biological productivity of the Bank also attracts a seasonal variety of large and small cetaceans, several of which are classified as endangered species. The Stellwagen Bank environment provides feeding and nursery areas for humpback, fin, and northern right whales, the latter being the most critically endangered of all large cetacean species. The photo-identification at Stellwagen Bank of 100 or more individual right whales from a total North Atlantic population estimated in 1990 at approximately 300 to 350 indicates the importance of the Bank to this species. The predictable seasonal presence of these and other cetacean species has generated a growing commercial whalewatch industry, involving more than 40 vessels (over 1.5 million passengers), and producing revenues in excess of $17 million in 1988.

A vessel traffic separation scheme (VTSS) crosses directly over Stellwagen Bank, and accommodates approximately 2,700 commercial vessels annually in and out of Boston, Massachusetts. Existing or potential additional human activities involving the Stellwagen Bank environment include dredged materials disposal; sand and gravel extraction; offshore mariculture development; and offshore fixed artificial platform construction.

The uniqueness of the Stellwagen Bank environment as well as its accessibility draws the continuing interest of area scientific institutions, including the Center for Coastal Studies, Cetacean Research Unit, University of Massachusetts, Woods Hole Oceanographic Institution, Marine Biological Laboratory, Manomet Bird Observatory, New England Aquarium, University of Rhode Island and the National Marine Fisheries Service (NOAA). In light of the increasing levels of human activities, several issues such as: interactions between marine mammals and commercial/recreational vessels; immediate, long-term and cumulative impacts on marine mammals from whale-watching vessel activity; and the immediate, long-term and cumulative effects of discharge/disposal operations on the Bank's resources and qualities require coordinated and comprehensive monitoring and research.

Article IV. Scope of Regulations

SECTION 1. ACTIVITIES SUBJECT TO REGULATION

The following activities are subject to regulation under the Act, including prohibition, to the extent necessary and reasonable to ensure the protection and management of the conservation, recreational, ecological, historical, research, educational or esthetic resources and qualities of the area:

a. Discharging or depositing, from within the boundary of the Sanctuary, any material or other matter;

b. Discharging or depositing, from beyond the boundary of the Sanctuary, any material or other matter;

c. Exploring for, developing, or producing oil, gas or minerals (e.g. clay, stone, sand, gravel, metalliferous ores and nonmetalliferous ores or any other solid material or other matter of commercial value ["industrial materials"]) in the Sanctuary;

d. Drilling into, dredging or otherwise altering the seabed of the Sanctuary; or constructing, placing or abandoning any structure, material or other matter on the seabed of the Sanctuary;

e. Development or conduct in the Sanctuary of mariculture activities;

f. Taking, removing, moving, catching, collecting, harvesting, feeding, injuring, destroying or causing the loss of, or attempting to take, remove, move, catch, collect, harvest, feed, injure, destroy or cause the loss of, a marine mammal, marine reptile, seabird, historical resource or other Sanctuary resource;

g. Transferring of petroleum-based products or materials from vessel-to-vessel or "lightering," in the Sanctuary;

h. Operation of a vessel (i.e., water craft of any description capable of being used as a means of transportation) in the Sanctuary;

i. Possessing within the Sanctuary a Sanctuary resource or any other resource, regardless of where taken, removed, moved, caught, collected or harvested, that, if it had been found within the Sanctuary, would be a Sanctuary resource;

j. Interfering with, obstructing, delaying or preventing an investigation, search, seizure or disposition of seized property in connection with enforcement of the Act or any regulation or permit issued under the Act.

SECTION 2. EMERGENCIES

Where necessary to prevent or minimize the destruction of, loss of, or injury to a Sanctuary resource or quality; or minimize the imminent risk of such destruction, loss or injury, any activity, including those not listed in Section 1 of this Article , is subject to immediate temporary regulation, including prohibition.

Article V. Effect on Leases, Permits, Licenses, and Rights

If any valid regulation issued by any Federal, State or local authority of competent jurisdiction, regardless of when issued, conflicts with a Sanctuary regulation, the regulation deemed by the Director, Office of Ocean and Coastal Resource Management, National Oceanic and Atmospheric Administration, or his or her designee to be more protective of Sanctuary resources and qualities shall govern.

Pursuant to section 304(c)(1) of the Act, 16 U.S.C. §1434(c)(1), no valid lease, permit, license, approval or other authorization issued by any Federal, State or local authority of competent jurisdiction, or any right of subsistence use or access, may be terminated by the Secretary of Commerce, or his or her designee, as a result of this designation, or as a result of any Sanctuary regulation, if such authorization or right was in existence on the effective date of this designation. However, the Secretary of Commerce, or designee, may regulate the exercise (including, but not limited to, the imposition of terms and conditions) of such authorization or right consistent with the purposes for which the Sanctuary is designated.

In no event may the Secretary or designee issue a permit authorizing, or otherwise approving: (1) the exploration for, development of, or production of industrial materials within the Sanctuary; or (2) the disposal of dredged material within the Sanctuary (except by a certification, pursuant to Section 940.10, of valid authorizations in existence on the effective date of Sanctuary designation). Any purported authorizations issued by other authorities after the effective date of Sanctuary designation for any of these activities within the Sanctuary shall be invalid.

Article VI. Alteration of this Designation

The terms of designation, as defined under Section 304(a) of the Act, may be modified only by the procedures outlined in section 304(a) of the MPRSA, including public hearings, consultation with interested Federal, State, and local agencies, review by the appropriate Congressional committees, and Governor of the Commonwealth of Massachusetts, and approval by the Secretary of Commerce or designee.

Accordingly, for the reasons set forth above, 15 CFR Chapter IX is amended as set forth below.

1. A subchapter B heading is added to read as follows: Subchapter B — Ocean and Coastal Resource Management
2. A new part 940 is added to subchapter B to read as follows:

Part 940 — Stellwagen Bank National Marine Sanctuary

SECTION

940.1   Purpose.
940.2   Boundary.
940.3   Definitions.
940.4   Allowed Activities.
940.5   Prohibited Activities.
940.6   Emergency Regulations.
940.7   Penalties for Violations of Regulations.
940.8   Response Costs and Damages.
940.9   National Marine Sanctuary Permits — Application Procedures and Issuance Criteria.
940.10 Certification of Pre-existing Leases, Licenses, Permits, Approvals, Other Authorizations, or Rights to Conduct a Prohibited Activity.
940.11 Notification and Review of Applications for Leases, Licenses, Permits, Approvals, or Other Authorizations to Conduct a Prohibited Activity.
940.12 Appeals of Administrative Action.

Authority: Sections 302, 303, 304, 305, 307, 310, and 312 of Title III of the Marine Protection, Research and Sanctuaries Act of 1972, as amended, 16 U.S.C. 1431 *et seq.*

§940.1 Purpose.

The purpose of the regulations in this Part is to implement the designation of the Stellwagen Bank National Marine Sanctuary by regulating activities affecting the

Sanctuary consistent with the terms of that designation in order to protect and manage the conservation, ecological, recreational, research, educational, historical, cultural, and esthetic resources and qualities of the area.

§940.2 Boundary.

The Stellwagen Bank National Marine Sanctuary consists of an area of approximately 638 square nautical miles of Federal marine waters and the submerged lands thereunder, over and around Stellwagen Bank and other submerged features off the coast of Massachusetts. The boundary encompasses the entirety of Stellwagen Bank; Tillies Bank, to the northeast of Stellwagen Bank; and portions of Jeffreys Ledge, to the north of Stellwagen Bank. The Sanctuary boundary is identified by the following coordinates, indicating the most northeast, southeast, southwest, west-northwest, and north-northwest points: 42°45′59.83″N × 70°13′01.77″W (NE); 42°05′35.51″N × 70°02′08.14″W (SE); 42°07′44.89″N × 70°28′15.44″W; (SW); 42°32′53.52″N × 70°35′52.38″W (WNW); and 42°39′04.08″N × 70°30′11.29″W (NNW). The western border is formed by a straight line connecting the most southwest and the west-northwest points of the Sanctuary. At the most west-northwest point, the Sanctuary border follows a line contiguous with the three-mile jurisdictional boundary of Massachusetts to the most north-northwest point. From this point, the northern border is formed by a straight line connecting the most north-northwest point and the most northeast point. The eastern border is formed by a straight line connecting the most northeast and the most southeast points of the Sanctuary. The southern border follows a straight line between the most southwest point and a point located at 42°06′54.57″N × 70°16′42.71″W. From that point, the southern border then continues in a west-to-east direction along a line contiguous with the three-mile jurisdictional boundary of Massachusetts until reaching the most southeast point of the Sanctuary. The boundary coordinates of the Sanctuary, provided in latitude/longitude and LORAN, appear in Appendix I following section 940.12.

§940.3 Definitions.

(a)   (1) *Act* means Title III of the Marine Protection, Research and Sanctuaries Act of 1972, as amended, 16 U.S.C. 1431 *et seq.*
   (2) *Administrator* or *Under Secretary* means the Administrator of the National Oceanic and Atmospheric Administration/Under Secretary of Commerce for Oceans and Atmosphere.

(3) *Assistant Administrator* means the Assistant Administrator for Ocean Services and Coastal Zone Management, National Oceanic and Atmospheric Administration.

(4) *Director* means the Director of the Office of Ocean and Coastal Resource Management, National Oceanic and Atmospheric Administration.

(5) *Effective date of Sanctuary designation* means the enactment date of Public Law 102-587, or November 4, 1992.

(6) *Fish wastes* means waste materials resulting from commercial fish processing operations.

(7) *Historical resource* means a resource possessing historical, cultural, archaeological, or paleontological significance, including sites, structures, districts, and objects significantly associated with or representative of earlier people, cultures, and human activities and events. Historical resources also include "historical properties," as defined in the National Historic Preservation Act, as amended, and implementing regulations, as amended.

(8) *Industrial material* means clay, stone, sand, gravel, metalliferous ore, nonmetalliferous ore or any other solid material or other matter of commercial value.

(9) *Injure* means to change adversely, either in the long or short term, a chemical, biological, or physical attribute of, or the viability of. To "injure" therefore includes, but is not limited to, to cause the loss of and to destroy.

(10) *Lightering* means the at-sea transfer of petroleum-based products or materials from vessel to vessel.

(11) *Person* means any private individual, partnership, corporation, or other entity; or any officer, employee, agent, department, agency, or instrumentality of the Federal Government or of any State, regional, or local unit of government, or any foreign government.

(12) *Sanctuary* means the Stellwagen Bank National Marine Sanctuary.

(13) *Sanctuary quality* means a particular and essential characteristic of the Sanctuary, including but not limited to, water quality, sediment quality and air quality.

(14) *Sanctuary resource* means any living or non-living resource of the Sanctuary that contributes to its conservation, recreational, ecological, historical, research, educational or esthetic value, including, but not limited to, the substratum of the Stellwagen Bank and other submerged features, and the surrounding seabed, phytoplankton, zooplankton, invertebrates, fish, marine reptiles, marine mammals, seabirds, and historical and cultural resources.

(15) *Take* or *taking* means the following:

(i) For any marine reptile, marine mammal or seabird listed as either endangered or threatened pursuant to the Endangered Species Act, the term means to harass, harm, pursue, hunt, shoot, wound, kill, trap, capture, collect or injure, or to attempt to engage in any such conduct;

(ii) For any other marine reptile, marine mammal or seabird, the term means to harass, harm, pursue, hunt, shoot, wound, kill, trap, capture, collect or injure, or to attempt to engage in any such conduct.

For the purpose of both subsections (i) and (ii), the term includes, but is not limited to, any of the following activities: collecting any dead or injured marine reptile, marine mammal or seabird, or any part thereof; restraining or detaining any marine reptile, marine mammal or seabird, or any part thereof, no matter how temporarily; tagging any marine reptile, marine mammal or seabird; operating a vessel or aircraft or doing any other act that results in the disturbing or molesting of any marine reptile, marine mammal or seabird.

(16) *Traditional fishing* means those commercial or recreational fishing methods which have been conducted in the past within the Sanctuary.

(17) *Vessel* means a watercraft of any description capable of being used as a means of transportation in/on the waters of the Sanctuary.

(b) Other terms appearing in the regulations in this Part are defined at 15 CFR 922.2, and/or in the Marine Protection, Research and Sanctuaries Act of 1972, as amended, 33 U.S.C. 1401 *et seq.* and 16 U.S.C. 1431 *et seq.*

§940.4 Allowed activities.

All activities except those prohibited by §940.5 may be undertaken subject to any emergency regulations promulgated pursuant to §940.6, subject to all prohibitions, restrictions, and conditions validly imposed by any other authority of competent jurisdiction, and subject to the liability established by Section 312 of the Act (see §940.8).

If any valid regulation issued by any Federal, State, or local authority of competent jurisdiction, regardless of when issued, conflicts with a Sanctuary regulation, the regulation deemed by the Director or designee as more protective of Sanctuary resources and qualities shall govern.

Fishing activities are allowed and there are no fishing regulations under §940.5. As required by §304(a)(5) of the Act, the appropriate Regional Fishery Management Council shall be provided with the opportunity to prepare draft regulations applicable to fishing within the Sanctuary, and shall have the opportunity to incorporate such regulations in any existing Fishery Management Plan and implementing regulations. The Secretary shall prepare the fishing regulations in accordance with 15 CFR §922.31, which implements the requirements for drafting fishing regulations.

§940.5 Prohibited Activities.

(a) Except as specified in paragraphs (c) through (g) of this §940.5, the following activities are prohibited and thus unlawful for any person to conduct or cause to be conducted:

(1) Discharging or depositing, from within the boundary of the Sanctuary, any material or other matter except:

(i) fish, fish wastes, chumming materials or bait used in or resulting from traditional fishing operations in the Sanctuary;

(ii) biodegradable effluent incidental to vessel use and generated by marine sanitation devices approved in accordance with Section 312 of the Federal Water Pollution Control Act, as amended, (FWPCA), 33 U.S.C. 1322 *et seq.*;

(iii) water generated by routine vessel operations (e.g., cooling water, deck wash down and graywater as defined by Section 312 of the FWPCA) excluding oily wastes from bilge pumping; or

(iv) engine exhaust.

(2) Discharging or depositing, from beyond the boundary of the Sanctuary, any material or other matter, except those listed in paragraph (a)(1)(i)–(iv) above, that subsequently enters the Sanctuary and injures a Sanctuary resource or quality;

(3) Exploring for, developing, or producing industrial materials in the Sanctuary;

(4) Drilling into, dredging or otherwise altering the seabed of the Sanctuary; or constructing, placing or abandoning any structure or material or other matter on the seabed of the Sanctuary, except as an incidental result of:

(i) anchoring vessels;

(ii) traditional fishing operations; or

(iii) installation of navigation aids.

(5) Moving, removing, or injuring, or attempting to move, remove, or injure, a Sanctuary historical resource. This prohibition does not apply to moving, removing, or injury resulting incidentally from traditional fishing operations.

(6) Taking any marine reptile, marine mammal, or seabird in or above the Sanctuary, except as permitted by regulations, as amended, promulgated under the Marine Mammal Protection Act, as amended, (MMPA), 16 U.S.C. 1361 *et seq.*, the Endangered Species Act, as amended, (ESA), 16 U.S.C. 1531 *et seq.*, and the Migratory Bird Treaty Act, as amended, (MBTA), 16 U.S.C. 703 *et seq.*

(7) Lightering in the Sanctuary.

(8) Possessing within the Sanctuary (regardless of where taken, moved or removed from), except as necessary for valid law enforcement purposes, any

historical resource, or any marine mammal, marine reptile or seabird taken in violation of regulations, as amended, promulgated under the MMPA, ESA, or MBTA.

(9) Interfering with, obstructing, delaying or preventing an investigation, search, seizure or disposition of seized property in connection with enforcement of the Act or any regulation or permit issued under the Act.

(b) The regulations in this Part shall be applied to foreign persons and foreign vessels in accordance with generally recognized principles of international law, and in accordance with treaties, conventions and other international agreements to which the United States is a party.

(c) The prohibitions in paragraphs (a)(1)–(2) and (4)–(9) of this §940.5 do not apply to any activity necessary to respond to an emergency threatening life, property, or the environment.

(d)   (1) All Department of Defense military activities shall be carried out in a manner that avoids to the maximum extent practicable any adverse impacts on Sanctuary resources and qualities. Department of Defense military activities may be exempted from the prohibitions in paragraphs (a)(1)–(2) and (4)–(8) of this §940.5 by the Director or designee after consultation between the Director or designee and the Department of Defense. If it is determined that an activity may be carried out, such activity shall be carried out in a manner that avoids to the maximum extent practicable any adverse impacts on Sanctuary resources and qualities. Civil engineering and other civil works projects conducted by the U.S. Army Corps of Engineers are excluded from the scope of this paragraph (d)(1).

(2) In the event of threatened or actual destruction of, loss of, or injury to a Sanctuary resource or quality resulting from an untoward incident, including but not limited to spills and groundings caused by the Department of Defense, the Department of Defense shall promptly coordinate with the Director or designee for the purpose of taking appropriate actions to respond to and mitigate the harm and, if possible, restore or replace the Sanctuary resource or quality.

(e) The prohibitions in paragraphs (a)(1)–(2) and (4)–(8) do not apply to any activity executed in accordance with the scope, purpose, terms, and conditions of a National Marine Sanctuary permit issued pursuant to §940.9 or a Special Use permit issued pursuant to Section 310 of the Act.

(f) The prohibitions in paragraph (a)(1)–(2) and (4)–(8) do not apply to any activity authorized by a valid lease, permit, license, approval or other authorization in existence on the effective date of Sanctuary designation and issued by any Federal, State or local authority of competent jurisdiction, or by any valid right of subsistence use or access in existence on the effective date of Sanctuary designation, provided that the holder of such authorization or right complies with §940.10 and with any terms and conditions on the exercise of such authorization or right imposed by the Director or designee as a condition of certification as he or she deems necessary to achieve the purposes for which the Sanctuary was designated.

(g) The prohibitions in paragraphs (a)(1)–(2) and (4)–(8) of this §940.5 do not apply to any activity authorized by any lease, permit, license, approval or other authorization issued after the effective date of Sanctuary designation and issued by any Federal, State or local authority of competent jurisdiction, provided that the applicant complies with §940.11, the Director or designee notifies the applicant and authorizing agency that he or she does not object to issuance of the authorization, and the applicant complies with any terms and conditions the Director or designee deems necessary to protect Sanctuary resources and qualities. Amendments, renewals and extensions of authorizations in existence on the effective date of designation constitute authorizations issued after the effective date.

(h) Notwithstanding paragraphs (e) and (g) of this §940.5, in no event may the Director or designee issue a permit under §940.9 of these regulations, or under Section 310 of the Act, authorizing, or otherwise approving, the exploration for, development or production of industrial materials within the Sanctuary, or the disposal of dredged material within the Sanctuary (except by a certification, pursuant to §940.10, of valid authorizations in existence on the effective date of Sanctuary designation) and any purported authorizations issued by other authorities after the effective date of Sanctuary designation for any of these activities within the Sanctuary shall be invalid.

§940.6 Emergency Regulations.

Where necessary to prevent or minimize the destruction of, loss of, or injury to a Sanctuary resource or quality, or to minimize the imminent risk of such destruction, loss or injury, any and all activities, are subject to immediate temporary regulation, including prohibition.

§940.7 Penalties for Violations of Regulations.

(a) Each violation of the Act, any regulation in this Part, or any permit issued pursuant thereto, is subject to a civil penalty of not more than $100,000. Each day of a continuing violation constitutes a separate violation.

(b) Regulations setting forth the procedures governing the administrative proceedings for assessment of civil penalties, permit sanctions and denials for enforcement reasons, issuance and use of written warnings, and release or forfeiture of seized property appear at 15 CFR Part 904.

§940.8 Response Costs and Damages.

Under Section 312 of the Act, any person who destroys, causes the loss of, or injures any Sanctuary resource is liable to the United States for response costs and damages resulting from such destruction, loss or injury, and any vessel used to destroy, cause the loss of, or injure any Sanctuary resource is liable in rem to the United States for response costs and damages resulting from such destruction, loss, or injury.

§940.9 National Marine Sanctuary Permits — Application Procedures and Issuance Criteria.

(a) A person may conduct an activity prohibited by paragraphs (a)(1)–(2) and (4)–(8) of §940.5 if conducted in accordance with the scope, purpose, manner, terms and conditions of a permit issued under this §940.9.

(b) Applications for such permits should be addressed to the Director of the Office of Ocean and Coastal Resource Management; ATTN: Sanctuaries and Reserves Division, Office of Ocean and Coastal Resource Management, National Ocean Service, National Oceanic and Atmospheric Administration, 1305 East-West Highway, Silver Spring, Maryland 20910. An application must include a detailed description of the proposed activity including a timetable for completion of the activity and the equipment, personnel and methodology to be employed. The qualifications and experience of all personnel must be set forth in the application. The application must set forth the potential effects of the activity, if any, on Sanctuary resources and Sanctuary qualities. Copies of all other required licenses, permits, approvals or other authorizations must be attached.

(c) Upon receipt of an application, the Director or designee may request such additional information from the applicant as he or she deems necessary to act on the application and may seek the views of any persons.

(d) The Director or designee, at his or her discretion, may issue a permit, subject to such terms and conditions as he or she deems appropriate, to conduct an activity prohibited by paragraphs (a)(1)–(2) and (4)–(8) of §940.5, if the Director or designee finds that the activity will have only negligible short-term adverse effects on Sanctuary resources and qualities and will: further research related to Sanctuary resources and qualities; further the educational, natural or historical resource value of the Sanctuary; further salvage or recovery operations in or near the Sanctuary in connection with a recent air or marine casualty; assist in managing the Sanctuary. In deciding whether to issue a permit, the Director or designee may also consider such factors as: the professional qualifications and financial ability of the applicant as related to the proposed activity; the duration of the activity and the duration of its effects; the appropriateness of the methods and procedures proposed by the applicant for the conduct of the activity; the extent to which the conduct of the activity may diminish or enhance Sanctuary resources and qualities; the cumulative effects of the activity; and the end value of the activity. In addition, the Director or designee may consider such other factors as he or she deems appropriate.

(e) A permit issued pursuant to this §940.9 is nontransferable.

(f) The Director or designee may amend, suspend or revoke a permit issued pursuant to this §940.9 for good cause. The Director or designee may deny a permit application pursuant to this §940.9, in whole or in part, if it is determined that the permittee or applicant has acted in violation of the terms or conditions of a permit or of these regulations or for other good cause. Any such action shall be communicated in writing to the permittee or applicant by certified mail and shall set forth the reason(s) for the action taken. Procedures governing permit sanctions and denials for enforcement reasons are set forth in Subpart D of 15 CFR Part 904.

(g) It shall be a condition of any permit issued that the permit or a copy thereof be displayed on board all vessels or aircraft used in the conduct of the activity.

(h) The Director or designee may, *inter alia*, make it a condition of any permit issued that any data or information obtained under the permit be made available to the public.

(i) The Director or designee may, *inter alia*, make it a condition of any permit issued that a NOAA official be allowed to observe any activity conducted under the permit and/or that the permit holder submit one or more reports on the status, progress or results of any activity authorized by the permit.

(j) The applicant for or holder of a National Marine Sanctuary permit may appeal the denial, conditioning, amendment, suspension or revocation of the permit in accordance with the procedures set forth in §940.12.

§940.10 Certification of Pre-existing Leases, Licenses, Permits, Approvals, Other Authorizations, or Rights to Conduct a Prohibited Activity.

(a) The prohibitions in paragraphs (a)(1)–(2) and (4)–(8) of §940.5 do not apply to any activity authorized by a valid lease, permit, license, approval or other authorization in existence on the effective date of Sanctuary designation and issued by any Federal, State or local authority of competent jurisdiction, or by any valid right of subsistence use or access in existence on the effective date of Sanctuary designation, provided that: (1) the holder of such authorization or right notifies the Director or designee, in writing, within 90 days of the effective date of Sanctuary regulations, of the existence of such authorization or right and requests certification of such authorization or right; (2) the holder complies with the other provisions of this §940.10;

and (3) the holder complies with any terms and conditions on the exercise of such authorization or right imposed as a condition of certification, by the Director or designee, to achieve the purposes for which the Sanctuary was designated.

(b) The owner or holder of a valid lease, permit, license, approval or other authorization in existence on the effective date of Sanctuary designation and issued by any Federal, State or local authority of competent jurisdiction, or of any valid right of subsistence use or access in existence on the effective date of Sanctuary designation, authorizing an activity prohibited by paragraphs (a)(1)–(2) and (4)–(8) of §940.5 may conduct the activity without being in violation of §940.5, pending final agency action on his or her certification request, provided the holder is in compliance with this §940.10.

(c) Any holder of a valid lease, permit, license, approval or other authorization in existence on the effective date of Sanctuary designation and issued by any Federal, State or local authority of competent jurisdiction, or any holder of a valid right of subsistence use or access in existence on the effective date of Sanctuary designation may request the Director or designee to issue a finding as to whether the activity for which the authorization has been issued, or the right given, is prohibited under paragraphs (a)(1)–(2) and (4)–(8) of §940.5.

(d) Requests for findings or certifications should be addressed to the Director, Office of Ocean and Coastal Resource Management; ATTN: Sanctuaries and Reserves Division, Office of Ocean and Coastal Resource Management, National Ocean Service, National Oceanic and Atmospheric Administration, 1305 East-West Highway, Silver Spring, Maryland 20910. A copy of the lease, permit, license, approval or other authorization must accompany the request.

(e) The Director or designee may request additional information from the certification requester as he or she deems necessary to condition appropriately the exercise of the certified authorization or right to achieve the purposes for which the Sanctuary was designated. The information requested must be received by the Director or designee within 45 days of the postmark date of the request. The Director or designee may seek the views of any persons on the certification request.

(f) The Director or designee may amend any certification made under this §940.10 whenever additional information becomes available justifying such an amendment.

(g) The Director or designee shall communicate any decision on a certification request or any action taken with respect to any certification made under this §940.10, in writing, to both the holder of the certified lease, permit, license, approval, other authorization or right, and the issuing agency, and shall set forth the reason(s) for the decision or action taken.

(h) Any time limit prescribed in or established under this §940.10 may be extended by the Director or designee for good cause.

(i) The holder may appeal any action conditioning, amending, suspending or revoking any certification in accordance with the procedures set forth in §940.12.

(j) Any amendment, renewal or extension not in existence on the effective date of Sanctuary designation of a lease, permit, license, approval, other authorization or right is subject to the provisions of §940.11.

§940.11 Notification and Review of Applications for Leases, Licenses, Permits, Approvals, or Other Authorizations to Conduct a Prohibited Activity.

(a) The prohibitions set forth in paragraphs (a)(1)–(2) and (4)–(8) of §940.5 do not apply to any activity authorized by any valid lease, permit, license, approval or other authorization issued after the effective date of Sanctuary designation by any Federal, State or local authority of competent jurisdiction, provided that: (1) the applicant notifies the Director or designee, in writing, of the application for such authorization (and of any application for an amendment, renewal or extension of such authorization) within fifteen (15) days of the date of application or of the effective date of Sanctuary regulations, whichever is later; (2) the applicant complies with the other provisions of this §940.11; 3) the Director or designee notifies the applicant and authorizing agency that he or she does not object to issuance of the authorization (or amendment, renewal or extension); and (4) the applicant complies with any terms and conditions the Director or designee deems necessary to protect Sanctuary resources and qualities.

(b) Any potential applicant for a lease, permit, license, approval or other authorization from any Federal, State or local authority (or for an amendment, renewal or extension of such authorization) may request the Director or designee to issue a finding as to whether the activity for which an application is intended to be made is prohibited by paragraphs (a)(1)–(2) and (4)–(8) of §940.5.

(c) Notification of filings of applications and requests for findings should be addressed to the Director, Office of Ocean and Coastal Resource Management; ATTN: Sanctuaries and Reserves Division, Office of Ocean and Coastal Resource Management, National Ocean Service, National Oceanic and Atmospheric Administration, 1305 East-West Highway, Silver Spring, Maryland 20910. A copy of the application must accompany the notification.

(d) The Director or designee may request additional information from the applicant as he or she deems necessary to determine whether to object to issuance of such lease, license, permit, approval or other authorization (or to issuance of an amendment, extension or renewal of such authorization), or what terms and conditions are necessary to protect Sanctuary resources and qualities. The information requested must be received by the Director or designee within 45 days of the postmark date of the request. The Director or designee may seek the views of any persons on the application.

(e) The Director or designee shall notify, in writing, the agency to which application has been made of his or her review of the application and possible objection to issuance. After review of the application and information received with respect thereto, the Director or designee shall notify both the agency and applicant, in writing, whether he or she has an objection to issuance and what terms and conditions he or she deems necessary to protect Sanctuary resources and qualities. The Director or designee shall state the reason(s) for any objection or the reason(s) that any terms and conditions are deemed necessary to protect Sanctuary resources and qualities.

(f) The Director or designee may amend the terms and conditions deemed necessary to protect Sanctuary resources and qualities whenever additional information becomes available justifying such an amendment.

(g) Any time limit prescribed in or established under this §940.11 may be extended by the Director or designee for good cause.

(h) The applicant may appeal any objection by, or terms or conditions imposed by, the Director or designee to the Assistant Administrator of designee in accordance with the provisions set forth in §940.12.

§940.12 Appeals of Administrative Action.

(a) Except for permit actions taken for enforcement reasons (see Subpart D of 15 CFR Part 904 for applicable procedures), an applicant for, or a holder of, a §940.9 National Marine Sanctuary permit, an applicant for, or a holder of, a Section 310 of the Act Special Use permit, a §940.10 certification requester or a §940.11 applicant (hereinafter appellant) may appeal to the Assistant Administrator or designee: (1) the grant, denial, conditioning, amendment, suspension or revocation by the Director or designee of a National Marine Sanctuary or Special Use permit; (2) the conditioning, amendment, suspension or revocation of a certification under §940.10; or (3) the objection to issuance or the imposition of terms and conditions under §940.11.

(b) An appeal under paragraph (a) of this §940.12 must be in writing, state the action(s) by the Director or designee appealed and the reason(s) for the appeal, and be received within 30 days of receipt of notice of the action by the Director or designee. Appeals should be addressed to the Assistant Administrator, Office of Ocean and Coastal Resource Management, ATTN: Sanctuaries and Reserves Division, Office of Ocean and Coastal Resource Management, National Ocean Service, National Oceanic and Atmospheric Administration, 1305 East-West Highway, Silver Spring, Maryland 20910.

(c) While the appeal is pending, appellants requesting certification pursuant to §940.10 who are in compliance with such section may continue to conduct their activities without being in violation of the prohibitions in paragraphs (a)(1)–(2) and (4)–(8) of § 940.5. All other appellants may not conduct their activities without being subject to the prohibitions in paragraphs (a)(1)–(2) and (4)–(9) of §940.5.

(d) The Assistant Administrator or designee may request the appellant to submit such information as the Assistant Administrator or designee deems necessary in order for him or her to decide the appeal. The information requested must be received by the Assistant Administrator or designee within 45 days of the postmark date of the request. The Assistant Administrator may seek the views of any other persons. The Assistant Administrator or designee may hold an informal hearing on the appeal. If the Assistant Administrator or designee determines that an informal hearing should be held, the Assistant Administrator or designee may designate an officer before whom the hearing shall be held. The hearing officer shall give notice in the *Federal Register* of the time, place, and subject matter of the hearing. The appellant and the Director or designee may appear personally or by counsel at the hearing and submit such material and present such arguments as deemed appropriate by the hearing officer. Within 60 days after the record for the hearing closes, the hearing officer shall recommend a decision in writing to the Assistant Administrator or designee.

(e) The Assistant Administrator or designee shall decide the appeal using the same regulatory criteria as for the initial decision and shall base the appeal decision on the record before the Director or designee and any information submitted regarding the appeal, and, if a hearing has been held, on the record before the hearing officer and the hearing officer's recommended decision. The Assistant Administrator or designee shall notify the appellant of the final decision and the reason(s) therefor in writing. The Assistant Administrator or designee's decision shall constitute final agency action for the purposes of the Administrative Procedure Act.

(f) Any time limit prescribed in or established under this §940.12 other than the 30 day limit for filing an appeal may be extended by the Assistant Administrator, designee, or hearing officer for good cause.

Commercially Important Species of New England

American lobster   *Homarus americanus*
American plaice (sand dab)   *Hippoglossoides platessoides*
American shad   *Alosa sapidissima*
Atlantic bluefin tuna   *Thunnus thynnus*
Atlantic cod   *Gadus morhua*
Atlantic herring   *Clupea harengus*
Atlantic mackerel   *Scomber scombrus*
Atlantic wolffish   *Anarhichas lupus*
Black sea bass   *Centropristis striata*
Bluefish (snapper) *Pomatomus saltatrix*
Butterfish   *Peprilus triacanthus*
Cusk   *Brosme brosme*
Haddock   *Melanogrammus aeglefinus*
Little skate   *Raja erinacea*
Northern shrimp   *Pandalus borealis*
Ocean pout   *Macrozoarces americanus*
Ocean quahog   *Arctica islandica*
Pollack   *Pollachius virens*
Redfish (Ocean perch)   *Sebastes* spp.
Red hake   *Urophycis chuss*
Scup (Porgy)   *Stenotomus chrysops*
Sea scallop   *Placopecten magellanicus*
Silver hake (Whiting)   *Merluccius bilinearis*
Spiny Dogfish   *Squalus acanthias*
Squids   *Illex* spp.
Striped bass (Rockfish)   *Morone saxatilis*
Summer flounder   *Paralichthys dentatus*
White hake   *Urophycis tenuis*
Winter flounder   *Pseudopleuronectes americanus*
Winter skate   *Raja ocellata*
Witch flounder (Gray flounder, Torbay sole)   *Glyptocephalus cynoglossus*
Yellowtail flounder   *Limanda ferruginea*

Source: National Marine Fisheries Service

Organizational Members of the Stellwagen Bank Coalition (as of April 1991)

A.C.E. (Acting to Conserve Earth)
American Littoral Society
Aquaculture and Bio-Marine Resources — AVA
Association for the Preservation of Cape Cod
Atlantic Cetacean Research Center
Barnstable Conservation Foundation
Blue Water Pursuits Scuba Club
Boston Shipping Association
Cape Cod Aquarium — Atlantic Education Center
Cape Cod Museum of Natural History
Cape Cod National Seashore
Cape Outdoor Discovery
Capt. John Boats, Inc.
Capt. Tim Brady and Sons, Inc.
Center for Coastal Studies
Center for Marine Conservation
Cetacean Research Unit
Cetacean Society International
City of Boston (Environment Department)
Compact of the Cape Cod Conservation Trusts
Delaware Nature Society
Fishermen's Wives Association
Gloucester Fishermen's Program
Gloucester Inshore Fisheries Association
Hull Public Schools
International Fund for Animal Welfare
International Wildlife Coalition
League of Women Voters (New England Chapter)
Manomet Bird Observatory
Marine Mammal Conservation Program
Mass Bay Consortium
Massachusetts Audubon Society

Massachusetts Wildlife Coalition
Mingan Island Cetacean Society
MIT Sea Grant College Program
National Aquarium in Baltimore
New England Aquarium
New England Hebrew Academy
New England Whalewatch, Inc.
New England Wildlife Center
Northeast Charterboat Captain's Association
Outdoor Environmental Education Center
Peabody Museum
Plymouth Marine Mammal Research Center
Regis College Earth Club
Salt Water Sportsman
Save Our Harbor/Save Our Bay
Sierra Club (New England Chapter)
South Shore National Science Center
Southampton Elementary School
Stellwagen Bank Commercial Fisheries Cooperative
SWIM (Safer Waters in Massachusetts)
The Coastlines Project
Tiverton Garden Club
University of Massachusetts, Boston
Waquoit Bay National Estuarine Research Reserve
Whale and Dolphin Conservation Society
Woods Hole Oceanographic Institution, Coastal Research Center
World Society for the Protection of Animals

Source: Provincetown Center for Coastal Studies

Marine Protected Areas

Executive Order 13158 of May 26, 2000

By the authority vested in me as President by the Constitution and the laws of the United States of America and in furtherance of the purposes of the National Marine Sanctuaries Act (16 U.S.C. 1431 *et seq.*), National Wildlife Refuge System Administration Act of 1966 (16 U.S.C. 668dd-ee), National Park Service Organic Act (16 U.S.C. 1 *et seq.*), National Historic Preservation Act (16 U.S.C. 470 *et seq.*), Wilderness Act (16 U.S.C. 1131 *et seq.*), Magnuson-Stevens Fishery Conservation and Management Act (16 U.S.C. 1801 *et seq.*), Coastal Zone Management Act (16 U.S.C. 1451 *et seq.*), Endangered Species Act of 1973 (16 U.S.C. 1531 *et seq.*), Marine Mammal Protection Act (16 U.S.C. 1362 *et seq.*), Clean Water Act of 1977 (33 U.S.C. 1251 *et seq.*), National Environmental Policy Act, as amended (42 U.S.C. 4321 *et seq.*), Outer Continental Shelf Lands Act (42 U.S.C. 1331 *et seq.*), and other pertinent statutes, it is ordered as follows:

Section 1. Purpose.

This Executive Order will help protect the significant natural and cultural resources within the marine environment for the benefit of present and future generations by strengthening and expanding the Nation's system of marine protected areas (MPAs). An expanded and strengthened comprehensive system of marine protected areas throughout the marine environment would enhance the conservation of our Nation's natural and cultural marine heritage and the ecologically and economically sustainable use of the marine environment for future generations. To this end, the purpose of this order is to, consistent with domestic and international law:

(a) strengthen the management, protection, and conservation of existing marine protected areas and establish new or expanded MPAs;

(b) develop a scientifically based, comprehensive national system of MPAs representing diverse U.S. marine ecosystems, and the Nation's natural and cultural resources; and

(c) avoid causing harm to MPAs through federally conducted, approved, or funded activities.

Sec. 2. Definitions. For the purposes of this order:

(a) "Marine protected area" means any area of the marine environment that has been reserved by Federal, State, territorial, tribal, or local laws or regulations to provide lasting protection for part or all of the natural and cultural resources therein.

(b) "Marine environment" means those areas of coastal and ocean waters, the Great Lakes and their connecting waters, and submerged lands thereunder, over which the United States exercises jurisdiction, consistent with international law.

(c) The term "United States" includes the several States, the District of Columbia, the Commonwealth of Puerto Rico, the Virgin Islands of the United States, American Samoa, Guam, and the Commonwealth of the Northern Mariana Islands.

Sec. 3. MPA Establishment, Protection, and Management.

Each Federal agency whose authorities provide for the establishment or management of MPAs shall take appropriate actions to enhance or expand protection of existing MPAs and establish or recommend, as appropriate, new MPAs. Agencies implementing this section shall consult with the agencies identified in subsection 4(a) of this order, consistent with existing requirements.

Sec. 4. National System of MPAs.

(a) To the extent permitted by law and subject to the availability of appropriations, the Department of Commerce and the Department of the Interior, in consultation with the Department of Defense, the Department of State, the United States Agency for International Development, the Department of Transportation, the Environmental Protection Agency, the National Science Foundation, and other pertinent Federal agencies shall develop a national system of MPAs. They shall coordinate and share information, tools, and strategies, and provide guidance to enable and encourage the use of the following in the exercise of each agency's respective authorities to further enhance and expand protection of existing MPAs and to establish or recommend new MPAs, as appropriate:

(1) science-based identification and prioritization of natural and cultural resources for additional protection;

(2) integrated assessments of ecological linkages among MPAs, including ecological reserves in which consumptive uses of resources are prohibited, to provide synergistic benefits;

(3) a biological assessment of the minimum area where consumptive uses

would be prohibited that is necessary to preserve representative habitats in different geographic areas of the marine environment;

(4) an assessment of threats and gaps in levels of protection currently afforded to natural and cultural resources, as appropriate;

(5) practical, science-based criteria and protocols for monitoring and evaluating the effectiveness of MPAs;

(6) identification of emerging threats and user conflicts affecting MPAs and appropriate, practical, and equitable management solutions, including effective enforcement strategies, to eliminate or reduce such threats and conflicts;

(7) assessment of the economic effects of the preferred management solutions; and

(8) identification of opportunities to improve linkages with, and technical assistance to, international marine protected area programs.

(b) In carrying out the requirements of section 4 of this order, the Department of Commerce and the Department of the Interior shall consult with those States that contain portions of the marine environment, the Commonwealth of Puerto Rico, the Virgin Islands of the United States, American Samoa, Guam, and the Commonwealth of the Northern Mariana Islands, tribes, Regional Fishery Management Councils, and other entities, as appropriate, to promote coordination of Federal, State, territorial, and tribal actions to establish and manage MPAs.

(c) In carrying out the requirements of this section, the Department of Commerce and the Department of the Interior shall seek the expert advice and recommendations of non-Federal scientists, resource managers, and other interested persons and organizations through a Marine Protected Area Federal Advisory Committee. The Committee shall be established by the Department of Commerce.

(d) The Secretary of Commerce and the Secretary of the Interior shall establish and jointly manage a website for information on MPAs and Federal agency reports required by this order. They shall also publish and maintain a list of MPAs that meet the definition of MPA for the purposes of this order.

(e) The Department of Commerce's National Oceanic and Atmospheric Administration shall establish a Marine Protected Area Center to carry out, in cooperation with the Department of the Interior, the requirements of subsection 4(a) of this order, coordinate the website established pursuant to subsection 4(d) of this order, and partner with governmental and nongovernmental entities to conduct necessary research, analysis, and exploration. The goal of the MPA Center shall be, in cooperation with the Department of the Interior, to develop a framework for a national system of MPAs, and to provide Federal, State, territorial, tribal, and local governments with the information, technologies, and strategies to support the system. This national system framework and the work of the MPA Center is intended to support, not interfere with, agencies' independent exercise of their own existing authorities.

(f) To better protect beaches, coasts, and the marine environment from pollution, the Environmental Protection Agency (EPA), relying upon existing Clean Water Act authorities, shall expeditiously propose new science-based regulations, as necessary, to ensure appropriate levels of protection for the marine environment. Such regulations may include the identification of areas that warrant additional pollution protections and the enhancement of marine water quality standards. The EPA shall consult with the Federal agencies identified in subsection 4(a) of this order, States, territories, tribes, and the public in the development of such new regulations.

Sec. 5. Agency Responsibilities.

Each Federal agency whose actions affect the natural or cultural resources that are protected by an MPA shall identify such actions. To the extent permitted by law and to the maximum extent practicable, each Federal agency, in taking such actions, shall avoid harm to the natural and cultural resources that are protected by an MPA. In implementing this section, each Federal agency shall refer to the MPAs identified under subsection 4(d) of this order.

Sec. 6. Accountability.

Each Federal agency that is required to take actions under this order shall prepare and make public annually a concise description of actions taken by it in the previous year to implement the order, including a description of written comments by any person or organization stating that the agency has not complied with this order and a response to such comments by the agency.

Sec. 7. International Law.

Federal agencies taking actions pursuant to this Executive Order must act in accordance with international law and with Presidential Proclamation 5928 of December 27, 1988, on the Territorial Sea of the United States of America, Presidential Proclamation 5030 of March 10, 1983, on the Exclusive Economic Zone of the United States of America, and Presidential Proclamation 7219 of September 2, 1999, on the Contiguous Zone of the United States.

Sec. 8. General.

(a) Nothing in this order shall be construed as altering existing authorities regarding the establishment of Federal MPAs in areas of the marine environment subject to the jurisdiction and control of States, the District of Columbia, the Commonwealth of Puerto Rico, the Virgin Islands of the United States, American Samoa, Guam, the Commonwealth of the Northern Mariana Islands, and Indian tribes.

(b) This order does not diminish, affect, or abrogate Indian treaty rights or United States trust responsibilities to Indian tribes.

(c) This order does not create any right or benefit, substantive or procedural, enforceable in law or equity by a party against the United States, its agencies, its officers, or any person.

Bill Clinton
The White House
May 26, 2000

Notes

Introduction (pages xiii–xviii)

1 The German chancellor Otto von Bismark (1815–1898) is purported to have said, "Those with an appetite for law or sausage should not watch either being made."

2 Pew Oceans Commission, *America's Living Oceans: Charting a Course for Sea Change* (Arlington, Va.: Pew Oceans Commission, 2003).

3 National Marine Sanctuaries Act (NMSA), 16 U.S.C. §1431 *et seq.*

4 NOAA, Sanctuaries and Reserves Division, *Stellwagen Bank National Marine Sanctuary Final Environmental Impact Statement/Management Plan*, vol. 1 (Silver Spring, Md.: NOAA, July 1993), 4.

5 The U.S. EEZ is the area of oceans over which the United States exercises exclusive economic jurisdiction. It extends 200 nautical miles from the shoreline of U.S. territory and encompasses approximately 4.5 million square miles — an area about 23 percent larger than the nation's land area.

6 Ernest Barker, trans., *The Politics of Aristotle* (New York: Oxford University Press, 1958). Book II, chap. 3, §4, p. 44.

7 Peter A. A. Berle, *Does the Citizen Stand a Chance? The Politics of a State Legislature: New York* (Hauppague, N.Y.: Barrons Educational Series, 1978). Berle was a former New York State representative and commissioner of environmental conservation, and president of the National Audubon Society.

8 The U.S. Commission on Ocean Policy was established by the Oceans Act of 2000. Its work constituted the first comprehensive examination of ocean policy since the 1969 Stratton Commission. Its final report, "An Ocean Blueprint for the 21st Century," was issued in 2004.

Chapter 1. Middle Bank (pages 3–9)

1 Letter to A. D. Bache, superintendent of the Coast Survey, October 22, 1854, Boston. NOAA Coast Survey. For full text see http://stellwagen.noaa.gov/about/letters.html.

2 Ibid.

3 Robert M. Browning, Jr., writes that the attempt to utilize sail and steam propulsion resulted in "the final product being a combination of the bad qualities of each." Browning, "The Lasting Injury: The Revenue Marine's First Steam Cutters," *The American Neptune* 52, no. 1 (Winter 1992): 25–37.

4 See William P. Cumming, "The Colonial Charting of the Massachusetts Coast," in *Seafaring in Colonial Massachusetts*, ed. Philip C. F. Smith (Boston: The Colonial Society of Massachusetts, 1980), 67–118.

5 See Sinclair Hitchings, "Guarding the New England Coast: The Naval Career of Cyprian Southack," in Smith, *Seafaring in Colonial Massachusetts*.

6 See Osher Map Library and Smith Center for Cartographic Education, *The Cartographic Creation of New England* (Portland: University of Southern Maine, 1996).

7 While the discovery of Middle Bank may not compare with the discoveries of Lewis and Clark, the two can be traced to the insatiable curiosity and inventive genius of Thomas Jefferson. Six years before he became president, Jefferson chaired a committee of the Continental Congress that recommended a public survey of all U.S. land not settled at the time. A year later, the Continental Congress created the Public Land Survey System that laid out the rectangular grid system that to this day shapes much of the mapped western landscape.

Among his many talents, Jefferson was an extraordinary naturalist constantly making observations about the land around him and beyond. He studied maps all the time and envisioned a transcontinental water passage. It may have helped that his father, Peter, was a planter and surveyor. In between affairs of state, Thomas is recorded as receiving a surveyor's license in Virginia shortly before the revolution. Jefferson carried his enthusiasm for discovery and western expansion with him to the White House, beginning with the Louisiana Purchase in 1803. He then asked Congress to authorize the Corps of Discovery, forever after known as the Lewis and Clark Expedition (1804–1806) to map and explore the Northwest and Pacific coast.

Jefferson then turned his attention to the American coastline and offshore waters and asked Congress to create an agency to gather hydrographic data and create nautical charts. The idea was acted upon quickly, and in 1807 Jefferson signed the law authorizing the formation of a Survey of the Coast, which eventually became known as the Coast Survey.

The Survey of the Coast, which was to be administered by the Treasury Department, was appropriated $50,000 and charged with conducting "a survey ... of the coasts of the United States, in which shall be designated the islands and shoals, with the roads or places of anchorage, within twenty leagues of any part of the shores of the United States." Jefferson personally selected a Swiss immigrant by the name of Ferdinand Hassler, trained in geodetic survey methods, to head the new agency. The survey was to be based on a network of triangles that eventually would cover the entire continent. The first such triangle was located on Long Island, New York. Thus began what is considered the oldest scientific agency in U.S. government.

Hassler directed the agency until he died in 1843, before any survey data had been converted to nautical charts. He was succeeded by Alexander Dallas Bache, a great-grandson of Benjamin Franklin. Like Hassler before him, he was well grounded in European scientific methods and demanded the highest standards of everyone associated with the Coast Survey. He authored an eight-volume work on European scientific academies, especially the German polytechnic schools, and recruited German scientists to work on the survey. Bache's influence over the development of science in the United States cannot be underestimated. By the time of his death in 1867, the National Academy of Sciences, American Association for the Advancement of Science, and Smithsonian Institution had been created, due in no small measure to Bache's leadership.

8 References for this book vary widely from scientific papers and technical reports that traditionally employ the metric system of weights and measures to government reports, popularly written books, and news articles that generally employ U.S. equivalents. Unless specifically noted, measurements in this book are in U.S. equivalents.

9 See Robert N. Oldale, *Cape Cod and the Islands, The Geologic Story* (East Orleans, Mass.: Parnassus Imprints, 1992).

10 See Brian E. Tucholke and Charles D. Hollister, "Late Wisconsin Glaciation of the Southwestern Gulf of Maine: New Evidence from the Marine Environment," *Geological Society of America Bulletin* 84 (1983): 3279–96.

11 The size of the Gulf of Maine is approximately 36,000 square miles. The size of the Gerry E. Studds Stellwagen Bank National Marine Sanctuary, of which Stellwagen Bank represents only about 50 percent, is 842 square miles — less than 3 percent the size of the Gulf of Maine.

12 The Merrimack River is formed by the confluence of the Pemigewasset River, which originates at Profile Lake in Franconia Notch, New Hampshire, and the Winnipesaukee River, which has its source in the lake by the same name in central New Hampshire.

13 The density of sea water varies as a function of temperature and salinity, with temperature being the primary factor. On Stellwagen Bank, the water column generally is stratified during the period from late spring through early fall, as cold water sinks to the bottom and surface waters are heated by the sun. The internal wave phenomenon in Massachusetts Bay was first described in the 1980s by Loren R. Haury et al., "Tidally Generated High-Frequency Internal Wave Packets and Their Effects on Plankton in Massachusetts Bay," *Journal of Marine Research* 41 (1983): 65–112.

14 Tim Battista, Randy Clark, and Simon Pittman, eds., *An Ecological Characteriza-*

tion of the Stellwagen Bank National Marine Sanctuary Region. NOAA Technical Memorandum 45. National Centers for Coastal Ocean Science (NCCOS), 2006.

15 Maine Maritime Museum, *Notes from the Orlop*, no. 15; see http://www.maine maritimemuseum.org.

Chapter 2. A Special Place (pages 10–17)

1 John Smith's 1614 voyage to what was then considered the northern coast of Virginia was financed by a group of English merchants. Smith's 1616 map depicted islands, capes, harbors, and bays from Penobscot Bay to Cape Cod but was otherwise lacking in any nautical information.

2 For a brief and excellent history of the groundfishing industry of New England, visit the Northeast Fisheries Science Center's website at http://www.nefsc.noaa .gov/history/stories/groundfish.

3 NOAA, National Marine Sanctuary Program, *Stellwagen Bank National Marine Sanctuary Draft Management Plan/Draft Environmental Impact Assessment* (Silver Spring, Md.: NOAA: April 2008), 144–53.

4 Ibid. The landings value is based on vessel trip reports (VTRs). The figure includes landings of bluefin tuna and lobster caught within the Stellwagen Bank area by commercial vessels operating outside the sanctuary in Offshore Area 19 (for lobsters) and Federal Area 4 (for bluefin tuna).

5 Party boats are defined as commercial sport fishing vessels 50 feet in length or longer carrying 20 to 80 paying passengers. Charter boats are 25 to 30 feet in length and carry up to 6 paying passengers. Private boats are 20 feet or longer and generally carry 1 to 3 anglers.

6 As cited in NOAA, *Stellwagen Bank NMS Draft Management Plan*, p. ii.

7 NOAA, *Stellwagen Bank NMS Draft Management Plan.*

8 Endangered Species Act, 16 U.S.C. §§1531–1543.

9 This estimate is based on an international study known as YoNAH (Years of the North Atlantic Humpback) conducted in 1992 and 1993 utilizing photo identification and molecular genetics, summarized in "Genetic Tagging of Humpback Whales," Per J. Palsbøl et al., *Nature* 388 (August 21, 1993): 767–69.

10 Personal communication with Dr. Jooke Robbins, director of humpback studies, Provincetown Center for Coastal Studies, and a participant in the YoNAH study, January 2008.

11 According to Peter Trull, a popular naturalist, researcher, and teacher on Cape Cod.

12 National Marine Sanctuaries Act, 33 U.S.C. §§1401 *et seq.*; Endangered Species Act, 16, U.S.C. §§1431 *et seq.*

13 During the first decade of the National Marine Sanctuaries Act, any person could nominate an area for designation. The list of recommended areas (LRA) grew rapidly, primarily to limit offshore oil and gas exploration and leasing, and soon included some very large areas, including nearly 22,500 square miles of Georges Bank. The size of the LRA alarmed the administration and members of Congress and overwhelmed NOAA. To tighten the selection process, NOAA eliminated the open-ended nomination process and in 1982 contracted with a Washington, D.C., consulting firm to assemble "regional resource evaluation teams" to make recommendations to the secretary of commerce, who would then determine which areas would be placed on a site evaluation list (SEL). The contractor was the Chelsea International Corporation, which incorporated Mayo's recommendation, drawing the support of a number of regional organizations, agencies, and the Washington, D.C., advocacy group Defenders of Wildlife.

Chelsea International's final report included five areas in the North Atlantic: approximately 1,200 square miles of near-shore waters and barrier island bays of Virginia and Maryland, Narragansett Bay and Block Island Sound, Nantucket Shelf (including the federal waters of Nantucket Sound now proposed for wind-energy development), Stellwagen Bank, and Frenchmen's Bay, Maine. Stellwagen Bank was the only site evaluated by the North Atlantic evaluation team — comprised of independent marine scientists — as a "special" rather than representative site. NOAA, Sanctuaries and Reserves Division, *National Marine Sanctuary Site Evaluations: Recommendations and Final Reports*, NA-82-SAC-00647 (Silver Spring, Md.: NOAA, 1983).

14 Representative Gerry Studds, quoted in the 138 Congressional Record, 20909.

15 The issue of casino gambling resurfaced in February 2007 when the Mashpee (Massachusetts) Wampanoag Indian tribe was granted federal recognition as a sovereign nation. Mashpee Wampanoag tribal leaders immediately announced plans to build a casino in Middleboro outside of tribal lands. In an effort to control the growth of the industry and capture tax revenues, Governor Deval Patrick filed a casino bill in October that would have given him control of a seven-member gaming authority that would have licensed and controlled three casinos in Massachusetts. Presumably, the Mashpee Wampanoag's and their casino investors would have received some form of preferential treatment in applying for a state license. The controversial measure was unceremoniously defeated in the House of Representatives in March 2008 but is expected to be taken up again in 2009. The only other federally recognized tribe in Massachusetts is the Wampanoag tribe of Gay Head–Aquinnah on Martha's Vineyard. It too plans to get into the casino business and has formed a partnership with the Seneca Nation of Upstate New York, which currently owns and operates three casinos.

16 Letter dated February 23, 1991, to Susan Durden, Regional Manager of the Great

Lakes and Atlantic Region, Sanctuaries and Reserves Division, National Ocean Service, reprinted in NOAA, Sanctuaries and Reserves Division, *Stellwagen Bank National Marine Sanctuary Final Environmental Impact Statement/Management Plan*, vol. 2 (Silver Spring, Md.: NOAA, July 1993).

Chapter 3. Designation (pages 18–27)

1 The five marine sanctuaries established by 1972 were the USS *Monitor* (North Carolina), Channel Islands (California), Gulf of the Farallones (California), Gray's Reef (Georgia), and Fagatele Bay (American Samoa).

2 The rationale for including the site within the sanctuary was that greater oversight of activities at the site would thus occur.

3 Oceans Act of 1992, P.L. 102-587, §2202 of Title II of that Act, known as the National Marine Sanctuaries Program Amendments Act of 1992, designated "an area of waters and submerged lands, including the living and non-living resources within those waters, as described in Article II, as the Stellwagen Bank National Marine Sanctuary."

4 Designation Document and Regulations, chapter ix §940.5; http://stellwagen .noaa.gov/management/1993plan/appenda.html. See appendix D for the complete text. Exceptions to the prohibitions included emergency response activities, Department of Defense activities carried out in a manner that avoids to the maximum extent practicable any adverse impacts on the sanctuary, response to spills and groundings, activities allowed under special use permits, and any activities authorized by valid lease, permit, license, approval, or other authorization in existence on the effective date of the sanctuary designation.

5 Ibid., §940.4.

6 NOAA, Sanctuaries and Reserves Division, *Stellwagen Bank National Marine Sanctuary Final Environmental Impact Statement/Management Plan*, vol. 2 (Silver Spring, Md.: NOAA, July 1993), G13. [Hereafter referred to as NOAA, FEIS/MP.]

7 Equivalent to 453 square nautical miles. References for this work are inconsistent in their use of measurements of distance and surface area at sea. The National Marine Sanctuary Program, which is administered by NOAA within the Department of Commerce, tends to measure distance in nautical miles and area in nautical square miles in technical documents but in statute miles and square (statute) miles in nontechnical documents, frequently generating confusion. Further complicating matters, the Marine Protected Area Center within the Department of Interior uses square (statute) miles in determining the size of several thousand areas now included in the national inventory of marine protected areas.

The nautical mile is a unit of measure based on the length of a minute of arc of a great circle of the Earth. In 1959, the United States officially adopted the international unit equal to 6,076.115 feet. It is used primarily for sea and air navigation. However, since most of the distances used in this book are relatively short, marking distances between known points of land along the Massachusetts coastline to locations within Massachusetts Bay (where the curvature of the Earth is not relevant), I have used the more familiar statute mile, equal to 5,280 feet as a unit of distance and square miles (as opposed to nautical square miles) as a measure of sea surface area. A square mile is equal to 640 acres. To convert from square nautical miles to square statute miles (or simply square miles), the conversion is 1 square nautical mile = 1.32 square statute miles.

8 There are five ocean sanctuaries in Massachusetts, including the Cape Cod, Cape Cod Bay, Cape and Islands, North Shore, and South Essex Ocean sanctuaries, where structures and activities that significantly alter the marine ecosystem are generally prohibited. Ocean Sanctuaries Act, M.G.L. c. 132A, passed in 1970.

9 NOAA, FEIS/MP, vol. 1, 107.

10 Letter from Robert A. Jones dated April 5, 1991, in ibid., vol. 2, G81.

11 Letter from Janice Comeau Anderson dated March 13, 1991, in ibid.

12 See appendix F for a list of organizational members of the Stellwagen Bank Coalition.

13 Equivalent to 702 square nautical miles.

14 NOAA, FEIS/MP, vol. 2, G83.

15 Letter from EOEA Secretary Susan Tierney dated April 1, 1991, reprinted in ibid., G40.

16 Oceans Act of 1992 P.L. 102-587 §202, November 4, 1992.

17 The act also created the 3,310-square-mile Hawaiian Islands Humpback Whale National Marine Sanctuary and prohibited oil and gas exploration and development in the Monterey Bay National Marine Sanctuary.

18 Equivalent to 638 square nautical miles.

Chapter 4. If Not Wilderness, What? (pages 28–37)

1 Stewart L. Udall, *The Quiet Crisis* (New York: Holt, Rinehart & Winston, 1963), 173–91. In its day, Udall's book had much the same sobering effect as Al Gore's *An Inconvenient Truth*, with the notable exception that he had the ear of two presidents willing to take action. Udall's encouragement of citizen action helped fuel the environmental revolution that was building.

2 Kennedy signed the bill establishing the 43,500-acre Cape Cod National Seashore on August 7, 1961. Although the first national seashore was authorized in 1937 at

Cape Hatteras (North Carolina), it was not established until 1953. The national system of seashores that Kennedy hoped for was first proposed in the mid-1950s. That system now includes Padre Island (Texas), Point Reyes (California), Fire Island (New York), Assateague Island (Virginia and Maryland), Cape Lookout (North Carolina), Gulf Islands (Florida and Mississippi), Canaveral (Florida), and Cumberland Island (Georgia).

3 Wilderness Act of 1964, P.L. 88-577; Title 16, U.S. Code §1131–1136). The acreage listed is as of April 2004.

4 The term "preservationist," as legal scholar Joseph Sax once noted "is often used in an uncomplimentary way." I use it here and throughout this book in much the same way that Sax did in *Mountains without Handrails* to mean "those whose inclinations are to retain parklands largely (though not absolutely) as natural areas, without industrialization, commercialized recreation, or urban influences." While specific issues pertaining to management and use may divide the general public, I believe that the general public thinks of national marine sanctuaries as areas that should be preserved largely in their natural state. Sax, *Mountains without Handrails: Reflections on the National Parks* (Ann Arbor: University of Michigan Press, 1980), 115.

5 Lyndon B. Johnson, "Natural Beauty — Message from the President of the United States," *Congressional Record*, 89th Congress, 1st Session, vol. 111, pt. 2, 2085–89, February 8, 1965.

6 Daniel S. Greenberg, "Oceanography: PSAC Panel Calls for Setting Up New Agency," *Science*, July 22, 1966, 91–93.

7 President's Science Advisory Committee, Panel on Oceanography, *Effective Use of the Sea* (Washington, D.C.: GPO, 1966).

8 Ibid., 18.

9 Commission on Marine Science, Engineering, and Resources, *Our Nation and the Sea: A Plan for National Action* (Washington, D.C.: GPO, 1969).

10 The first major reorganization based on recommendations of the Ash Commission was the establishment of the Office of Management and Budget (OMB), which Ash, chairman of Litton Industries, directed from 1973 to 1979.

11 John Whitaker, Interview with the Center of the American West, Boulder, Colorado, November 19, 2003.

12 Title 5, U.S. Code §901(a)(1).

13 Reorganization Plans No. 3 and No. 4 of 1970. 116 Congressional Record H 6523 (H. Doc. nos. 91-364, 91-365, 91-366).

14 For a detailed account of the role played by Richard Nixon in establishing most of the major post–Earth Day environmental reforms, see J. Brooks Flippen, *Nixon and the Environment* (Albuquerque: University of New Mexico Press, 2000).

15 Outer Continental Shelf Lands Act, Title 43, U.S. Code §§1331 *et seq.*

16 Authorized by the National Wildlife Refuge System Act of 1966 and administered by the U.S. Fish and Wildlife Service.

17 Wilderness Act of 1964, P.L. 88-577, Title 16 U.S. Code 1131–1136.

18 I am indebted to William Chandler and Hannah Gillelan of the Marine Conservation Biology Institute for their excellent study, "The History and Evolution of the National Marine Sanctuaries Act," *Environmental Law Reporter* 34 (2004): 10505–65. A shorter version accompanied by illustrations and useful charts and graphs entitled "The Makings of the National Marine Sanctuaries Act: A Legislative History and Analysis" was published by the Marine Conservation Biology Institute in 2005 and is available online at http://www.mcbi.org/publications/pub_pdfs/The%20Makings%20of%20National%20Marine%20Sanctuaries%20Booklet.pdf.

19 Council on Environmental Quality, *Ocean Dumping, A National Policy* (Washington, D.C.: GPO, 1970).

20 Public Law 92-532. Titles I and II codified at 33 U.S. Code §401 *et seq.* Title III codified at 16 U.S. Code §1431 *et seq.*

21 National Marine Sanctuaries Act, 16 U.S.C 1431–1445, as amended by P.L. 106-513, November 2000.

22 See note 2 above.

23 NMSA, 16 U.S.C 1431–1445, §301(b)(3).

Chapter 5. An Ocean Runs Through It (pages 41–50)

1 NOAA, National Marine Sanctuary Program, *Gerry E. Studds Stellwagen Bank National Marine Sanctuary Condition Report 2007* (Silver Spring, Md.: NOAA, April, 2007).

2 Ibid.

3 Ibid.

4 Brian MacQuarrie, "Humans a Threat to Ocean Preserve: Stellwagen Bank Deemed at Risk," *Boston Globe*, May 28, 2007, B1.

5 Ibid.

6 NOAA, *Stellwagen Bank Condition Report 2007*, p. ii.

7 Stormy Mayo, personal communication, February 2008.

8 The Gulf of Maine Council on the Marine Environment defines the Gulf of Maine as the semi-enclosed area boarded on the west by Massachusetts, Maine, New Hampshire, New Brunswick, and Nova Scotia, including the Bay of Fundy and flanked on the east by Browns Bank and Georges Bank, encompassing a total area of approximately 36,000 square miles (90,700 square kilometers). The sanctuary is a subset of this biogeographic region or ecosystem.

9 Charles A. Mayo in *Stellwagen Bank: A Guide to the Whales, Sea Birds, and Marine Life of the Stellwagen Bank National Marine Sanctuary*, ed. Nathalie Ward (Camden, Me.: Down East Books, 1995), 45.

10 Massachusetts Water Resources Authority, *State of Boston Harbor: Mapping the Harbor's Recovery* (Boston: MWRA, 2002).

11 NOAA Condition Report, 2007, 12–13. Sampling coordinated by NOAA National Status and Trends Bioeffects Program and National Benthic Surveillance Program, 2004 (in prep.)

12 Michael H. Bothner and Bradford Butner, eds., "Processes Influencing the Transport and Fate of Contaminated Sediments in the Coastal Ocean — Boston Harbor and Massachusetts Bay," USGS Circular 1302 (Reston, Va.: U.S. Geological Survey, 2007).

13 The computer model used by USGS's Richard Signell and others is described by Signell (quoted in ibid., Section 5) as:

> a modified version of the Estuarine and Coastal Ocean Model (ECOM) originally developed by George Mellor and Alan Blumberg at Princeton University. . . . The model simulates currents and water properties in three dimensions (and time), driven by wind, river runoff, offshore discharges of freshwater, surface heating and cooling, tides, and sea-level fluctuations in the open ocean. In Massachusetts Bay, the model was used to study the flushing characteristics of Boston Harbor, to provide input for a bay-wide, water-quality model, and to assess the effect of possible chlorination failure at the new outfall location, as well as to predict effluent dilution.
>
> The ECOM model was configured to encompass all of Massachusetts and Cape Cod bays, with a resolution that varied from approximately 1 kilometer in western Massachusetts Bay to about 6 kilometers in the open ocean outside Massachusetts Bay. The three-year period from 1990 to 1992 was simulated, including an 18-month period from January 1990 to July 1991 of intense oceanographic data collection by the USEPA-funded Massachusetts Bays Estuary Program. . . .
>
> Comparing simulation results to measured oceanographic data showed that the model reproduced the development of seasonal stratification in the bay and the statistics for currents responsible for effluent transport in western Massachusetts Bay. . . . The model was therefore judged to be appropriate for use in simulating effluent fields produced by continuous discharge in this region. Comparative dilution simulations for the existing outfalls and for the new outfall projected that effluent concentrations in Boston Harbor would be reduced greatly by using the new outfall site, without significantly increasing concentrations in most of Massachusetts Bay. . . . Thus, the model simula-

tions supported relocation of the outfall from Boston Harbor to the site 15.2 km offshore.

14 Ibid, Section 11.

Chapter 6. Business as Usual (pages 51–61)

1 At the time of the Stellwagen Bank NMS designation, NOAA in part built the case for further protection by documenting the importance of the fishery, noting: "From the time of Colonial settlement, this area has supported an abundant and varied array of fisheries, which continue to provide livelihoods for an active commercial fleet. Important fisheries include bluefin tuna, herring, cod, haddock, winter and summer flounder, silver hake, pollock, ocean pout, lobster, shrimp, surf clam, and sea scallop. The commercial value of fish caught (exclusive of bluefin tuna) within Sanctuary waters exceeded $15 million in 1990." NOAA, Sanctuaries and Reserves Division, *Stellwagen Bank National Marine Sanctuary Final Environmental Impact Statement/Management Plan*, vols. 1 and 2 (Silver Spring, Md.: NOAA, July 1993).

2 H.R.4310 and S.2788 (102nd Congress).

3 16 U.S.C. 1431, §301(b)(3).

4 Dick Russell, "Hitting Bottom," *Amicus Journal* (Winter 1997): 21–25.

5 Ocean Studies Board, *Effects of Trawling and Dredging on Seafloor Habitat* (Washington, D.C.: National Research Council, 2002).

6 Peter Auster et al., "The Impacts of Mobile Fishing Gear on Seafloor Habitats in the Gulf of Maine (Northwest Atlantic): Implications for Conservation of Fish Populations," *Reviews in Fisheries Science* 4, no. 2 (1996): 185–202.

7 Hardin used the word "tragedy" as the philosopher Alfred North Whitehead used it. Tragedy, wrote Whitehead, "resides in the solemnity of the remorseless working of things." A. N. Whitehead, *Science and the Modern World* (New York: Mentor, 1948), 17

8 Garrett Hardin, "The Tragedy of the Commons," *Science* 162 (1968): 1243.

9 The cable is now owned and operated by Columbia Ventures Corp.

10 15 C.F.R. ch. ix §921.143 as authorized by 16 U.S.C. §1441.

11 NOAA, Environmental Assessment of Stellwagen Bank National Marine Sanctuary Submarine Cable, July 20, 2000.

12 NOAA has attempted to promote the concept of unity by renaming NMFS the NOAA Fisheries Service, but the new name has not caught on.

13 Sustainable Fisheries Act of 1996, 16 U.S.C. 1801, Public Law 104-297.

14 Mark Forest, personal communication, January 2008.

15 Personal communication, February 2006.

16 Joining CLF in the lawsuit were the Center for Marine Conservation, National Audubon Society, and Natural Resources Defense Council.

17 Northeast Fisheries Science Center, "Assessment of 19 Northeast Groundfish Stocks through 2004." Woods Hole, Mass., August 2005.

18 The most recent assessment of Northeast groundfish stocks, released as this book went to press, offers a glimmer of hope for haddock, which were reported to have rebuilt on Georges Bank, while Gulf of Maine haddock are expected to rebuild in 2009. However, according to the Northeast Fisheries Science Center, "Eleven of the stocks are now both overfished and experiencing overfishing compared to seven in 2004. Pollock, witch flounder, Georges Bank winter flounder, Gulf of Maine winter flounder and northern windowpane have deteriorated in status, while Gulf of Maine cod has improved. NEFSC, "Assessment of 19 Northeast Groundfish Stocks through 2007." Report of the Third Groundfish Assessment Review Meeting, Woods Hole, Mass., August 2008.

19 The species were white hake, goosefish, pollock, winter flounder, silver hake, cod, windowpane flounder, yellowtail flounder, haddock, American plaice, redfish, ocean pout, witch flounder, red hake, and dogfish.

20 J. D. Crawford and R. Cook, "Historical Trends in Adult Size among Common Groundfishes in Stellwagen Bank National Marine Sanctuary and Environs" (in preparation). Cited in NOAA *Draft Management Plan*, 2008, p. 79.

21 Kenneth T. Frank et al., "Trophic Cascades in a Formerly Cod-Dominated Ecosystem," *Science* 308 (June 10, 2005): 1621–23.

Chapter 7. Whales Ho! (pages 62–73)

1 Misty Nelson et al., "Mortality and Serious Injury Determinations for Baleen Whale Stocks along the U.S. Eastern Seaboard and Adjacent Canadian Maritimes 2001–2005," Northeast Fisheries Science Center Reference Document 07-05, February 2007.

2 Some tankers are fitted with bulbs that extend beyond the bow below the level of their cargo compartments to protect the cargo in the case of collision or grounding. If a whale were struck broadside, its vertebrae would snap and the limp body in most instances would slide away or it could wrap around the hull and rest on top of the bulb.

3 Jooke Robbins and David K. Mattila, "Establishing Humpback Whale (*Megaptera novaeangliae*) Entanglement Rates on the Basis of Scar Evidence," Provincetown Center for Coastal Studies, Report to the Northeast Fisheries Science Center, National Marine Fisheries Service, 2004.

4 A 1999 study predicts that if current trends continue, the right whale will become extinct in approximately two centuries. Hal Caswell, Masami Fujiwara, and Solange Brault, "Declining Survival Probability Threatens the North Atlantic Right Whale," *Proceedings of the National Academy of Sciences* 96: 3308–13.

5 CFR, Title 50, §229.2. The potential biological removal level is the product of the following factors: (1) The minimum population estimate of the stock; (2) one-half the maximum theoretical or estimated net productivity rate of the stock at a small population size; and (3) a recovery factor of between 0.1 and 1.0.

6 PBR for humpback whales is only 1.3, which means that for the period 2001 to 2005, it was exceeded (7 fatal ship strikes + 8 fatal entanglements) by almost a factor of three each year, based solely on the number of known mortalities and verified causes of death. For fin whales, PBR is 4.7.

7 In U.S. waters, the North Atlantic right whale is listed as an *endangered* species under the Endangered Species Act and as a *depleted* species under the Marine Mammal Protection Act. Internationally, the first effort to protect right whales from commercial whaling took effect in 1935, by which time the species was already commercially extinct.

8 Scott D. Kraus and Rosalind M. Rolland, "Right Whales in the Urban Ocean," in *The Urban Whale: North Atlantic Whales at the Crossroads*, ed. Scott D. Kraus and Rosalind M. Rolland (Cambridge, Mass.: Harvard University Press, 2007), 4.

9 *Strahan v. Coxe*, 939F Supp. 963 (D. Mass. 1996). See also chapter 8 on fixed-gear modifications ordered by the court.

10 Amy Knowlton and Moira Brown, "Running the Gauntlet: Right Whales and Vessel Strikes," in Kraus and Rolland, *The Urban Whale*, 409–35.

11 The IMO is a specialized agency of the United Nations with 167 member states tasked with developing and maintaining a regulatory framework that addresses shipping safety, security, and environmental concerns.

12 Ten knots equals 11.5 miles per hour.

13 NMFS Proposed Rule, June 26, 2006. 71 FR 36299.

14 David W. Laist et al., "Collisions between Ships and Whales," *Marine Mammal Science* 17, no. 1 (2001): 35–75.

15 Christopher W. Clark, Douglas Gillespie, Douglas Nowacek, and Susan Parks, "Listening to Their World: Acoustics for Monitoring and Protecting Right Whales in an Urbanized Ocean," in Kraus and Rolland, *The Urban Whale*, 333–57. The full hearing range of right whales has been predicted by Susan E. Parks to be between 12 Hz and 22 kHz, the approximate hearing range of humans. Susan Parks, "Response of North Atlantic Right Whales (*Eubalaena glacialis*) to Playback of Calls Recorded from Surface Active Groups in Both the North and South Atlantic," *Marine Mammal Science* 19 (2003): 563–80.

16 Susan E. Parks and Christopher Clark, "Acoustic Communication: Social Sounds

and the Potential Impacts of Noise," in Kraus and Rolland, *The Urban Whale,*
310–32.

17 As a condition of its approval, Excelerate Energy agreed to a $23.5-million com-
pensatory mitigation package that included $3.25 million for the acoustic array.
Other payments included $6.3 million to the Gloucester Fishing Community
Preservation Fund, $1.7 million to lobster fishermen for alleged losses, $5.3 million to the Island Alliance for improvements to the Boston Harbor Islands, $3 mil-
lion to Massachusetts Office of Coastal Zone Management for seafloor mapping
and habitat characterization, and $4 million for low-income energy assistance.
Neptune LNG has agreed to a similar package.

18 *Federal Register* vol. 73, no. 60, March 27, 2008.

Chapter 8. The Accidental Hunt (pages 74–85)

1 Marine Mammal Protection Act (MMPA), 16 U.S.C. 1371, §101(2).

2 Misty Nelson et al., "Mortality and Serious Injury Determinations for Baleen
Whale Stocks along the U.S. Eastern Seaboard and Adjacent Canadian Maritimes
2001–2005," Northeast Fisheries Science Center Reference Document 07-05,
February 2007.

3 Amy R. Knowlton et al., "Analysis of Scarring on North Atlantic Right Whales
(*Eubalaena glacialis*): Monitoring Rates of Entanglement Interaction: 1980–
2002," Final Report to the National Marine Fisheries Service, 2005; Jooke Robbins and David K. Mattila, "Monitoring Entanglements of Humpback Whales in
the Gulf of Maine on the Basis of Caudal Peduncle Scarring," Report to the 53rd
Scientific Committee meeting of the International Whaling Commission. Hammersmith, London. Document #C/53/NAH25, 2001.

4 Scott D. Kraus and Rosalind M. Rolland, "Right Whales in the Urban Ocean," in
The Urban Whale: North Atlantic Whales at the Crossroads, ed. Scott D. Kraus and
Rosalind M. Rolland (Cambridge, Mass.: Harvard University Press, 2007), 4.

5 Minke whales are not listed as endangered or threatened under the Endangered
Species Act but are a protected species under the Marine Mammal Protection
Act. The best estimate of abundance for the Canadian East Coast stock is 2,998.
Northeast Fisheries Science Center, NMFS, "Minke Whale (Canadian East Coast
Stock) 2006 Stock Assessment Report," March 2007.

6 David N. Wiley, Just C. Moller, and Kristin A. Zillnskas, "The Distribution and
Density of Commercial Fisheries and Baleen Whales within the Stellwagen Bank
National Marine Sanctuary: July 2001–June 2002," *Marine Technology Society Jour-
nal* 37, no. 1 (2003): 35–53.

7 MMPA, §118 (f)(2).

8 MMPA, §13.

9 In April 1995, Richard Max Strahan representing himself and an organization called Green World, Inc., filed suit in U.S. District Court for the District of Massachusetts against the Commonwealth of Massachusetts (*Strahan v. Coxe*) alleging that the state was in violation of the Endangered Species Act (ESA) and Marine Mammal Protection Act (MMPA) consequent to its issuance of licenses and permits to gillnet and lobster pot fishermen whose gear was entangling North Atlantic right whales. Strahan sought a preliminary injunction ordering the state to revoke existing licenses and permits and enjoining the state from the issuance of any further permits until such time as it had applied to NMFS for an incidental take permit under the ESA. The district court declined to grant the injunctive relief sought by Strahan but did order the state to apply for an incidental take permit under the ESA and to convene a working group to address the issue of entanglement.

10 Statistics on entanglements often are misinterpreted. A relatively high number of reports come in from the SBNMS, especially during the spring and summer, when there are many whale watchers and commercial and recreational fishermen on the water. However, this does not mean that the whales were entangled in the sanctuary. That can only be determined by an examination of the gear (and not always even then).

11 Record of Decision. Final Environmental Impact Statement, Amendments to the ALWTRP, NMFS, 2007.

12 939 F. Supp. 963, 984 D Mass 1996.

13 127 F3d at 163.

14 For a more detailed account of take cases confirming this interpretation of the ESA, see David E. Filippi and Ann Gravatt, "Section 9(g) Litigation: 'Take' Cases and Permitting Agencies," November 1, 2000, on Stoel & Rives LLP website at http://www.stoel.com/showarticle.aspx?Show=907.

Chapter 9. Ecotourism Unlimited (pages 86–98)

1 The actual number of commercial vessels has varied from year to year and throughout the season. In July and August, if the whales are abundant and the weather is good, some companies run multiple trips aboard several vessels. In addition to those companies that are primarily conducting whale watches in the summer, a number of motorized and sailing charter vessels engage in whale watching.

2 The International Fund for Animal Welfare and Greenpeace have effectively lobbied nations directly and through the International Whaling Commission to consider the economic advantages of ecotourism over exploitation.

3 In the spirit of full disclosure, the author was executive director of the Provincetown Center for Coastal Studies from 1995 to 2007. Naturalists and researchers either trained or employed by the Center at one time or another have conducted research and whale watches aboard commercial whale-watch companies since 1976.

4 Coast Guard safety regulations, on the other hand, do require captains to keep passenger counts.

5 David N. Wiley, Just C. Moller, Richard M. Pace III, and Carole Carlson, "Effectiveness of Voluntary Conservation Agreements: Case Study of Endangered Whales and Commercial Whale Watching," *Conservation Biology* 19 (April 2008): 450–57.

6 National Marine Sanctuaries Act, 16 U.S.C. §1431(a)(4)(C).

7 Ibid., §1431(b)(6).

8 Alison Hawthorne Deming, "Brief Encounters on the Savanna," *onearth* (Summer 2008): 64

9 Robert Underwood Johnson, "The Neglect of Beauty in the Conservation Movement," *Century* 79 (1910): 637–38, reprinted in *The American Environment*, ed. Roderick Nash (Reading, Mass.: Addison-Wesley Publishing Co., 1968).

10 NMFS Director William Hogarth, *Federal Register* vol. 67, no. 20 (January 30, 2002): 4380.

11 MMPA, §3(18)(A).

12 Joseph Petulla, *American Environmentalism: Values, Tactics, Priorities* (College Station: Texas A&M Press, 1980), 51, quoted in Roderick Nash, *The Rights of Nature: A History of Environmental Ethics* (Madison: University of Wisconsin Press, 1989).

13 May 20, 2006, aboard the *Portuguese Princess*, out of Provincetown, Mass.

14 William A. Watkins, "Whale Reactions to Human Activities in Cape Cod Waters," *Marine Mammal Science* 2, no. 4 (October 1986): 251–62.

15 Research for this study discovered no instances of fines or penalties having been levied in the past five years.

16 Peter Tyack, quoted in Bob Holmes, "Noises Off: "The Cacophony of Human Noise in the Ocean Grows Louder by the Year," *New Scientist*, March 1, 1997.

17 Jon Lien, "The Conservation Basis for the Regulation of Whale Watching in Canada by the Department of Fisheries and Oceans: A Precautionary Approach," *Canadian Technical Report of Fisheries and Aquatic Sciences* 2363 (2001): 1–38.

18 The Scientific Committee of the IWC in 1997 adopted the following general principles for allowing cetaceans "to control the nature and duration of interactions": (i) operators should have a sound understanding of the behavior of the cetaceans and be aware of behavioral changes which may indicate disturbance; (ii) in approaching or accompanying cetaceans, maximum platform speed should be

determined relative to that of the cetacean, and should not exceed it once on station; (iii) use appropriate angles and distances of approach; species may react differently, and most existing guidelines preclude head-on approaches; (iv) friendly
whale behavior should be welcomed, but not cultivated; do not instigate direct
contact; (v) avoid sudden changes in speed direction or noise; (vi) do not alter
platform speed or direction to counteract avoidance behavior by cetaceans;
(vii) do not pursue, head-off, or encircle cetaceans or cause groups to separate;
(viii) approaches to mother/calf pairs and solitary calves and juveniles should
be undertaken with special care; there may be an increased risk of disturbance to
these animals, or risk of injury if vessels are approached by calves; (ix) cetaceans
should be able to detect a platform at all times.

Chapter 10. Purposes and Policies Revisited (pages 101–10)

1 The Oceans Act of 1992, Pub. L. 102-587. Section 2202 of Title II of that act, known
   as the National Marine Sanctuaries Program Act of 1992, designated an area of
   waters and submerged lands, including the living and nonliving resources within
   those waters, as the Stellwagen Bank National Marine Sanctuary

2 Proponents of a prohibition at the time included the Stellwagen Bank Coalition,
   Stellwagen Bank Commercial Fisheries Cooperative, American Cetacean Society,
   Urban Harbors Institute, Conservation Law Foundation, Massachusetts Audu-
   bon, and Center for Marine Conservation (now the Ocean Conservancy).

3 Throughout its history, the national marine sanctuary program has been buried
   deep within the NOAA bureaucracy, often making it difficult to understand how
   and by whom major policy decisions have been made. The final environmental
   impact statement and management plan (FEIS/MP) for the Stellwagen Bank
   NMS were prepared by the Sanctuaries and Reserves Division within the Office
   of Ocean and Coastal Resource Management administered by the National Ocean
   Service (NOS). NOS is a line office within NOAA and a functional equivalent
   of the National Marine Fisheries Service and National Weather Service. Among
   NOS's other responsibilities are the Office of Coast Survey, Coastal Zone Management Program, National Undersea Research Program, and National Geodetic
   Survey.

4 NOAA, Sanctuaries and Reserves Division, Stellwagen Bank National Marine
   Sanctuary Final Environmental Impact Statement/Management Plan, vols. 1 and 2
   (Silver Spring, Md.: NOAA, July 1993), Appendices, G7.

5 Ibid., G7–G8.

6 Ibid., G42. Tierney appears to have been referring to the authority that rests with
   the Interior Department under the Outer Continental Shelf Lands Act to protect

sensitive areas from any adverse effects of both minerals extraction and oil and gas development. Why prohibit one activity and not the other? The answer quite clearly was that Congress specifically chose to prohibit sand and gravel mining and to avoid unnecessary controversy over an oil and gas prohibition, since at the time a presidential moratorium on oil and gas exploration and development was already in place.

7 Ibid.

8 The two sanctuaries are located northwest of San Francisco. The Gulf of Farallones NMS was designated in 1981 and is comprised of 1,255 square miles. Cordell Bank NMS was designated in 1989 and is comprised of 526 square miles. The primary mission of the two sanctuaries is to protect the California Current Coastal Upwelling area centered off Point Arena, which works as a conveyor belt of food and nutrients to areas as far as 250 miles down the coast. This coastal upwelling pumps cold, nutrient-rich water from the deep ocean up to the surface, where it acts as fertilizer for tens of thousands of square miles of ocean. Environment California.

9 54 FR 22417, May 24, 1989.

10 Marine Sanctuaries Review Team, "National Marine Sanctuaries: Challenges and Opportunities." Reprinted in hearings before Subcommittee on Oceanography and Subcommittee on Fisheries, Wildlife Conservation and the Environment, House Committee of Merchant Marine and Fisheries, 102nd Congress 87 140 (1992). Cited in David Owen, "The Disappointing History of the National Marine Sanctuaries Act," *NYU Environmental Law Journal* 11, no.3 (2003): 734.

11 See chapter 4. President Nixon rejected the recommendation of the Stratton Commission to create an independent NASA-like agency and opted instead to place NOAA within an existing department. The Interior Department, which administers the national park and national wildlife refuge systems, was probably the more logical choice in the long run, but pressure from Commerce Secretary Stans and the President's animosity toward Interior Secretary Hickel, whom he fired within months of creating NOAA, have been cited by contemporaries as reasons for NOAA being set up within the Commerce Department.

12 National Marine Sanctuaries Act (NMSA), 16 U.S.C. 1431, §301(b)(1).

13 NOAA, National Marine Sanctuaries website, http://sanctuaries.noaa.gov/nmsp.swf. The fourteen "gems" refer to thirteen sanctuaries and one national monument. The National Marine Sanctuaries Amendments Act of 2000 (P.L. 106-513) gave the President authority to establish a Northwestern Hawaiian Islands Coral Reef Ecosystem Reserve, which President Bill Clinton did by Executive Order 13178 on December 4, 2000. In June 2006, President George H. Bush, also by executive order, "upgraded" and renamed the area the Papahānaumokuākea National Marine National Monument.

14 NMSA, 16 U.S.C. 1431, §301(b)(2).

15 For an excellent discussion of the redundancy issue, see William T. Chandler and Hannah Gillelan, "The History and Evolution of the National Marine Sanctuaries Act," *Environmental Law Reporter* 34 (2004): 10505–65. During the Reagan years, a few congressional critics of the program were emboldened enough by the administration's hostility toward the program to suggest that the sanctuaries act be abolished. One such critic was Louisiana congressman John Breaux, who became chairman of the House Subcommittee on Fisheries, Wildlife Conservation and the Environment. Breaux saw the sanctuaries program as nothing more than a program designed to stop oil and gas leasing. While he was unable to advance abolition legislation, as chair of the subcommittee he was able to call upon the Government Accounting Office in 1981 to study the issue of "redundancy." The GAO concluded that the sanctuary program fulfilled a necessary purpose.

16 NMSA, 16 U.S.C. 1431, §301(a)(3).

17 Ibid., §301(b)(3).

18 Aldo Leopold, "The Land Ethic," in *A Sand County Almanac* (New York: Oxford University Press, 1949), 224–25.

19 NMSA, 16 U.S.C. 1431, §301(b)(4).

20 *America's Underwater Treasures* was produced in collaboration with KQED, northern California's PBS affiliate and first aired in September 2006.

21 NOAA, National Marine Sanctuaries website, http://sanctuaries.noaa.gov/news/features/0906_jmcousteau_bio.html.

22 NMSA, 16 U.S.C. 1431, §301(b)(5).

23 Ibid., §301(b)(6).

24 Ibid., §301(b)(7).

25 Ibid., §301(b)(8).

26 Ibid., §301(b)(9).

27 The movement of the Boston shipping lanes was preceded in 2002 by IMO approval of a realignment scheme in the Bay of Fundy.

28 Oceans Act of 1992, P.L. 102-587, §2202.

Chapter 11. The Plan (pages 111–21)

1 Wallace Fowlie, "Waiting for Godot," in *Dionysus in Paris* (New York: Meridian Books, 1960), 210–14.

2 At the time of his retirement in 1997, Representative Don Young (R-Alaska), in recognition of Studds' leadership on a wide array of fisheries and ocean legislation, introduced a congressional resolution renaming the sanctuary the Gerry E. Studds Stellwagen Bank National Marine Sanctuary.

3 Studds never denied making such a "promise," but he did so in the firm belief that

the aims of the National Marine Sanctuaries Act and Magnuson-Stevens Act were compatible; that protection of the ecosystem and maintenance of a commercially viable and sustainable fishery could be achieved in the long run. As an author of both pieces of legislation and elected representative to many communities that would be affected, he also knew that the transition from past practices might be lengthy and painful. Personal communication, 2005.

4 Members of the SAC in place at the time of the release of the draft management plan on May 6, 2008, included representatives of the National Undersea Research Center, Whale Center of New England, Recreational Fishing Alliance, Dolphin Fleet of Provincetown, Massachusetts Lobstermen's Association, Massachusetts Fishermen's Partnership, Peabody & Lane Corp./Mediterranean Shipping Company, Brewer Plymouth Marine, Conservation Law Foundation, Ocean Conservancy, Provincetown Center for Coastal Studies, Cape Cod Museum of Natural History, and three members at large. The governmental members include representatives from the National Marine Fisheries Service, New England Regional Fishery Management Council, U.S. Coast Guard, Massachusetts Office of Coastal Zone Management, Massachusetts Division of Marine Fisheries, and the Massachusetts Division of Law Enforcement.

5 NOAA, Office of Inspector General, "National Marine Sanctuary Program Protects Certain Resources But Further Actions Could Increase Protection," Final Report, IPE-18591, February 2008.

6 NOAA, National Marine Sanctuary Program, *Stellwagen Bank National Marine Sanctuary Draft Management Plan and Draft Environmental Assessment* (Silver Spring, Md.: NOAA, April 2008).

7 Gib Chase, personal communication, March 5, 2008.

8 National Marine Sanctuaries Act, §301(C)(b)(3); and Designation Document for the Stellwagen Bank National Marine Sanctuary, Article IV, §1. See appendixes B and D.

9 Email alert to members, June 2008.

10 Public hearing, Plymouth, Mass., June 11, 2008.

11 Public hearing, Hyannis, Mass., June 12, 2008.

12 NOAA, *Stellwagen Bank Draft MP/EA*, p. iii.

13 Susan Playfair, *Vanishing Species: Saving the Fish, Sacrificing the Fisherman* (Lebanon, N.H.: University Press of New England, 2003).

Chapter 12. Potential Actions (pages 122–32)

1 NOAA, National Marine Sanctuary Program, *Stellwagen Bank National Marine Sanctuary Draft Management Plan and Environmental Assessment* (Silver Spring, Md.: NOAA, April 2008), 6. Hereafter, NOAA, SBNMS DMP/EA.

2 The plan identified a total of 102 strategies synthesized from 244 contained in the SAC's 2004 action plans. According to assistant superintendent Ben Cowie-Haskell, the synthesis faithfully reflected all of the SAC's recommendations. Personal communication, May 2008.

3 The marine mammal behavioral disturbance working group included representatives of whale-watching companies, conservation groups, tuna fishermen, research institutions, and NMFS.

4 Jon Lien, "The Conservation Basis for the Regulation of Whale Watching in Canada by the Department of Fisheries and Oceans: A Precautionary Approach." *Canadian Technical Report of Fisheries and Aquatic Sciences* 2363 (2001): 1–38.

5 Personal communication, January 2008.

6 Peter J. Auster and Lance L. Stewart, "Species Profiles: Life Histories and Environmental Requirements of Coastal Fishes and Invertebrates: Sand Lance," U.S. Fish & Wildlife Service Biological Report 82, 1986.

7 Atlantic States Marine Fisheries Commission; http://www.asmfc.org/species Documents/herring/speciesProfileNov07.pdf

8 David K. Stevenson and Marcy L. Scott, *Essential Fish Habitat Source Document: Atlantic Herring, Clupea harengus, Life History and Habitat Characteristics*, 2nd ed. NOAA Technical Memorandum NMFS-NE-192 (Woods Hole, Massachusetts: National Marine Fisheries Service, Northeast Fisheries Science Center, 2005).

9 Ibid. and Atlantic States Marine Fisheries Commission (see note 7).

10 Andrew J. Read and Carrie R. Brownstein, "Considering Other Consumers: Fisheries, Predators, and Atlantic Herring in the Gulf of Maine," *Conservation Ecology* 7, no. 1 (2003).

11 Ibid.

12 NOAA, SBNMS DMP/EA, 215.

13 Ibid. The source for this spatial comparison is a 1996 study conducted by Peter Auster et al., "The Impacts of Mobile Fishing Gear on Seafloor Habitats in the Gulf of Maine (Northwest Atlantic): Implications for Conservation of Fish Populations," *Reviews in Fisheries Science* 4, no. 2 (1996): 185–202.

14 "Essential fish habitat can consist of both the water column and the underlying surface (e.g. seafloor) of a particular area. Areas designated as EFH contain habitat essential to the long-term survival and health of our nation's fisheries. Certain properties of the water column, such as temperature, nutrients, or salinity, are essential to various species. Some species may require certain bottom types such as sandy or rocky bottoms, vegetation such as sea grasses or kelp, or structurally complex coral or oyster reefs." NOAA, Office of Habitat Conservation, Habitat Protection Division, as authorized by Magnuson-Stevens Act §1802 (10) and NMFS EFH Rule §600.10.

15 Ibid., NMFS EFH Rule §600.815(a)(8).

16 Minutes of June 2007 NEFMC meeting. The HAPC motion failed by a vote of

8–9, with NOAA Fisheries, Massachusetts Division of Marine Fisheries, and Massachusetts Office of Coastal Zone Management voting for approval.

17 Ibid.

Chapter 13. Vision and Goals (pages 133–45)

1 National Marine Sanctuaries Act, 16 U.S.C. §1431(b)(6).

2 Designation Document and Regulations, P.L. 102-587, Title II, Article IV, Section 1.

3 Public Law 86-517.

4 Public Law 88-607.

5 The vision statement was adopted on July 11, 2005, by William Adler, Massachusetts Lobstermen's Association; Judith Pedersen, MIT Sea Grant; Peter Borrelli, Provincetown Center for Coastal Studies; Priscilla Brooks, Conservation Law Foundation; Steven Tucker, Cape Cod Commission; Susan Farady, The Ocean Conservancy; Barry Gibson, Recreational Fishing Alliance; Steven Milliken, Dolphin Fleet Whale Watch; Mason Weinrich, Whale Center of New England; Richard Wheeler, Cape Cod Museum of Natural History; John Williamson, At-Large Fishing Community Activist; Dale Brown, At-Large Gloucester Community Representative. Minutes of 16th Sanctuary Advisory Council meeting, Scituate, Massachusetts.

6 Personal communication, January 2008.

7 Provisions of the plan include reductions in allocation of days at sea for fishing vessels, establishment of permanent essential fish habitat closed areas, continuation of existing rolling closures, and reduction of bycatch.

8 The wilderness subcommittee was comprised of Boston University marine biologist Les Kaufman, John Williamson, a fishing advocate and SAC chairman, and Deidre Kimball with the northeast regional office of NMFS. The definition appeared in Appendix A, p. 16, of the June 3, 2004, minutes of the ecosystem-based management working group.

9 Julie Palakovich and Les Kaufman, "Estimating the Importance of Maternal Age, Size, and Spawning Experience to Recruitment of Atlantic cod (*Gaus morhua*)," *Conservation Biology*, in review.

10 Ibid.

11 Personal communication, January 2008.

12 The remaining cod, some of which may pass through the sanctuary, are either wildly transient or migratory.

13 Sustainable Fisheries Act, §28(A).

14 Appendix B, p. 19, of the June 3, 2004, minutes of the ecosystem-based management working group.

15 NOAA, Office of Inspections and Program Evaluations, "National Marine Sanctuary Program Protects Certain Resources, But Further Actions Could Increase Protection." Final Report No. IPE-18591, February 2008.

16 Kurkul at June 2007 meeting of the New England Fisheries Management Council.

17 Stellwagen wilderness group meeting of May 12, 2004, found in Appendix A of the June 3, 2004, minutes of the ecosystem-based management working group.

18 Draft Ecosystem-Based Management Action Plan, A-2.

19 Ibid.

20 Marine Protected Areas, Executive Order 13158 of May 26, 2000. Presidential Documents 34909, *Federal Register*, vol. 65, no. 105, Wednesday, May 31, 2000. See appendix G for the full text of the executive order.

21 Presidential Document 111,1 June 1998. Existing leases in the Channel Islands and Flower Garden Bank were not affected by the order.

22 National Marine Sanctuaries Amendments Act of 2000 (P.L. 106-513).

23 Presidential Proclamation 8031, June 15, 2006, invoked a century-old law known as the Antiquities Act.

24 Personal communication, June 2008.

25 MSNBC, June 16, 2006.

References

Auster, Peter J., Randy Clark, and Rachael E. S. Reid. "Marine Fishes." In *An Ecological Characterization of the Stellwagen Bank National Marine Sanctuary Region.* National Centers for Coastal Ocean Science (NCCOS), NOAA Technical Memorandum 45, 2006.

Auster, Peter J., and Richard W. Langton. "The Effects of Fishing on Fish Habitat." *American Fisheries Society Symposium* 22 (1999): 150–87.

Auster, Peter J., R. J. Malatesta, R. W. Langton, L. Watling, P. C. Valentine, C. L. S. Donaldson, E. W. Langton, A. N. Shepard, and I. G. Babb. "The Impacts of Mobile Fishing Gear on Seafloor Habitats in the Gulf of Maine (Northwest Atlantic): Implications for Conservation of Fish Populations." *Reviews in Fisheries Science* 4, no. 2 (1996): 185–202.

Auster, Peter J., and Lance L. Stewart. "Species Profiles: Life Histories and Environmental Requirements of Coastal Fishes and Invertebrates: Sand Lance." U.S. Fish and Wildlife Service Biological Report 82, 1986.

Backus, Richard H., ed. *Georges Bank.* Cambridge, Mass.: MIT Press, 1987.

Barker, Ernest, trans. *The Politics of Aristotle.* New York: Oxford University Press, 1958.

Battista, Tim, Randy Clark, and Simon Pittman, eds. *An Ecological Characterization of the Stellwagen Bank National Marine Sanctuary Region.* NOAA Technical Memorandum 45. National Centers for Coastal Ocean Science (NCCOS), 2006.

Beardsley R., E. E. Adams, D. Harleman, A. E. Giblin, J. R Kelly, J. E. O'Reilly, and J. F. Paul. *Report of the MWRA Hydrodynamic and Water Quality Model Evaluation Group.* Boston: Massachusetts Water Resources Authority, 1995.

Berle, Peter A. A. *Does the Citizen Stand a Chance? The Politics of a State Legislature: New York.* Hauppague, N.Y.: Barrons Educational Series, 1978.

Bothner, Michael H., and Bradford Butman, eds. "Processes Influencing the Transport and Fate of Contaminated Sediments in the Coastal Ocean — Boston Harbor and Massachusetts Bay." Section 11, USGS Circular 1302. Reston, Va.: U.S. Geological Survey, 2005.

Browning, Robert M., Jr. "The Lasting Injury: The Revenue Marine's First Steam Cutters." *The American Neptune* 52, no. 1 (Winter 1992) : 25–37.

Buck, Eugene H. "Marine Mammal Protection Act Amendments of 1994." Congressional Research Service, September 28, 1994. Reprinted by National Council for Science and the Environment, http://www.ncseonline.org.

Carey, Richard Adams. *Against the Tide: The Fate of the New England Fisherman*. Boston: Houghton Mifflin, 1999.

Caswell, Hal, Masami Fujiwara, and Solange Brault. "Declining Survival Probability Threatens the North Atlantic Right Whale." *Proceedings of the National Academy of Sciences* 96: 3308–13.

Center of the American West. Interview with John C. Whitaker, Boulder, Co., November 19, 2003. http://www.centerwest.org/projects/secretaries/interviewpdg/Whitaker.pdf.

Chandler, William T., and Gillelan, Hannah. "The History and Evolution of the National Marine Sanctuaries Act." *Environmental Law Reporter* 34: 10505–65. Washington, D.C.: Environmental Law Institute, 2004.

———. "The Makings of the National Marine Sanctuaries Act: A Legislative History and Analysis." Redmond, Wash.: Marine Conservation Biology Institute, 2005. Online at http://www.mcbi.org/publications/pub_pdfs/The%20Makings%20of%20National%20Marine%20Sanctuaries%20Booklet.pdf.

Clapham, Philip J., Lisa S. Baraff, Carole A. Carlson, Margaret A. Christian, David K. Mattila, Charles A. Mayo, Margaret A. Murphy, and Sharon Pittman. "Seasonal Occurrence and Annual Return of Humpback Whales, *Megaptera novaeangliae*, in the Southern Gulf of Maine." *Canadian Journal of Zoology* 71, no. 2 (1993): 440–43.

Clark, Christopher W., Douglas Gillespie, Douglas Nowacek, and Susan Parks. "Listening to Their World: Acoustics for Monitoring and Protecting Right Whales in an Urbanized Ocean." In *The Urban Whale: North Atlantic Whales at the Crossroads*, ed. Scott D. Kraus and Rosalind M. Rolland (Cambridge, Mass.: Harvard University Press, 2007), 333–57.

Clarke, K.C. and Jeffrey Hemphill. "The Santa Barbara Oil Spill, A Retrospective." *Yearbook of the Pacific Coast Geographers* 64: 157–62. Honolulu: University of Hawaii Press, 2002.

Cloud, John. "The 200th Anniversary of the Survey of the Coast." *Prologue: Quarterly of the National Archives and Records Administration* 39, no. 1 (2007).

Commission on Marine Science, Engineering, and Resources. *Our Nation and the Sea: A Plan for National Action*. Washington, D.C.: GPO, 1969.

Corkeron, Peter J. "Humpback Whales (*Megaptera novaeangliae*) in Hervey Bay, Queensland: Behaviour and Responses to Whale-Watching Vessels." *Canadian Journal of Zoology* 73, no. 7 (1995): 1290–99.

Council on Environmental Quality. *Ocean Dumping: A National Policy*. Washington, D.C.: GPO, 1970.

Cox, Tara M., Andrew J. Read, Andrew Solow, and Nick Tregenza. "Will Harbor Porpoises Habitutate to Pingers?" *Journal of Cetacean Research and Management* 3, no. 1 (2001): 81–86.

Crawford, Jud. "An Analysis of Change in Maximum Fish Length of Commercially Important Fish Species." Stellwagen Bank National Marine Sanctuary, in press.

Cumming, William P. "The Colonial Charting of the Massachusetts Coast." In *Seafaring in Colonial Massachusetts*, ed. Philip C. F. Smith (Boston: The Colonial Society of Massachusetts and University Press of Virginia, 1980).

Deming, Alison Hawthorne. "Brief Encounters on the Savanna." *onearth* (Summer 2008): 64.

Eames, Thomas Harrison. "The Wreck of the Steamer *Portland*." *The New England Quarterly* 13, no. 2 (1940): 191–206.

David E. Filippi and Ann Gravatt, "Section 9(g) Litigation: 'Take' Cases and Permitting Agencies." November 1, 2000. Available online at Stoel & Rives LLP website http://www.stoel.com/showarticle.aspx?Show=907.

Flippen, J. Brooks. *Nixon and the Environment*. Albuquerque: University of New Mexico Press, 2000.

Foote, Andrew D., Richard W. Osborne, and A. Rus Hoelzel. "Environment: Whale-Call Response to Masking Boat Noise." *Nature* 428, no. 6986 (2004): 910.

Fowlie, Wallace. "Waiting for Godot." In *Dionysus in Paris* (New York: Meridian Books, 1960): 210–14.

Frank, Kenneth T., Brian Petrie, Jae S. Choi, and William C. Leggett. "Trophic Cascades in a Formerly Cod-Dominated Ecosystem." *Science* 308 (June 10, 2005): 1621–23.

Greenberg, Daniel S. "Oceanography: PSAC Panel Calls for Setting Up New Agency." *Science* 153 (July 22, 1966): 91–93.

Hardin, Garrett. "The Tragedy of the Commons." *Science* 162 (1968) 1243–48.

Haury, Loren R., Peter H. Wiebe, Marshall H. Orr, and Melbourne G. Briscoe. "Tidally Generated High-Frequency Internal Wave Packets and Their Effects on Plankton in Massachusetts Bay." *Journal of Marine Research* 41 (1983): 65–112.

Hitchings, Sinclair. "Guarding the New England Coast: The Naval Career of Cyprian Southack." In *Seafaring in Colonial Massachusetts*, ed. Philip C. F. Smith (Boston: The Colonial Society of Massachusetts and University Press of Virginia, 1980).

Holmes, Bob. "Noises Off: "The Cacophony of Human Noise in the Ocean Grows Louder by the Year." *New Scientist*, March 1, 1997.

International Whaling Commission (IWC). Report of the Whale Watching Working Group. *Report of the International Whaling Commission* 47 (1997): 250–56.

Jackson, Jeremy B. C., Michael X. Kirby, Wolfgang H. Berger, Karen A. Bjorndal, Louis W. Botsford, Bruce J. Bourque, Roger H. Bradbury, et al. "Historical Overfishing and the Recent Collapse of Coastal Ecosystems." *Science* 293 (2001): 629–37.

Jensen, Aleria S., and Gregory K. Silber. "Large Whale Ship Strike Database." NOAA Technical Memorandum NMFS-OPR 25, 2003.

Johnson, Lyndon B. "Natural Beauty — Message from the President of the United States." *Congressional Record*, 89th Congress, 1st Session, vol. 111, pt. 2, 2085–89, February 8, 1965.

Johnson, Robert Underwood. "The Neglect of Beauty in the Conservation Movement." *Century* 79 (1910): 637–38. Reprinted in *The American Environment*, ed. Roderick Nash (Reading, Mass.: Addison-Wesley Publishing Co., 1968).

Knowlton, Amy R., and Moira Brown. "Running the Gauntlet: Right Whales and Vessel Strikes." In *The Urban Whale: North Atlantic Right Whales at the Crossroads*, ed. Scott D. Kraus and Rosalind M. Rolland (Cambridge, Mass.: Harvard University Press, 2007), 409–35.

Knowlton, Amy R., Marilyn K. Marx, Heather M. Pettis, Philip K. Hamilton, and Scott D. Kraus. "Analysis of Scarring on North Atlantic Right whales (*Eubalaena glacialis*): Monitoring Rates of Entanglement Interaction: 1980–2002." Final Report to the National Marine Fisheries Service, 2005.

Kraus, Scott D., and Rosalind M. Rolland, eds. *The Urban Whale: North Atlantic Whales at the Crossroads*. Cambridge, Mass.: Harvard University Press, 2007.

Laist, David W., Amy R. Knowlton, James G. Mead, Anne S. Collet, and Michela Podesta. "Collisions between Ships and Whales." *Marine Mammal Science* 17, no. 1 (2001): 35–75.

Leopold, Aldo. *A Sand County Almanac*. New York: Oxford University Press, 1949.

Lien, Jon. "The Conservation Basis for the Regulation of Whale Watching in Canada by the Department of Fisheries and Oceans: A Precautionary Approach." *Canadian Technical Report of Fisheries and Aquatic Sciences* 2363 (2001): 1–38.

MacQuarrie, Brian. "Humans a Threat to Ocean Preserve: Stellwagen Bank Deemed at Risk." *Boston Globe*, May 28, 2007, B1.

Marine Sanctuaries Review Team. "National Marine Sanctuaries: Challenges and Opportunities." Reprinted in hearings before Subcommittee on Oceanography and Subcommittee on Fisheries, Wildlife Conservation and the Environment, House Committee of Merchant Marine and Fisheries, 102nd Congress 87 140, 1992.

Massachusetts Water Resources Authority. *State of Boston Harbor: Mapping the Harbor's Recovery*. Boston: MWRA, 2002.

Mayo, Charles A. "Stellwagen Bank: Whales and Environmental Information." NOAA Contract No. NA83-AAA03071, Office of Ocean and Coastal Resource Management, 1986.

———. "Marine Mammals in the Mosaic of Stellwagen Bank." Presented at Stellwagen Bank Conference, University of Massachusetts, Boston, April 26–27, 1990.

Merchant, Carolyn. *Ecological Revolutions: Nature, Gender, and Science in New England*. Chapel Hill: University of North Carolina Press, 1989.

Nash, Roderick. *The Rights of Nature: A History of Environmental Ethics.* Madison: University of Wisconsin Press, 1989.

National Oceanic and Atmospheric Administration (NOAA), National Marine Fisheries Service. *2006 Gulf of Maine Humpback Whale Stock Assessment.* Silver Spring, Md.: NOAA, 2007.

NOAA, National Marine Sanctuary Program. *Gerry E. Studds Stellwagen Bank National Marine Sanctuary Condition Report 2007.* Silver Spring, Md.: NOAA, April 2007.

———. *Stellwagen Bank National Marine Sanctuary Draft Management Plan and Environmental Assessment.* Silver Spring, Md.: NOAA, April 2008.

NOAA, Office of Inspector General. "National Marine Sanctuary Program Protects Certain Resources, But Further Actions Could Increase Protection." Final Report No. IPE-18591, February 2008.

NOAA, Sanctuaries and Reserves Division. *National Marine Sanctuary Site Evaluations: Recommendations and Final Reports.*" NA-82-SAC-00647. Silver Spring, Md.: NOAA, 1983.

———. *Stellwagen Bank National Marine Sanctuary Draft Environmental Impact Statement/Management Plan.* Silver Spring, Md.: NOAA, February 1991.

———. *Stellwagen Bank National Marine Sanctuary Final Environmental Impact Statement/Management Plan,* vols. 1 and 2. Silver Spring, Md.: NOAA, July 1993.

National Research Council. *Marine Mammal Populations and Ocean Noise: Determining When Noise Causes Biologically Significant Effects.* Washington, D.C.: National Academy Press, 2005.

Nelson, Misty, Mendy Garron, Richard L. Merrick, Richard M. Pace III, and Timothy V. N. Cole. "Mortality and Serious Injury Determinations for Baleen Whale Stocks along the U.S. Eastern Seaboard and Adjacent Canadian Maritimes 2001–2005." Northeast Fisheries Science Center Reference Document 07-05, February 2007.

Northeast Fisheries Science Center. "Assessment of 19 Northeast Groundfish Stocks through 2004." Report of the 2nd Groundfish Assessment Review Meeting, Woods Hole, Mass., August 2005.

———. "Humpback Whale Gulf of Maine Stock Assessment." December 2005.

———. "Minke Whale (Canadian East Coast Stock) 2006 Stock Assessment Report," March 2007.

———. "Assessment of 19 Northeast Groundfish Stocks through 2007." Report of the 3rd Groundfish Assessment Review Meeting, Woods Hole, Mass., August 2008.

Nowacek, Douglas P., Lesley H. Thorne, David W. Johnston, and Peter L. Tyack. "Responses of Cetaceans to Anthropogenic Noise." *Mammal Review* 37, no. 2 (April 2007): 81–115.

Ocean Studies Board. *Effects of Trawling and Dredging on Seafloor Habitat.* Washington, D.C.: National Research Council, 2002.

———. *Dynamic Changes in Marine Ecosystems: Fishing, Food Webs, and Future Options.* Washington, D.C. National Academy Press, 2006.

Oldale, Robert N. *Cape Cod and the Islands: The Geologic Story.* East Orleans, Mass.: Parnassus Imprints, 1992.

Osher Map Library and Smith Center for Cartographic Education. *The Cartographic Creation of New England.* Portland: University of Southern Maine, 1996.

Owen, David. "The Disappointing History of the National Marine Sanctuaries Act," *NYU Environmental Law Journal* 11, no. 3 (2003): 734.

Palakovich, Julie, and Les Kaufman. "Estimating the Importance of Maternal Age, Size, and Spawning Experience to Recruitment of Atlantic Cod (*Gaus morhua*)." *Conservation Biology,* in review.

Parks, Susan E. "Response of North Atlantic Right Whales (*Eubalaena glacialis*) to Playback of Calls Recorded from Surface Active Groups in Both the North and South Atlantic." *Marine Mammal Science* 19 (2003): 563–80.

Parks, Susan E., and Christopher Clark. "Acoustic Communication: Social Sounds and the Potential Impacts of Noise." In *The Urban Whale: North Atlantic Right Whales at the Crossroads,* ed. Scott D. Kraus and Rosalind M. Rolland (Cambridge, Mass.: Harvard University Press, 2007), 310–32.

Petulla, Joseph. *American Environmentalism: Values, Tactics, Priorities.* College Station: Texas A&M Press, 1980.

Pew Oceans Commission. *America's Living Oceans: Charting a Course for Sea Change.* Arlington, Va.: Pew Oceans Commission, 2003.

———. 2003. *Marine Reserves: A Tool for Ecosystem Management and Conservation.* Arlington, Va.: Pew Oceans Commission, 2003.

Pierce, Wesley George. *Going Fishing: The Story of the Deep Sea Fishermen of New England.* Marine Research Company, 1934; reprint, Camden, Me.: International Marine Publishing Company, 1989.

Pinet, Paul R. *Oceanography: An Introduction to the Planet Oceanus.* St. Paul, Minn.: West Publishing Co., 1992.

Playfair, Susan. *Vanishing Species: Saving the Fish, Sacrificing the Fisherman.* Lebanon, N.H.: University Press of New England, 2003.

President's Science Advisory Committee, Panel on Oceanography. "Effective Use of the Sea." Washington, D.C. GPO, 1966.

Read, Andrew J., and Carrie R. Brownstein. "Considering Other Consumers: Fisheries, Predators, and Atlantic Herring in the Gulf of Maine," *Conservation Ecology* 7, no. 1 (2003): 2.

Roberts, Callum. *The Unnatural History of the Sea.* Washington, D.C.: Island Press, 2007.

Robbins, Jooke, and David K. Mattila. "Establishing Humpback Whale (*Megaptera novaeangliae*) Entanglement Rates on the Basis of Scar Evidence." Provincetown Center for Coastal Studies, Report to the Northeast Fisheries Science Center, National Marine Fisheries Service, 2004.

———. "Monitoring Entanglements of Humpback Whales in the Gulf of Maine on the Basis of Caudal Peduncle Scarring." Report to the 53rd Scientific Committee meeting of the International Whaling Commission. Hammersmith, London. Document #C/53/NAH25, 2001.

Robbins, Julie. 2007. "Structure and Dynamics of the Gulf of Maine Humpback Whale Population." Ph.D. diss., School of Biology, University of St. Andrew.

Russell, Dick. "Hitting Bottom." *Amicus Journal* (Winter 1997): 21–25.

Sax, Joseph L. *Mountains without Handrails: Reflections on the National Parks*. Ann Arbor: University of Michigan Press, 1980.

Scheiber, Harry N. "The Stratton Commission: An Historical Perspective on Policy Studies in Ocean Governance, 1969–1998." The Stratton Roundtable, Washington, D.C., 1998.

Scheidat, Meike, Cristina Castro, Janira González, and Rob Williams. "Behavioral Responses of Humpback Whales (*Megaptera novaeangliae*) to Whalewatching Boats near Isla de la Plata, Machalilla National Park, Ecuador." *Journal of Cetacean Research and Management* 6, no. 1 (2004): 63–68.

Stevenson, David K., and Marcy L. Scott. *Essential Fish Habitat Source Document: Atlantic Herring, Clupea harengus, Life History and Habitat Characteristics*, 2nd ed. NOAA Technical Memorandum NMFS-NE-192. Woods Hole, Mass.: National Marine Fisheries Service, Northeast Fisheries Science Center, 2005.

Tension Technology International. "Analysis of Non-Buoyant Lobster Line: New, Used, and Machine Tested." Report to Massachusetts Division of Marine Fisheries and Atlantic Lobstermen's Association, 2006.

Tucholke, Brian E., and Charles D. Hollister. "Late Wisconsin Glaciation of the Southwestern Gulf of Maine: New Evidence from the Marine Environment." *Geological Society of America Bulletin* 84 (1983): 3279–96.

Udall, Stewart L. *The Quiet Crisis*. New York: Holt, Rinehart & Winston, 1963.

U.S. Commission on Ocean Policy. *An Ocean Blueprint for the 21st Century*. Washington, D.C.: U.S. Commission on Ocean Policy, 2004.

U.S. Geological Survey. *USGS Stellwagen Bank Mapping Project*. USGS Fact Sheet 078-98, 1998.

Valentine, Page, ed. "Sea Floor Image Maps Showing Topography, Sun-Illuminated Topography, Backscatter Intensity, Ruggedness, Slope and Distribution of Boulder Ridges and Bedrock Outcrops in the Stellwagen Bank National Marine Sanctuary Region." USGS Scientific Investigations Map 2840, 2005.

Van Dyke, Jon N., Durwood Zaelke, and Grant Hewison, eds. *Freedom for the Seas in the 21st Century: Ocean Governance and Environmental Harmony*. Washington, D.C.: Island Press, 1993.

Ward, Nathalie, ed. *Stellwagen Bank: A Guide to the Whales, Sea Birds, and Marine Life of the Stellwagen Bank National Marine Sanctuary*. Camden, Me.: Center for Coastal Studies & Down East Books, 1995.

Watkins, William A. "Whale Reactions to Human Activities in Cape Cod Waters." *Marine Mammal Science* 2, no. 4 (October 1986): 251–62.

Weinrich, Mason, Malcolm Martin, Rachel Griffiths, Jennifer Bove, and Mark Schilling. "A Shift in Distribution of Humpback Whales in Response to Prey in the Southern Gulf of Maine." *Fishery Bulletin* 95 (1997): 826–36.

Whitehead, Alfred North. *Science and the Modern World*. New York: Mentor, 1948.

Wiley, David N., Just C. Moller, Richard M. Pace III, and Carole Carlson. "Effectiveness of Voluntary Conservation Agreements: Case Study of Endangered Whales and Commercial Whale Watching." *Conservation Biology* 19 (April 2008): 450–57.

Wiley, David N., Just C. Moller, and Kristin A. Zillnskas. "The Distribution and Density of Commercial Fisheries and Baleen Whales within the Stellwagen Bank National Marine Sanctuary: July 2001–June 2002." *Marine Technology Society Journal* 37, no. 1 (2003): 35–53.

Index